Sweet & Maxwell

Criminal Law Statutes 2003/04

AUSTRALIA
Law Book Co.
Sydney

CANADA and USA
Carswell
Toronto

HONG KONG
Sweet & Maxwell Asia

NEW ZEALAND
Brookers
Wellington

SINGAPORE and MALAYSIA
Sweet & Maxwell Asia
Singapore and Kuala Lumpur

Sweet & Maxwell's

Criminal Law Statutes 2003/04

6th Edition

IAN DENNIS M.A. Ph.D.
of Gray's Inn, Barrister
Professor of English Law, University College London

LONDON
SWEET & MAXWELL
2003

First Edition........... 1982
Second Edition........ 1989
Reprinted 1990
Reprinted 1994
Third Edition.......... 1995
Fourth Edition......... 1998
Fifth Edition........... 2002
Sixth Edition 2003

Published in 2003 by Sweet & Maxwell Ltd
of 100 Avenue Road, London NW3 3PF
Typeset by Sweet & Maxwell Ltd, 100 Avenue Road, London NW3 3PF
and Mendip Communications Ltd, Frome, Somerset
Printed in Great Britain by Ashford Colour Printers Hants

No natural forests were destroyed to make this product; only farmed timber was used and replanted

ISBN 0 421 84740 9

PREFACE

The sixth edition of Sweet & Maxwell's Criminal Law Statutes is the first of the annual updates in this volume of the relaunched Statutes Series. The new volume incorporates a number of amendments to existing legislation made by the Police Reform Act 2002 and the Adoption and Children Act 2002. Also included are changes effected by statutory instrument. The use of secondary legislation as a device for amending the substantive criminal law may have bureaucratic advantages, but it does nothing to improve the accessibility of the law. The sooner the criminal law is codified, with periodic updates made by primary legislation, the better. Textual amendments apart, this has been a quite year in terms of Parliamentary activity. The thrust of Government reform in the criminal justice area has been mainly directed to reform of policing (Police Reform Act 2002) and an overhaul of the regime for recovering the fruits of crime (Proceeds of Crime Act 2002). Next year will be different. The law on sexual offences will be heavily revised by the Sexual Offences Bill currently before Parliament, and the Criminal Justice Bill is set to introduce a major new exception to the common law rule against double jeopardy. At the time of writing it is impossible to predict the final form of either of these controversial measures, hence the Bills have not been appended to this volume.

Ian Dennis
Faculty of Laws, University College London
July 7, 2003

CONTENTS

CHRONOLOGICAL CONTENTS

STATUTES

CODES OF PRACTICE

ALPHABETICAL CONTENTS

STATUTES

CODES OF PRACTICE

Accessories and Abettors Act 1861

(24 AND 25 VICT. C. 94)

AS TO ABETTORS IN MISDEMEANORS:

Abettors in misdemeanors

8. Whosoever shall aid, abet, counsel, or procure the commission of [any indictable offence][1], whether the same be [an offence][2] at common law or by virtue of any Act passed or to be passed, shall be liable to be tried, indicted, and punished as a principal offender. **1-001**

Offences against the Person Act 1861

(24 AND 25 VICT. C. 100)

Homicide

Conspiring or soliciting to commit murder

4. [...][3] whosoever shall solicit, encourage, persuade, or endeavour to persuade, or shall propose to any person, to murder any other person, whether he be a subject of Her Majesty or not, and whether he be within the Queen's dominions or not, shall be guilty of an offence,[...][4] and being convicted thereof shall be liable [...][5] to [imprisonment for life][6] [...][7] **2-001**

Manslaughter

5. Whosoever shall be convicted of manslaughter shall be liable, at the discretion of the court, to imprisonment [...][8] for life [...][9] **2-002**

Murder or manslaughter abroad

9. Where any murder or manslaughter shall be committed on land out of the United Kingdom, whether within the Queen's dominions or without, and whether the person killed were a subject of Her Majesty or not, every offence committed by any subject of Her Majesty in respect of any such case, whether the **2-003**

---

[1] Words substituted by Criminal Law Act 1977 c.45 s 65 (7) Sch 12
[2] Words substituted by Criminal Law Act 1977 c.45 s 65 (7) Sch 12
[3] Words repealed by Criminal Law Act 1977 c.45 Sch 13
[4] Throughout this Act, the terms "Felony" and "misdemeanor" have been replaced by the term "an offence".
[5] Words repealed by Statute Law Revision Act 1892 c.19
[6] Words substituted by Criminal Law Act 1977 c.45 s 5 (10) (b)
[7] Words repealed by Statute Law Revision Act 1892 c.19)
[8] Throughout this Act, the expression "be kept in penal servitude" has been replaced by the term "imprisonment".
[9] Words repealed by Statute Law Revision Act 1892 c.19 and Criminal Justice Act 1948 c.58 Sch 10 Pt I

same shall amount to the offence of murder or of manslaughter, [...][1], may be dealt with, inquired of, tried, determined, and punished [...][2] in England or Ireland [...][3] Provided, that nothing herein contained shall prevent any person from being tried in any place out of England or Ireland for any murder or manslaughter committed out of England or Ireland, in the same manner as such person might have been tried before the passing of this Act.

Provision for the trial of murder and manslaughter where the death or cause of death only happens in England or Ireland

2-004 **10.** Where any person being [criminally][4] stricken, poisoned, or otherwise hurt upon the sea, or at any place out of England or Ireland, shall die of such stroke, poisoning, or hurt in England or Ireland, or, being [criminally][5] stricken, poisoned, or otherwise hurt in any place in England or Ireland, shall die of such stroke, poisoning, or hurt upon the sea, or at any place out of England or Ireland, every offence committed in respect of any such case, whether the same shall amount to the offence of murder or of manslaughter, [...][6] may be dealt with, inquired of, tried, determined, and punished [...][7] in England or Ireland [...][8]

Letters threatening to murder

[Threats to Kill

2-005 **16.** A person who without lawful excuse makes to another a threat, intending that that other would fear it would be carried out, to kill that other or a third person shall be guilty of an offence and liable on conviction on indictment to imprisonment for a term not exceeding ten years.][9]

Acts causing or tending to cause Danger to Life or Bodily Harm or to resist apprehension

Impeding a person endeavouring to save himself from shipwreck

2-006 **17.** Whosoever shall unlawfully and maliciously prevent or impede any person, being on board of or having quitted any ship or vessel which shall be in distress, or wrecked, stranded, or cast on shore, in his endeavour to save his life, or shall unlawfully and maliciously prevent or impede any person in his endeavour to save the life of any such person as in this section first aforesaid, shall be guilty of an offence, and being convicted thereof shall be liable [...][10] to imprisonment for life [...][11]

---

[1] Words repealed by Criminal Law Act 1967 c.58 Sch 3 Pt III
[2] Words repealed by Criminal Law Act 1967 c.58 Sch 3 Pt III
[3] Words repealed by Criminal Law Act 1967 c.58 Sch 3 Pt III
[4] Word substituted by Criminal Law Act 1967 c.58 Sch 2 para 6
[5] Word substituted by Criminal Law Act 1967 c.58 Sch 2 para 6
[6] Words repealed by Criminal Law Act 1967 c.58 Sch 3 Pt III
[7] Words repealed by Criminal Law Act 1967 c.58 Sch 3 Pt III
[8] Words repealed by Criminal Law Act 1967 c.58 Sch 3 Pt. III
[9] Substituted by Criminal Law Act 1977 c.45 Sch 12
[10] Words repealed by Statute Law Revision (No. 2) Act 1893 c.54
[11] Words repealed by Statute Law Revision Act 1892 c.19 and Statute Law Revision (No. 2) Act 1893 c.54

Shooting or attempting to shoot, or wounding with intent to do grievous bodily harm or to resist apprehension

18. Whosoever shall unlawfully and maliciously by any means whatsoever wound or cause any grievous bodily harm to any person, [...][1] with intent, [...][2] to do some [...][3] grievous bodily harm to any person, or with intent to resist or prevent the lawful apprehension or detainer of any person, shall be guilty of an offence, and being convicted thereof shall be liable [...][4] to imprisonment for life [...][5] **2-007**

Inflicting bodily injury, with or without weapon

20. Whosoever shall unlawfully and maliciously wound or inflict any grievous bodily harm upon any other person, either with or without any weapon or instrument, shall be guilty of an offence and being convicted thereof shall be liable [...][6] to a term of imprisonment not exceeding five years[...][7] **2-008**

Attempting to choke, &c. in order to commit or assist in the committing of any indictable offence

21. Whosoever shall, by any means whatsoever, attempt to choke, suffocate, or strangle any other person, or shall by any means calculated to choke, suffocate, or strangle, attempt to render any other person insensible, unconscious, or incapable of resistance, with intent in any of such cases thereby to enable himself or any other person to commit, or with intent in any of such cases thereby to assist any other person in committing, any indictable offence, shall be guilty of an offence, and being convicted thereof shall be liable [...][8] to imprisonment for life [...][9] **2-009**

Using chloroform, &c. to commit or assist in the committing of any indictable offence

22. Whosoever shall unlawfully apply or administer to or cause to be taken by, or attempt to apply or administer to or attempt to cause to be administered to or taken by, any person, any chloroform, laudanum, or other stupefying or overpowering drug, matter, or thing, with intent in any of such cases thereby to enable himself or any other person to commit, or with intent in any of such cases thereby to assist any other person in committing, any indictable offence, shall be guilty of an offence, and being convicted thereof shall be liable [...][10] to imprisonment for life [...][11] **2-010**

Maliciously administering poison, &c. so as to endanger life or inflict grievous bodily harm

23. Whosoever shall unlawfully and maliciously administer to or cause to be administered to or taken by any other person any poison or other destructive or **2-011**

[1] Words repealed by Criminal Law Act 1967 c. 58 Sch 3 Pt III
[2] Words repealed by Criminal Law Act 1967 c.58 Sch 3 Pt III
[3] Words repealed by Criminal Law Act 1967 c.58 Sch 3 Pt III
[4] Words repealed by Statute Law Revision (No. 2) Act 1893 c.54
[5] Words repealed by Statute Law Revision Act 1892 c.19 and Statute Law Revision (No. 2) Act 1893 c.54
[6] Words repealed by Statute Law Revision Act 1892 c.19
[7] Words repealed by Statute Law Revision Act 1892 c.19
[8] Words repealed by Statute Law Revision Act 1892 c.19
[9] Words repealed by Statute Law Revision Act 1892 c.19
[10] Words repealed by Statute Law Revision Act 1892 c.19
[11] Words repealed by Statute Law Revision Act 1892 c.19

noxious thing, so as thereby to endanger the life of such person, or so as thereby to inflict upon such person any grievous bodily harm, shall be guilty of an offence, and being convicted thereof shall be liable [...][1] to imprisonment for any term not exceeding ten years [...][2]

Maliciously administering poison, &c. with intent to injure, aggrieve, or annoy any other person

2-012 **24.** Whosoever shall unlawfully and maliciously administer to or cause to be administered to or taken by any other person any poison or other destructive or noxious thing, with intent to injure, aggrieve, or annoy such person, shall be guilty of a an offence and being convicted thereof shall be liable [...][3] to imprisonment for not more than five years[...][4]

Persons charged with [an offence] under s. 23 may be found guilty of [an offence] under s. 24.

2-013 **25.** If, upon the trial of any person for an offence in the last but one preceding section mentioned, the jury shall not be satisfied that such person is guilty thereof, but shall be satisfied that he is guilty of an offence in the last preceding section mentioned, then and in every such case the jury may acquit the accused of an offence under s.23, and find him guilty of an offence under s.24, and thereupon he shall be liable to be punished in the same manner as if convicted upon an indictment for an offence under s.24.

Not providing apprentices or servants with food, &c. or bodily harm whereby life is endangered, or health permanently injured

2-014 **26.** Whosoever, being legally liable, either as a master or mistress, to provide for any apprentice or servant necessary food, clothing, or lodging, shall wilfully and without lawful excuse refuse or neglect to provide the same, or shall unlawfully and maliciously do or cause to be done any bodily harm to any such apprentice or servant, so that the life of such apprentice or servant shall be endangered, or the health of such apprentice or servant shall have been or shall be likely to be permanently injured, shall be guilty of an offence, and being convicted thereof shall be liable [...][5] to imprisonment for any term not exceeding five years [...][6]

Exposing children whereby life is endangered

2-015 **27.** Whosoever shall unlawfully abandon or expose any child, being under the age of two years, whereby the life of such child shall be endangered, or the health of such child shall have been or shall be likely to be permanently injured, shall be guilty of an offence, and being convicted thereof shall be liable [...][7] to imprisonment for any term not exceeding five years [...][8]

[1] Words repealed by Statute Law Revision Act 1892 c.19
[2] Words repealed by Statute Law Revision Act 1892 c.19
[3] Words repealed by Statute Law Revision Act 1892 c.19
[4] Words repealed by Statute Law Revision Act 1892 c.19 and Statute Law Revision (No. 2) Act 1893 c.54
[5] Words repealed by Statute Law Revision Act 1892 c.19
[6] Words repealed by Statute Law Revision Act 1892 c.19 and Statute Law Revision (No. 2) Act 1893 c.54
[7] Words repealed by Statute Law Revision Act 1892 c.19
[8] Words repealed by Statute Law Revision Act 1892 c.19 and Statute Law Revision (No. 2) Act 1893 c.54

Causing bodily injury by gunpowder

28. Whosoever shall unlawfully and maliciously, by the explosion of gunpowder or other explosive substance, burn, maim, disfigure, disable, or do any grievous bodily harm to any person, shall be guilty of an offence, and being convicted thereof shall be liable, at the discretion of the court [...][1] to imprisonment for life [...][2] **2-016**

Causing gunpowder to explode, or sending to any person an explosive substance, or throwing corrosive fluid on a person, with intent to do grievous bodily harm

29. Whosoever shall unlawfully and maliciously cause any gunpowder or other explosive substance to explode, or send or deliver to or cause to be taken or received by any person any explosive substance or any other dangerous or noxious thing, or put or lay at any place, or cast or throw at or upon or otherwise apply to any person, any corrosive fluid or any destructive or explosive substance, with intent in any of the cases aforesaid to burn, maim, disfigure, or disable any person, or to do some grievous bodily harm to any person, shall, whether any bodily injury be effected or not, be guilty of am offence, and being convicted thereof shall be liable, at the discretion of the court, [...][3] to imprisonment for life [...][4] **2-017**

Placing gunpowder near a building, with intent to do bodily injury to any person

30. Whosoever shall unlawfully and maliciously place or throw in, into, upon, against, or near any building, ship, or vessel any gunpowder or other explosive substance, with intent to do any bodily injury to any person, shall, whether or not any explosion take place, and whether or not any bodily injury be effected, be guilty of an offence, and being convicted thereof shall be liable, at the discretion of the court, to imprisonment for any term not exceeding fourteen years [...][5] [...][6] **2-018**

Setting spring guns, &c., with intent to inflict grievous bodily harm, or allowing the same to remain

31. Whosoever shall set or place, or cause to be set or placed, any spring gun, man trap, or other engine calculated to destroy human life or inflict grievous bodily harm, with the intent that the same or whereby the same may destroy or inflict grievous bodily harm upon a trespasser or other person coming in contact therewith, shall be guilty of an offence, and being convicted thereof shall be liable [...][7] to imprisonment for any term not exceeding five years [...][8]; and whosoever shall knowingly and wilfully permit any such spring gun, man trap, or other engine which may have been set or placed in any place then being in or afterwards coming into his possession or occupation by some other person to **2-019**

[1] Words repealed by Statute Law Revision Act 1892 c.19
[2] Words repealed by Statute Law Revision Act 1892 c.19, Statute Law Revision (No. 2) Act 1893 c.54 and Criminal Justice Act 1948 c.58 Sch 10 Pt I
[3] Words repealed by Statute Law Revision Act 1893 c.14
[4] Words repealed by Statute Law Revision Act 1893 c.14 Statute Law Revision (No. 2) Act 1893 c.54 and Criminal Justice Act 1948 c.58 Sch 10 Pt I
[5] Words repealed by Statute Law Revision Act 1892 c.19
[6] Words repealed by Statute Law Revision Act 1893 c.14 Statute Law Revision (No. 2) Act 1893 c.54 and Criminal Justice Act 1948 c.58 Sch 10 Pt I
[7] Words repealed by Statute Law Revision Act 1892 c.19
[8] Words repealed by Statute Law Revision Act 1892 c.19

continue so set or placed, shall be deemed to have set and placed such gun, trap, or engine with such intent as aforesaid:

Provided, that nothing in this section contained shall extend to make it illegal to set or place any gin or trap such as may have been or may be usually set or placed with the intent of destroying vermin:

Provided also, that nothing in this section shall be deemed to make it unlawful to set or place, or cause to be set or placed, or to be continued set or placed, from sunset to sunrise, any spring gun, man trap, or other engine which shall be set or placed, or caused or continued to be set or placed, in a dwelling house, for the protection thereof.

Placing wood, &c., on a railway, taking up rails, turning points, showing or hiding signals etc.,with intent to endanger passengers

2-020 **32.** Whosoever shall unlawfully and maliciously put or throw upon or across any railway any wood, stone, or other matter or thing, or shall unlawfully and maliciously take up, remove, or displace any rail, sleeper, or other matter or thing belonging to any railway, or shall unlawfully and maliciously turn, move, or divert any points or other machinery belonging to any railway, or shall unlawfully and maliciously make or show, hide or remove, any signal or light upon or near to any railway, or shall unlawfully and maliciously do or cause to be done any other matter or thing, with intent, in any of the cases aforesaid, to endanger the safety of any person travelling or being upon such railway, shall be guilty of an offence, and being convicted thereof shall be liable, at the discretion of the court, to imprisonment for life [...][1] [...][2]

Casting stone, &c. upon a railway carriage, with intent to endanger the safety of any person therein, or in any part of the same train

2-021 **33.** Whosoever shall unlawfully and maliciously throw, or cause to fall or strike, at, against, into, or upon any engine, tender, carriage, or truck used upon any railway, any wood, stone, or other matter or thing, with intent to injure or endanger the safety of any person being in or upon such engine, tender, carriage, or truck, or in or upon any other engine, tender, carriage, or truck of any train of which such first-mentioned engine, tender, carriage, or truck shall form part, shall be guilty of an offence, and being convicted thereof shall be liable [...][3] to imprisonment for life [...][4]

Doing or omitting anything so as to endanger passengers by railway

2-022 **34.** Whosoever, by any unlawful act, or by any wilful omission or neglect, shall endanger or cause to be endangered the safety of any person conveyed or being in or upon a railway, or shall aid or assist therein, shall be guilty of an offence, and being convicted thereof shall be liable, at the discretion of the court, to be imprisoned for any term not exceeding two years, [...][5]

Drivers of carriages injuring persons by furious driving

2-023 **35.** Whosoever, having the charge of any carriage or vehicle, shall by wanton or furious driving or racing, or other wilful misconduct, or by wilful neglect, do

[1] Words repealed by Statute Law Revision Act 1892 c.19
[2] Words repealed by Statute Law Revision Act 1892 c.19 and Criminal Justice Act 1948 c.58, Sch 10 Pt I
[3] Words repealed by Statute Law Revision Act 1892 c.19
[4] Words repealed by Statute Law Revision Act 1892 c.19
[5] Words repealed by Criminal Justice Act 1948 c.58 s 1 (2)

or cause to be done any bodily harm to any person whatsoever, shall be guilty of an offence, and being convicted thereof shall be liable, at the discretion of the court, to be imprisoned for any term not exceeding two years, [...][1]

Assaults

Obstructing or assaulting a clergyman or other minister in the discharge of his duties in place of worship or burial place, or on his way thither

36. Whosoever shall, by threats or force, obstruct or prevent or endeavour to obstruct or prevent, any clergyman or other minister in or from celebrating divine service or otherwise officiating in any church, chapel, meeting house, or other place of divine worship, or in or from the performance of his duty in the lawful burial of the dead in any churchyard or other burial place, or shall strike or offer any violence to, or shall, upon any civil process, or under the pretence of executing any civil process, arrest any clergyman or other minister who is engaged in, or to the knowledge of the offender is about to engage in, any of the rites or duties in this section aforesaid, or who to the knowledge of the offender shall be going to perform the same or returning from the performance thereof, shall be guilty of an offence, and being convicted thereof shall be liable, at the discretion of the court, to be imprisoned for any term not exceeding two years, [...][2] **2-024**

Assaulting a magistrate, &c. on account of his preserving wreck

37. Whosoever shall assault and strike or wound any magistrate, officer, or other person whatsoever lawfully authorized, in or on account of the exercise of his duty in or concerning the preservation of any vessel in distress, or of any vessel, goods, or effects wrecked, stranded, or cast on shore, or lying under water, shall be guilty of an offence, and being convicted thereof shall be liable, [...][3] at the discretion of the court, to be imprisoned for any term not exceeding seven years [...][4] **2-025**

Assault with intent to commit an offence, or on peace officers, &c

38. Whosoever [...][5] shall assault any person with intent to resist or prevent the lawful apprehension or detainer of himself or of any other person for any offence, shall be guilty of an offence, and being convicted thereof shall be liable, at the discretion of the court, to be imprisoned for any term not exceeding two years, [...][6] **2-026**

If the magistrates dismiss the complaint, they shall make out a certificate to that effect

44. If the justices, upon the hearing of any [...][7] case of assault or battery upon the merits, where the complaint was preferred by or on behalf of the party **2-027**

[1] Words repealed by Criminal Justice Act 1948 c.58 s 1 (2)
[2] Words repealed by Criminal Justice Act 1948 c.58 s 1 (2)
[3] Words repealed by Statute Law Revision Act 1892 c.19
[4] Words repealed by Statute Law Revision Act 1892 c.19
[5] Words repealed by Police Act 1964 c.48 Sch 10 Pt. I and Criminal Law Act 1967 c.58 Sch 3 Pt III
[6] Words repealed by Criminal Justice Act 1948 c.58 s 1 (2)
[7] Words repealed by Criminal Justice Act 1988 c.33 ss 123 (6), 170 Sch 8 para 16, Sch 15 para 3, Sch 16

aggrieved, [...][1] shall deem the offence not to be proved, or shall find the assault or battery to have been justified, or so trifling as not to merit any punishment, and shall accordingly dismiss the complaint, they shall forthwith make out a certificate under their hands stating the fact of such dismissal, and shall deliver such certificate to the party against whom the complaint was preferred.

Certificate or conviction shall be a bar to any other proceedings

2-028 **45.** If any person against whom any such complaint as is mentioned [in section 44 of this Act][2] shall have been preferred by or on the behalf of the party aggrieved shall have obtained such certificate, or, having been convicted, shall have paid the whole amount adjudged to be paid, or shall have suffered the imprisonment [...][3] awarded, in every such case he shall be released from all further or other proceedings, civil or criminal, for the same cause.

Assault occasioning bodily harm. Common assault

2-029 **47.** Whosoever shall be convicted upon an indictment of any assault occasioning actual bodily harm shall be liable [...][4] to imprisonment for not more than five years [...][5][...][6].

Bigamy

Bigamy. Offence may be dealt with where offender shall be apprehended. Not to extend to second marriages, &c. herein stated

2-030 **57.** Whosoever, being married, shall marry any other person during the life of the former husband or wife, whether the second marriage shall have taken place in England or Ireland or elsewhere, shall be guilty of an offence, and being convicted thereof shall be liable [...][7] to imprisonment for any term not exceeding seven years [...][8]:

Provided, that nothing in this section contained shall extend to any second marriage contracted elsewhere than in England and Ireland by any other than a subject of Her Majesty, or to any person marrying a second time whose husband or wife shall have been continually absent from such person for the space of seven years then last past, and shall not have been known by such person to be living within that time, or shall extend to any person who, at the time of such second marriage, shall have been divorced from the bond of the first marriage, or to any person whose former marriage shall have been declared void by the sentence of any court of competent jurisdiction.

---

[1] Words repealed by Criminal Justice Act 1988 c.33 ss 123 (6), 170, Sch 8 para 16, Sch 15 para 3, Sch 16
[2] Words substituted by Criminal Justice Act 1988 c.33 s 170, Sch 8 para 16, Sch 15 para 4
[3] Words repealed by Criminal Justice Act 1948 c.58 s 1 (2)
[4] Words repealed by Statute Law Revision Act 1892 c.19
[5] Words repealed by Statute Law Revision Act 1892 c.19
[6] Words repealed by Criminal Justice Act 1988 c.33 ss 123 (6), 170, Sch 8 para 16, Sch 16
[7] Words repealed by Statute Law Revision Act 1892 c.19
[8] Words repealed by Statute Law Revision Act 1892 c.19 and Criminal Law Act 1967 c.58 Sch 3 Pt III

Attempts to procure Abortion

Administering drugs or using instruments to procure abortion

58. Every woman, being with child, who, with intent to procure her own miscarriage, shall unlawfully administer to herself any poison or other noxious thing, or shall unlawfully use any instrument or other means whatsoever with the like intent, and whosoever, with intent to procure the miscarriage of any woman, whether she be or be not with child, shall unlawfully administer to her or cause to be taken by her any poison or other noxious thing, or shall unlawfully use any instrument or other means whatsoever with the like intent, shall be guilty of an offence, and being convicted thereof shall be liable [...][1] to imprisonment for life [...][2] **2-031**

Procuring drugs, &c. to cause abortion

59. Whosoever shall unlawfully supply or procure any poison or other noxious thing, or any instrument or thing whatsoever, knowing that the same is intended to be unlawfully used or employed with intent to procure the miscarriage of any woman, whether she be or be not with child, shall be guilty of an offence and being convicted thereof shall be liable [...][3] to imprisonment for any term not exceeding five years [...][4] **2-032**

Concealing the Birth of a Child

Concealing the birth of a child

60. If any woman shall be delivered of a child, every person who shall, by any secret disposition of the dead body of the said child, whether such child died before, at, or after its birth, endeavour to conceal the birth thereof, shall be guilty of an offence, and being convicted thereof shall be liable, at the discretion of the court, to be imprisoned for any term not exceeding two years, [...][5] **2-033**

Making Gunpowder to commit Offences, and searching for the same

Making or having gunpowder, &c., with intent to commit any felony against this Act

64. Whosoever shall knowingly have in his possession, or make or manufacture, any gunpowder, explosive substance, or any dangerous or noxious thing, or any machine, engine, instrument, or thing, with intent by means thereof to commit, or for the purpose of enabling any other person to commit, any of the offences in this Act mentioned shall be guilty of an offence, and being convicted **2-034**

[1] Words repealed by Statute Law Revision (No. 2) Act 1893 c.54
[2] Words repealed by Statute Law Revision Act 1892 c.19 and Statute Law Revision (No. 2) Act 1893 c.54
[3] Words repealed by Statute Law Revision Act 1892 c.19
[4] Words repealed by Statute Law Revision Act 1892 c.19
[5] Words repealed by Criminal Justice Act 1948 c.58 s 1 (2) and by Criminal Law Act 1967 c.58 Sch 2 para 13 (1) (a), Sch 13 Pt III

thereof shall be liable, at the discretion of the court, to be imprisoned for any term not exceeding two years, [...][1]

Explosive Substances Act 1883

(46 AND 47 VICT. C.3)

[Causing explosion likely to endanger life or property

3-001 **2.** A person who in the United Kingdom or (being a citizen of the United Kingdom and Colonies) in the Republic of Ireland unlawfully and maliciously causes by any explosive substance an explosion of a nature likely to endanger life or to cause serious injury to property shall, whether any injury to person or property has been actually caused or not, be guilty of an offence and on conviction on indictment shall be liable to imprisonment for life.][2]

[Attempt to cause explosion, or making or keeping explosive with intent to endanger life or property

3-002 **3.**—(1) A person who in the United Kingdom or a dependency or (being a citizen of the United Kingdom and Colonies) elsewhere unlawfully and maliciously—

(a) does any act with intent to cause, or conspires to cause, by an explosive substance an explosion of a nature likely to endanger life, or cause serious injury to property, whether in the United Kingdom or the Republic of Ireland, or

(b) makes or has in his possession or under his control an explosive substance with intent by means thereof to endanger life, or cause serious injury to property, whether in the United Kingdom or the Republic of Ireland, or to enable any other person so to do,

shall, whether any explosion does or does not take place, and whether any injury to person or property is actually caused or not, be guilty of an offence and on conviction on indictment shall be liable to imprisonment for [life][3] and the explosive substance shall be forfeited.

(2) In this section "dependency" means the Channel Islands, the Isle of Man and any colony, other than a colony for whose external relations a county other than the United Kingdom is responsible.][4]

Punishment for making or possession of explosive under suspicious circumstances

3-003 **4.**—(1) Any person who makes or knowingly has in his possession or under his control any explosive substance, under such circumstances as to give rise to a reasonable suspicion that he is not making it or does not have it in his possession or under his control for a lawful object, shall, unless he can show that he made it or had it in his possession or under his control for a lawful object, be

[1] Words repealed by Criminal Justice Act 1948 c.58 Sch 10 Pt I
[2] Substituted by Criminal Jurisdiction Act 1975 c.59 ss 7 (1) (3), 13 (3)
[3] Word substituted by Criminal Law Act 1977 c.45 s 33 Sch 12 and SI 1977/1249 (N.I. 16) art 5 (2)
[4] Substituted by Criminal Jurisdiction Act 1975 c.59 ss 7 (1) (3), 13 (3)

guilty of an offence, and, on conviction, shall be liable to imprisonment for a term not exceeding fourteen years, [...][1]

Punishment of accessories

5. Any person who within or (being a subject of Her Majesty) without Her Majesty's dominions by the supply of or solicitation for money, the providing of premises, the supply of materials, or in any manner whatsoever, procures, counsels, aids, abets, or is accessory to, the commission of any crime under this Act, shall be guilty of an offence, and shall be liable to be tried and punished for that crime, as if he had been guilty as a principal. **3-004**

Trial of Lunatics Act 1883

(46 AND 47 VICT. C. 38)

Special verdict where accused found guilty, but insane at date of act or omission charged, and orders thereupon

2.—(1) Where in any indictment or information any act or omission is charged against any person as an offence, and it is given in evidence on the trial of such person for that offence that he was insane, so as not to be responsible, according to law, for his actions at the time when the act was done or omission made, then, if it appears to the jury before whom such person is tried that he did the act or made the omission charged, but was insane as aforesaid at the time when he did or made the same, the jury shall return [a special verdict that the accused is not guilty by reason of insanity.][2] **4-001**

Perjury Act 1911

(1 AND 2 GEO. 5 C. 6)

Perjury

1.—(1) If any person lawfully sworn as a witness or as an interpreter in a judicial proceedings wilfully makes a statement material in that proceeding, which he knows to be false or does not believe to be true, he shall be guilty of perjury, and shall, on conviction thereof on indictment, be liable to imprisonment for a term not exceeding seven years,[...][3] or to a fine or to both imprisonment and a fine. **5-001**

(2) The expression "judicial proceeding" includes a proceeding before any court, tribunal, or person having by law power to hear, receive, and examine evidence on oath.

---

[1] Words repealed by Criminal Justice Act 1948 c.58 s 1 (2), Criminal Procedure (Scotland) Act 1975 c.21 s 221 (2)

[2] Words substituted by Criminal Procedure (Insanity) Act 1964 c.84 ss 1, 8 (3) (a)

[3] Words repealed by Criminal Justice Act 1948 c.58 s 1 (2)

Aiders, abettors, suborners, &c

5-002 7.—(1) Every person who aids, abets, counsels, procures, or suborns another person to commit an offence against this Act shall be liable to be proceeded against, indicted, tried and punished as if he were a principal offender.

(2) Every person who incites [...][1] another person to commit an offence[2] against this Act shall be guilty of a an offence, and, on conviction thereof on indictment, shall be liable to imprisonment, or to a fine, or to both such imprisonment and fine.

Official Secrets Act 1911

(1 AND 2 GEO. 5 C. 28)

Penalties for spying

6-001 1.—(1) If any person for any purpose prejudicial to the safety or interests of the State—

(a) approaches, [inspects, passes over][3] or is in the neighbourhood of, or enters any prohibited place within the meaning of this Act; or

(b) makes any sketch, plan, model, or note which is calculated to be or might be or is intended to be directly or indirectly useful to an enemy; or

(c) obtains, [collects, records, or publishes,][4] or communicates to any other person [any secret official code word, or pass word, or][5] any sketch, plan, model, article, or note, or other document or information which is calculated to be or might be or is intended to be directly or indirectly useful to an enemy;

he shall be guilty of an offence[6][...][7]

(2) On a prosecution under this section, it shall not be necessary to show that the accused person was guilty of any particular act tending to show a purpose prejudicial to the safety or interests of the State, and, notwithstanding that no such act is proved against him, he may be convicted if, from the circumstances of the case, or his conduct, or his known character as proved, it appears that his purpose was a purpose prejudicial to the safety or interests of the State; and if any sketch, plan, model, article, note, document, or information relating to or used in any prohibited place within the meaning of this Act, or anything in such a place [or any secret official code word or pass word][8], is made, obtained, [collected, recorded, published][9], or communicated by any person other than a person acting under lawful authority, it shall be deemed to have been made,

---

[1] Words repealed by Criminal Attempts Act 1981 c.47 Sch Pt I
[2] In s 7 of this Act, the term "misdemeanor" has been replaced by the term "an offence".
[3] Words inserted by Official Secrets Act 1920 c.75 Sch 1
[4] Words inserted by Official Secrets Act 1920 c.75 Sch 1
[5] Words inserted by Official Secrets Act 1920 c.75 Sch 1
[6] In this Act, the term "felony" has been replaced by the term "an offence".
[7] Words inserted by Official Secrets Act 1920 c.75 Sch 2
[8] Words inserted by Official Secrets Act 1920 c.75 Sch 1
[9] Words inserted by Official Secrets Act 1920 c.75 Sch 1

obtained, [collected, recorded, published][1] or communicated for a purpose prejudicial to the safety or interests of the State unless the contrary is proved.

Criminal Justice Act 1925

(15 AND 16 GEO. 5 C. 86)

Abolition of presumption of coercion of married woman by husband

47. Any presumption of law that an offence committed by a wife in the presence of her husband is committed under the coercion of the husband is hereby abolished, but on a charged against a wife for any offence other than treason or murder it shall be a good defence to prove that the offence was committed in the presence of, and under the coercion of, the husband. **7-001**

Infant Life (Preservation) Act 1929

(19 AND 20 GEO. 5 C. 34)

Punishment for child destruction

1.—(1) Subject as hereinafter in this subsection provided, any person who, with intent to destroy the life of a child capable of being born alive, by any wilful act causes a child to die before it has an existence independent of its mother, shall be guilty of an offence[2], to wit, of child destruction, and shall be liable on conviction thereof on indictment to imprisonment for life: **8-001**

Provided that no person shall be found guilty of an offence under this section unless it is proved that the act which caused the death of the child was not done in good faith for the purpose only of preserving the life of the mother.

(2) For the purposes of this Act, evidence that a woman had at any material time been pregnant for a period of twenty-eight weeks or more shall be prima facie proof that she was at that time pregnant of a child capable of being born alive.

Prosecution of offences

2.—(2) Where upon the trial of any person for the murder or manslaughter of any child, or for infanticide, or for an offence under section fifty-eight of the Offences against the Person Act 1861 (which relates to administering drugs or using instruments to procure abortion), the jury are of opinion that the person charged is not guilty of murder, manslaughter or infanticide, or of an offence under the said section fifty-eight, as the case may be, but that he is shown by the evidence to be guilty of the offence of child destruction, the jury may find him guilty of that offence, and thereupon the person convicted shall be liable to be punished as if he had been convicted upon an indictment for child destruction. **8-002**

[1] Words inserted by Official Secrets Act 1920 c.75 Sch 1

[2] Throughout this Act, the term "felony" has been replaced by the term "an offence".

(3) Where upon the trial of any person for the offence of child destruction the jury are of opinion that the person charged is not guilty of that offence, but that he is shown by the evidence to be guilty of an offence under the said section fifty-eight of the Offences against the Person Act 1861, the jury may find him guilty of that offence, and thereupon the person convicted shall be liable to be punished as if he had been convicted upon an indictment under that section.

Children and Young Persons Act 1933

(23 AND 24 GEO. 5 C. 12)

PART I

PREVENTION OF CRUELTY AND EXPOSURE TO MORAL AND PHYSICAL DANGER

Offences

Cruelty to persons under sixteen

9-001 **1.**—(1) If any person who has attained the age of sixteen years and [has responsibility for][1] any child or young person under that age, wilfully assaults, ill-treated, neglects, abandons, or exposes him, or causes or procures him to be assaulted, ill-treated, neglected, abandoned, or exposed, in a manner likely to cause him unnecessary suffering or injury to health (including injury to or loss of sight, or hearing, or limb, or organ of the body, and any mental derangement), that person shall be guilty of an offence, and shall be liable—

(a) on conviction on indictment, to a fine [...][2] or alternatively, [...][3], or in addition thereto, to imprisonment for any term not exceeding [ten][4] years;

(b) on summary conviction, to a fine not exceeding the prescribed sum, or alternatively, [...][5], or in addition thereto, to imprisonment for any term not exceeding six months.

(2) For the purposes of this section—

(a) a parent or other person legally liable to maintain a child or young person[, or the legal guardian of a child or young person,][6] shall be deemed to have neglected him in a manner likely to cause injury to his health if he has failed to provide adequate food, clothing, medical aid or lodging for him, or if, having been unable otherwise to provide such food, clothing, medical aid or lodging, he has failed to take steps to procure it to be provided under [the enactments applicable in that behalf][7];

---

[1] Words substituted by Children Act 1989 c.41 Sch 13 para 2
[2] Words repealed by Children Act 1975 c.72 Sch 4 Pt III
[3] Words repealed by Children and Young Persons Act 1963 c.37 s 64 Sch 5
[4] Words substituted by Criminal Justice Act 1988 c.33 s 45 (1) (2)
[5] Words repealed by Children and Young Persons Act 1963 c.37 s 64 Sch 5
[6] Words inserted by Children Act 1989 c.41 Sch 12 para 2
[7] Words substituted by S.I. 1951/174 (1951 I, p. 1369) Sch

(b) where it is proved that the death of an infant under three years of age was caused by suffocation (not being suffocation caused by disease or the presence of any foreign body in the throat or air passages of the infant) while the infant was in bed with some other person who has attained the age of sixteen years, that other person shall, if he was, when he went to bed, under the influence of drink, be deemed to have neglected the infant in a manner likely to cause injury to its health.

(3) A person may be convicted of an offence under this section—

(a) notwithstanding that actual suffering or injury to health, or the likelihood of actual suffering or injury to health, was obviated by the action of another person;

(b) notwithstanding the death of the child or young person in question.

(7) Nothing in this section shall be construed as affecting the right of any parent, [or (subject to section 548 of the Education Act 1996) any other person,][1] having the lawful control or charge of a child or young person to administer punishment to him.

Juvenile Offenders

Age of criminal responsibility

50. It shall be conclusively presumed that no child under the age of [ten][2] years can be guilty of any offence. **9-002**

Public Order Act 1936

(1 EDW. 8 AND 1 GEO. 6 C. 6)

Prohibition of uniforms in connection with political objects

1.—(1) Subject as hereinafter provided, any person who in any public place or at any public meeting wears uniform signifying his association with any political organisation or with the promotion of any political object shall be guilty of an offence: **10-001**

Provided that, if the chief officer of police is satisfied that the wearing of any such uniform as aforesaid on any ceremonial, anniversary, or other special occasion will not be likely to involve risk of public disorder, he may, with the consent of a Secretary of State, by order permit the wearing of such uniform on that occasion either absolutely or subject to such conditions as may be specified in the order.

Prohibition of quasimilitary organisations

2.—(1) If the members or adherents of any association of persons, whether incorporated or not, are— **10-002**

(a) organised or trained or equipped for the purposes of enabling them to be employed in usurping the functions of the police or of the armed forces of the Crown; or

[1] Words substituted by School Standards and Framework Act 1998 c.31 Sch 30 para 1
[2] Word substituted by Children and Young Persons Act 1963 c.37 s 16 (1)

(b) organised and trained or organised and equipped either for the purpose of enabling them to be employed for the use or display of physical force in promoting any political object, or in such manner as to arouse reasonable apprehension that they are organised and either trained or equipped for that purpose;

then any person who takes part in the control or management of the association, or in so organising or training as aforesaid any members or adherents thereof, shall be guilty of an offence under this section:

Provided that in any proceedings against a person charged with the offence of taking part in the control or management of such an association as aforesaid it shall be a defence to that charge to prove that he neither consented to nor connived at the organisation, training, or equipment of members or adherents of the association in contravention of the provisions of this section.

Enforcement

10-003 **7.**—(1) Any person who commits an offence under section two of this Act shall be liable on summary conviction to imprisonment for a term not exceeding six months or to a fine not exceeding the prescribed sum, or to both such imprisonment and fine, or, on conviction on indictment, to imprisonment for a term not exceeding two years or to a fine, or to both such imprisonment and fine.

(2) Any person guilty of [any offence under this Act other than an offence under section two [...][1]][2] shall be liable on summary conviction to imprisonment for a term not exceeding three months or to a fine not exceeding [level 4 on the standard scale][3] or to both such imprisonment and fine.

(3) A constable may without warrant arrest any person reasonably suspected by him to be committing an offence under section one [...][4] of this Act.

Infanticide Act 1938

(1 AND 2 GEO. 6 C. 36)

Offence of infanticide

11-001 **1.**—(1) Where a woman by any wilful act or omission causes the death of her child being a child under the age of twelve months, but at the time of the act or omission the balance of her mind was disturbed by reason of her not having fully recovered from the effect of giving birth to the child or by reason of the effect of lactation consequent upon the birth of the child, then, notwithstanding that the circumstances were such that but for this Act the offence would have amounted to murder, she shall be guilty of an offence, to wit of infanticide, and may for such offence be dealt with and punished as if she had been guilty of the offence of manslaughter of the child.

(2) Where upon the trial of a woman for the murder of her child, being a child under the age of twelve months, the jury are of opinion that she by any wilful act or omission caused its death, but that at the time of the act or omission the

---

[1] Words repealed by Public Order Act 1986 c.64 s 40 (3) Sch 3
[2] Words substituted by Public Order Act 1963 c.52 s 1 (2)
[3] Words substituted by (England, Wales) Criminal Justice Act 1982 c.48 s 46 and (Scotland) Criminal Procedure (Scotland) Act 1975 c.21 s 289G
[4] Words repealed by Public Order Act 1986 c.64 s 40 (3) Sch 3

balance of her mind was disturbed by reason of her not having fully recovered from the effect of giving birth to the child or by reason of the effect of lactation consequent upon the birth of the child, then the jury may, notwithstanding that the circumstances were such that but for the provisions of this Act they might have returned a verdict of murder, return in lieu thereof a verdict of infanticide.

(3) Nothing in this Act shall affect the power of the jury upon an indictment for the murder of a child to return a verdict of manslaughter, or a verdict of guilty but insane.

Prevention of Crime Act 1953

(1 AND 2 ELIZ, 2 C. 14)

Prohibition of the carrying of offensive weapons without lawful authority or reasonable excuse

1.—(1) Any person who without lawful authority or reasonable excuse, the proof whereof shall lie on him, has with him in any public place any offensive weapon shall be guilty of an offence, and shall be liable - **12-001**

(a) on summary conviction, to imprisonment for a term not exceeding six months or a fine not exceeding the prescribed sum or both

(b) on conviction on indictment, to [imprisonment for a term not exceeding four years][1] or a fine or both.

(2) Where any person is convicted of an offence under subsection (1) of this section the court may make an order for the forfeiture or disposal of any weapon in respect of which the offence was committed.

(4) In this section "public place" includes any highway and any other premises or place to which at the material time the public have or are permitted to have access, whether on payment or otherwise; and "offensive weapon" means any article made or adapted for use for causing injury to the person, or intended by the person having it with him for such use by him or by some other person.

---

[1] Words substituted by Offensive Weapons Act 1996 c.26 s 2

Sexual Offences Act 1956

(4 AND 5 ELIZ. 2 C. 69)

PART I

OFFENCES, AND THE PROSECUTION AND PUNISHMENT OF OFFENCES

Intercourse by force, intimidation, etc

[Rape of woman or man

13-001 **1.**—(1) It is an offence for a man to rape a woman or another man.

(2) A man commits rape if—

(a) he has sexual intercourse with a person (whether vaginal or anal) who at the time of the intercourse does not consent to it; and

(b) at the time he knows that the person does not consent to the intercourse or is reckless as to whether that person consents to it.

(3) A man also commits rape if he induces a married woman to have sexual intercourse with him by impersonating her husband.

(4) Subsection (2) applies for the purpose of any enactment.][1]

Procurement of woman by threats

13-002 **2.**—(1) It is an offence for a person to procure a woman, by threats or intimidation, to have [...][2] sexual intercourse in any part of the world.

Procurement of woman by false pretences

13-003 **3.**—(1) It is an offence for a person to procure a woman, by false pretences or false representations to have [...][3] sexual intercourse in any part of the world.

Administering drugs to obtain or facilitate intercourse

13-004 **4.**—(1) It is an offence for a person to apply or administer to, or cause to be taken by, a woman any drug, matter or thing with intent to stupefy or overpower her so as thereby to enable any man to have unlawful sexual intercourse with her.

Intercourse with girls under sixteen

Intercourse with girl under thirteen

13-005 **5.** It is an offence for a man to have unlawful sexual intercourse with a girl under the age of thirteen.

[1] Substituted by Criminal Justice and Public Order Act 1994 c.33 Pt XI s 142
[2] Words repealed by Criminal Justice and Public Order Act 1994 c.33 Sch 11 para 1
[3] Words repealed by Criminal Justice and Public Order Act 1994 c.33 Sch 11 para 1

Intercourse with girl between thirteen and sixteen

6.—(1) It is an offence, subject to the exceptions mentioned in this section, for a man to have unlawful sexual intercourse with a girl under the age of sixteen. **13-006**

(2) Where a marriage is invalid under section two of the Marriage Act 1949, or section one of the Age of Marriage Act 1929 (the wife being a girl under the age of sixteen), the invalidity does not make the husband guilty of an offence under this section because he has sexual intercourse with her, if he believes her to be his wife and has reasonable cause for the belief.

(3) A man is not guilty of an offence under this section because he has unlawful sexual intercourse with a girl under the age of sixteen, if he is under the age of twenty-four and has not previously been charged with a like offence, and he believes her to be of the age of sixteen or over and has reasonable cause for the belief.

In this subsection, "a like offence" means an offence under this section or an attempt to commit one, or an offence under paragraph (1) of section five of the Criminal Law Amendment Act 1885 (the provision replaced for England and Wales by this Section).

[Intercourse with defective

7.—(1) It is an offence, subject to the exception mentioned in this section for a man to have unlawful sexual intercourse with a woman who is a defective. **13-007**

(2) A man is not guilty of an offence under this section because he has unlawful sexual intercourse with a woman if he does not know and has no reason to suspect her to be a defective.][1]

Procurement of defective

9.—(1) It is an offence, subject to the exception mentioned in this section, for a person to procure a woman who is a defective to have unlawful sexual intercourse in any part of the world. **13-008**

(2) A person is not guilty of an offence under this section because he procures a defective to have unlawful sexual intercourse, if the does not know and has no reason to suspect her to be a defective.

Incest

Incest by a man

10.—(1) It is an offence for a man to have sexual intercourse with a woman he knows to be his grand-daughter, daughter, sister or mother. **13-009**

(2) In the foregoing subsection "sister"includes half-sister, and for the purposes of that subsection any expression importing a relationship between two people shall be taken to apply notwithstanding that the relationship is not traced through lawful wedlock.

Incest by a woman

11.—(1) It is an offence for a woman of the age of sixteen or over to permit a man whom she knows to be her grandfather, father, brother or son to have sexual intercourse with her by her consent. **13-010**

[1] Substituted by Mental Health Act 1959 c.72 s 127 (1)

(2) In the foregoing subsection "brother" includes half-brother, and for the purposes of that subsection any expression importing a relationship between two people shall be taken to apply notwithstanding that the relationship is not traced through lawful wedlock.

Unnatural offences

Buggery

13-011 **12.**—(1) It is an offence for a person to commit buggery with another person [otherwise than in the circumstances described in subsection (1A) [or (1AA)][1] below][2] or with an animal.

[(1A) The circumstances [first][3] referred to in subsection (1) are that the act of buggery takes place in private and both parties have attained the age of [sixteen][4].

[(1AA) The other circumstances so referred to are that the person is under the age of sixteen and the other person has attained that age.][5]

(1B) An act of buggery by one man with another shall not be treated as taking place in private if it takes place—

(a) when more than two persons take part or are present; or
(b) in a lavatory to which the public have or are permitted to have access, whether on payment or otherwise.

(1C) In any proceedings against a person for buggery with another person it shall be for the prosecutor to prove that the act of buggery took place otherwise than in private or that one of the parties to it had not attained the age of [sixteen][6].][7]

Indecency between men

13-012 **13.** It is an offence for a man to commit an act of gross indecency with another man [otherwise than in the circumstances described below][8], whether in public or private, or to be a party to the commission by a man of an act of gross indecency with another man, or to procure the commission by a man of an act of gross indecency with another man.

[The circumstances referred to above are that the man is under the age of sixteen and the other man has attained that age.][9]

Assaults

Indecent assault on a woman

13-013 **14.**—(1) It is an offence, subject to the exception mentioned in subsection (3) of this section, for a person to make an indecent assault on a woman.

(2) A girl under the age of sixteen cannot in law give any consent which would prevent an act being an assault for the purposes of this section.

[1] Words inserted by Sexual Offences (Amendment) Act 2000 c.44 s 2 (1) (a)
[2] Words inserted by Criminal Justice and Public Order Act 1994 c.33 Pt XI s 143 (2)
[3] Word inserted by Sexual Offences (Amendment) Act 2000 c.44 s 2 (1) (b)
[4] Word substituted by Sexual Offences (Amendment) Act 2000 c.44 s 1 (1) (a)
[5] Added by Sexual Offences (Amendment) Act 2000 c.44 s 2 (1) (c)
[6] Word substituted by Sexual Offences (Amendment) Act 2000 c.44 s 1 (1) (a)
[7] Added by Criminal Justice and Public Order Act 1994 c.33 Pt XI s 143 (3)
[8] Words inserted by Sexual Offences (Amendment) Act 2000 c.44 s 2 (2) (a)
[9] Words inserted by Sexual Offences (Amendment) Act 2000 c.44 s 2 (2) (b)

(3) Where a marriage is invalid under section two of the Marriage Act 1949, or section one of the Age of Marriage Act 1929 (the wife being a girl under the age of sixteen), the invalidity does not make the husband guilty of any offence under this section by reason of her incapacity to consent while under that age, if he believes her to be his wife and has reasonable cause for the belief.

(4) A woman who is a defective cannot in law give any consent which would prevent an act being an assault for the purposes of this section, but a person is only to be treated as guilty of an indecent assault on a defective by reason of that incapacity to consent, if that person knew or had reason to suspect her to be a defective.

Indecent assault on a man

15.—(1) It is an offence for a person to make an indecent assault on a man. **13-014**

(2) A boy under the age of sixteen cannot in law give any consent which would prevent an act being an assault for the purposes of this section.

(3) A man who is a defective cannot in law give any consent which would prevent an act being an assault for the purposes of this section, but a person is only to be treated as guilty of an indecent assault on a defective by reason of that incapacity to consent, if that person knew or had reason to suspect him to be a defective.

Assault with intent to commit buggery

16.—(1) It is an offence for a person to assault another person with intent to **13-015**
commit buggery.

Abduction

Abduction of woman by force or for the sake of her property

17.—(1) It is an offence for a person to take away or detain a woman against **13-016**
her will with the intention that she shall marry or have unlawful sexual intercourse with that or any other person, if she is so taken away or detained either by force or for the sake of her property or expectations of property.

(2) In the foregoing subsection, the reference to a woman's expectations of property relates only to property of a person to whom she is next of kin or one of the next of kin, and "property" includes any interest in property.

Abduction of unmarried girl under eighteen from parent or guardian

19.—(1) It is an offence, subject to the exception mentioned in this section, **13-017**
for a person to take an unmarried girl under the age of eighteen out of the possession of her parent or guardian against his will, if she is so taken with the intention that she shall have unlawful sexual intercourse with men or with a particular man.

(2) A person is not guilty of an offence under this section because he takes such a girl out of the possession of her parent or guardian as mentioned above, if he believes, her to be of the age of eighteen or over and has reasonable cause for the belief.

(3) In this section "guardian" means any person having [parental responsibility for or care of][1] the girl.

[1] Words substituted by Children Act 1989 c.41 Sch 12 para 11

Abduction of unmarried girl under sixteen from parent or guardian

13-018 **20.**—(1) It is an offence for a person acting without lawful authority or excuse to take an unmarried girl under the age of sixteen out of the possession of her parent or guardian against his will.

(2) In the foregoing subsection "guardian" means any person having [parental responsibility for or care of][1] the girl.

Abduction of defective from parent or guardian

13-019 **21.**—(1) It is an offence, subject to the exception mentioned in this section, for a person to take a woman who is a defective out of the possession of her parent or guardian against his will, if she is so taken with the intention that she shall have unlawful sexual intercourse with men or with a particular man.

(2) A person is not guilty of an offence under this section because he takes such a woman out of the possession of her parent or guardian as mentioned above, if he does not know and has no reason to suspect her to be a defective.

(3) In this section "guardian" means any person having [parental responsibility for or care of][2] the woman.

Prostitution, procuration etc

Causing prostitution of women

13-020 **22.**—(1) It is an offence for a person—

(a) to procure a woman to become, in any part of the world, a common prostitute; or

(b) to procure a woman to leave the United Kingdom, intending her to become an inmate of or frequent a brothel elsewhere; or

(c) to procure a woman to leave her usual place of abode in the United Kingdom, intending her to become an inmate of or frequent a brothel in any part of the world for the purposes of prostitution.

Procuration of girl under twenty-one

13-021 **23.**—(1) It is an offence for a person to procure a girl under the age of twenty-one to have unlawful sexual intercourse in any part of the world with a third person.

Detention of woman in brothel or other premises

13-022 **24.**—(1) It is an offence for a person to detain a woman against her will on any premises with the intention that she shall have unlawful sexual intercourse with men or with a particular man, or to detain a woman against her will in a brothel.

(2) Where a woman is on any premises for the purpose of having unlawful sexual intercourse or is in a brothel, a person shall be deemed for the purpose of the foregoing subsection to detain her there if, with the intention of compelling or inducing her to remain there, he either withholds from her clothes or any other property belonging to her or threatens her with legal proceedings in the event of her taking away clothes provided for her by him or on his directions.

(3) A woman shall not be liable to any legal proceedings, whether civil or criminal, for taking away or being found in possession of any clothes she needed

[1] Words substituted by Children Act 1989 c.41 Sch 12 para 12

[2] Words substituted by Children Act 1989 c.41 Sch 12 para 13

to enable her to leave premises on which she was for the purpose of having unlawful sexual intercourse or to leave a brothel.

Permitting girl under thirteen to use premises for intercourse

25. It is an offence for a person who is the owner or occupier of any premises, or who has, or acts or assists in, the management or control of any premises, to induce or knowingly suffer a girl under the age of thirteen to resort to or be on those premises for the purpose of having unlawful sexual intercourse with men or with a particular man. **13-023**

Permitting girl between thirteen and sixteen to use premises for intercourse

26. It is an offence for a person who is the owner or occupier of any premises, or who has, or acts or assists in, the management or control of any premises, to induce or knowingly suffer a girl [...][1] under the age of sixteen, to resort to or be on those premises for the purposes of having unlawful sexual intercourse with men or with a particular man. **13-024**

Permitting defective to use premises for intercourse

27.—(1) It is an offence, subject to the exception mentioned in this section, for a person who is the owner or occupier of any premises, or who has, or acts or assists in, the management or control of any premises, to induce or knowingly suffer a woman who is a defective to resort to or be on those premises for the purpose of having unlawful sexual intercourse with men or with a particular man. **13-025**

(2) A person is not guilty of an offence under this section because he induces or knowingly suffers a defective to resort to or be on any premises for the purpose mentioned, if he does not know and has no reason to suspect her to be a defective.

Causing or encouraging prostitution of, intercourse with, or indecent assault on, girl under sixteen

28.—(1) It is an offence for a person to cause or encourage the prostitution of, or the commission of unlawful sexual intercourse with, or of an indecent assault on, a girl under the age of sixteen for whom he is responsible. **13-026**

(2) Where a girl has become a prostitute, or has had unlawful sexual intercourse, or has been indecently assaulted, a person shall be deemed for the purposes of this section to have caused or encouraged it, if he knowingly allowed her to consort with, or to enter or continue in the employment of, any prostitute or person of known immoral character.

[(3) The persons who are to be treated for the purposes of this section as responsible for a girl are (subject to subsection (4) of this section)—

(a) her parents;

(b) any person who is not a parent of hers but who has parental responsibility for her; and

(c) any person who has care of her.

(4) An individual falling within subsection (3)(a) or (b) of this section is not to be treated as responsible for a girl if—

(a) a residence order under the Children Act 1989 is in force with respect to her and he is not named in the order as the person with whom she is to live; or

[1] Words repealed by Criminal Law Act 1967 c.58 Sch 2 para 14

(aa) a special guardianship order under that Act is in force with respect to her and he is not her special guardian; or[1]

(b) a care order under that Act is in force with respect to her.][2]

(5) If, on a charge of an offence against a girl under this section, the girl appears to the court to have been under the age of sixteen at the time of the offence charged, she shall be presumed for the purposes of this section to have been so, unless the contrary is proved.

Causing or encouraging prostitution of defective

13-027 **29.**—(1) It is an offence, subject to the exception mentioned in this section, for a person to cause or encourage the prostitution in any part of the world of a woman who is a defective.

(2) A person is not guilty of an offence under this section because he causes or encourages the prostitution of such a woman, if he does not know and has no reason to suspect her to be a defective.

Man living on earnings of prostitution

13-028 **30.**—(1) It is an offence for a man knowingly to live wholly or in part on the earnings of prostitution.

(2) For the purposes of this section a man who lives with or is habitually in the company of a prostitute, or who exercises control, direction or influence over a prostitute's movements in a way which shows he is aiding, abetting or compelling her prostitution with others, shall be presumed to be knowingly living on the earnings of prostitutions, unless he proves the contrary.

Woman exercising control over prostitute

13-029 **31.** It is an offence for a woman for purposes of gain to exercise control, direction or influence over a prostitute's movements in a way which shows she is aiding, abetting or compelling her prostitution.

Solicitation

Solicitation by men

13-030 **32.** It is an offence for a man persistently to solicit or importune in a public place for immoral purposes.

Suppression of brothels

Keeping a brothel

13-031 **33.** It is an offence for a person to keep a brothel, or to manage, or act or assist in the management of, a brothel.

Landlord letting premises for use as brothel

13-032 **34.** It is an offence for the lessor or landlord of any premises or his agent to let the whole or part of the premises with the knowledge that it is to be used, in whole or in part, as a brothel, or, where the whole or part of the premises is used as a brothel, to be wilfully a party to that use continuing.

[1] Inserted by Adoption and Children Act 2002, Sch 3 para 8
[2] Substituted by Children Act 1989 c.41 Sch 12 para 14

Tenant permitting premises to be used as brothel

35.—(1) It is an offence for the tenant or occupier, or person in charge, of any premises knowingly to permit the whole or part of the premises to be used as a brothel. **13-033**

(2) Where the tenant or occupier of any premises is convicted (whether under this section or, for an offence committed before the commencement of this Act, under section thirteen of the Criminal Law Amendment Act 1885) of knowingly permitting the whole or part of the premises to be used as a brothel, the First Schedule to this Act shall apply to enlarge the rights of the lessor or landlord with respect to the assignment or determination of the lease or other contract under which the premises are held by the person convicted.

(3) Where the tenant or occupier of any premises is so convicted, or was so convicted under the said section thirteen before the commencement of this Act, and either—

(a) the lessor or landlord, after having the conviction brought to his notice, fails or failed to exercise his statutory rights in relation to the lease or contract under which the premises are or were held by the person convicted; or

(b) The lessor or landlord, after exercising his statutory rights so as to determine that lease or contract, grants or granted a new lease or enters or entered into a new contract of tenancy of the premises to, with or for the benefit of the same person, without having all reasonable provisions to prevent the recurrence of the offence inserted in the new lease or contract;

then, if subsequently an offence under this section is committed in respect of the premises during the subsistence of the lease or contract referred to in paragraph (a) of this subsection or (where paragraph (b) applies) during the subsistence of the new lease or contract, the lessor or landlord shall be deemed to be a party to that offence unless he shows that he took all reasonable steps to prevent the recurrence of the offence.

References in this subsection to the statutory rights of a lessor or landlord refer to his rights under the First Schedule to this Act or under subsection (1) of section five of the Criminal Law Amendment Act 1912 (the provision replaced for England and Wales by that Schedule).

Tenant permitting premises to be used for prostitution

36. It is an offence for the tenant or occupier of any premises knowingly to permit the whole or part of the premises to be used for the purposes of habitual prostitution. **13-034**

Interpretation

Meaning of "sexual intercourse"

44. Where, on the trial of any offence under this Act, it is necessary to prove sexual intercourse (whether natural or unnatural), it shall not be necessary to prove the completion of the intercourse by the emission of seed, but the intercourse shall be deemed complete upon proof of penetration only. **13-035**

[Meaning of "defective"

13-036 **45.** In this Act "defective" means a person suffering from [a state of arrested or incomplete development of mind which includes severe impairment of intelligence and social functioning][1].][2]

Use of words "man", "boy", "woman" and "girl"

13-037 **46.** The use in any provision of this Act of the word "man" without the addition of the word "boy", or vice versa, shall not prevent the provision applying to any person to whom it would have applied if both words had been used, and similarly with the words "woman" and "girl".

[Meaning of 'parental responsibility'

13-038 **46A.** In this Act 'parental responsibility' has the same meaning as in the Children Act 1989.][3]

Proof of exceptions

13-039 **47.** Where in any of the foregoing sections the description of an offence is expressed to be subject to exceptions mentioned in the section, proof of the exception is to lie on the person relying on it.

Homicide Act 1957

(5 AND 6 ELIZ. 2 C. 11)

PART I

AMENDMENTS OF LAW OF ENGLAND AND WALES AS TO FACT OF MURDER

Abolition of "constructive malice"

14-001 **1.**—(1) Where a person kills another in the course or furtherance of some other offence, the killing shall not amount to murder unless done with the same malice aforethought (express or implied) as is required for a killing to amount to murder when not done in the course or furtherance of another offence.

(2) For the purposes of the foregoing subsection, a killing done in the course or for the purpose of resisting an officer of justice, or of resisting or avoiding or preventing a lawful arrest, or of effecting or assisting an escape or rescue from legal custody, shall be treated as a killing in the course or furtherance of an offence.

Persons suffering from diminished responsibility

14-002 **2.**—(1) Where a person kills or is a party to the killing of another, he shall not be convicted of murder if he was suffering from such abnormality of mind (whether arising from a condition of arrested or retarded development of mind or

[1] Words substituted by Mental Health (Amendment) Act 1982 c.51 Sch 3 para 29
[2] Substituted by Mental Health Act 1959 c.72 s 127 (1)
[3] Added by Children Act 1989 c.41 Sch 12 para 17

any inherent causes or induced by disease or injury) as substantially impaired his mental responsibility for his acts and omissions in doing or being a party to the killing.

(2) On a charge of murder, it shall be for the defence to prove that the person charged is by virtue of this section not liable to be convicted of murder.

(3) A person who but for this section would be liable, whether as principal or as accessory, to be convicted of murder shall be liable instead to be convicted of manslaughter.

(4) The fact that one party to a killing is by virtue of this section not liable to be convicted of murder shall not affect the question whether the killing amounted to murder in the case of any other party to it.

Provocation

3. Where on a charge of murder there is evidence on which the jury can find that the person charged was provoked (whether by things done or by things said or by both together) to lose his self-control, the question whether the provocation was enough to make a reasonable man do as he did shall be left to be determined by the jury; and in determining that question the jury shall take into account everything both done and said according to the effect which, in their opinion, it would have on a reasonable man. **14-003**

Suicide pacts

4.—(1) It shall be manslaughter, and shall not be murder, for a person acting in pursuance of a suicide pact between him and another to kill the other or be a party to the other [...][1] being killed by a third person. **14-004**

(2) Where it is shown that a person charged with the murder of another killed the other or was a party to his [...][2] being killed, it shall be for the defence to prove that the person charged was acting in pursuance of a suicide pact between him and the other.

(3) For the purposes of this section "suicide pact" means a common agreement between two or more persons having for its object the death of all of them, whether or not each is to take his own life, but nothing done by a person who enters into a suicide pact shall be treated as done by him in pursuance of the pact unless it is done while he has the settled intention of dying in pursuance of the pact.

Obscene Publications Act 1959

(7 AND 8 ELIZ. 2 C. 66)

Test of obscenity

1.—(1) For the purposes of this Act an article shall be deemed to be obscene if its effect or (where the article comprises two or more distinct items) the effect of any one of its items is, if taken as a whole, such as to tend to deprave and corrupt persons who are likely, having regard to all relevant circumstances, to read, see or hear the matter contained or embodied in it. **15-001**

[1] Words repealed by Suicide Act 1961 c.60 Sch 2
[2] Words repealed by Suicide Act 1961 c.60 Sch 2

(2) In this Act "article" means any description of article containing or embodying matter to be read or looked at or both, any sound record, and any film or other record of a picture or pictures.

(3) For the purposes of this Act a person publishes an article who—

(a) distributes, circulates, sells, lets on hire, gives, or lends it, or who offers it for sale or for letting on hire; or

(b) in the case of an article containing or embodying matter to be looked at or a record, shows, plays or projects it[, or, where the matter is data stored electronically, transmits that data][1]:

[(4) For the purposes of this Act a person also publishes an article to the extent that any matter recorded on it is included by him in a programme included in a programme service.

(5) Where the inclusion of any matter in a programme so included would, if that matter were recorded matter, constitute the publication of an obscene article for the purposes of this Act by virtue of subsection (4) above, this Act shall have effect in relation to the inclusion of that matter in that programme as if it were recorded matter.

(6) In this section "programme" and "programme service" have the same meaning as in the Broadcasting Act 1990.][2]

Prohibition of publication of obscene matter

15-002 **2.**—(1) Subject as hereinafter provided, any person who, whether for gain or not, publishes an obscene article [or who has an obscene article for publication for gain (whether gain to himself or gain to another)][3] shall be liable—

(a) on summary conviction to a fine not exceeding the prescribed sum or to imprisonment for a term not exceeding six months;

(b) on conviction on indictment to a fine or to imprisonment for a term not exceeding three years or both.

(3) A prosecution [...][4] for an offence against this section shall not be commenced more than two years after the commission of the offence.

[(3A) Proceedings for an offence under this section shall not be instituted except by or with the consent of the Director of Public Prosecutions in any case where the article in question is a moving picture film of a width of not less than sixteen millimetres and the relevant publication or the only other publication which followed or could reasonably have been expected to follow from the relevant publication took place or (as the case may be) was to take place in the course of a [film exhibition][5]; and in this subsection "the relevant publication" means —

(a) in the case of any proceedings under this section for publishing an obscene article, the publication in respect of which the defendant would be charged if the proceedings were brought; and

(b) in the case of any proceedings under this section for having an obscene article for publication for gain, the publication which, if the proceedings were brought, the defendant would be alleged to have had in contemplation.][6]

[1] Words inserted by Criminal Justice and Public Order Act 1994 c.33 Sch 9 para 3
[2] Inserted by Broadcasting Act 1990 c.42 s 162 (1) (b)
[3] Words inserted by Obscene Publications Act 1964 c.74 s 1 (1)
[4] Words repealed by Criminal Law Act 1977 c.45 s 65 (7) Sch 13
[5] Words substituted by Cinemas Act 1985 c.13 s 24 (1) Sch 2 para 6 (2)
[6] Inserted by Criminal Law Act 1977 c.45 s 53 (2)

(4) A person publishing an article shall not be proceeded against for an offence at common law consisting of the publication of any matter contained or embodied in the article where it is of the essence of the offence that the matter is obscene.

[(4A) Without prejudice to subsection (4) above, a person shall not be proceeded against for an offence at common law—

(a) in respect of a [film exhibition][1] or anything said or done in the course of a [film exhibition][2], where it is of the essence of the common law offence that the exhibition or, as the case may be, what was said or done was obscene, indecent, offensive, disgusting or injurious to morality; or

(b) in respect of an agreement to give a [film exhibition][3] or to cause anything to be said or done in the course of such an exhibition where the common law offence consists of conspiring to corrupt public morals or to do any act contrary to public morals or decency.][4]

(5) A person shall not be convicted of an offence against this section if he proves that he had not examined the article in respect of which he is charged and had no reasonable cause to suspect that it was such that his publication of it would make him liable to be convicted of an offence against this section.

(6) In any proceedings against a person under this section the question whether an article is obscene shall be determined without regard to any publication by another person unless it could reasonably have been expected that the publication by the other person would follow from publication by the person charged.

[(7) In this section "film exhibition" has the same meaning as in the Cinemas Act 1985.][5]

Powers of search and seizure

3.—(1) If a justice of the peace is satisfied by information on oath that there is reasonable ground for suspecting that, in any premises in the petty sessions area for which he acts, or on any stall or vehicle in that area, being premises or a stall or vehicle specified in the information, obscene articles are, or are from time to time, kept for publication for gain, the justice may issue a warrant under his hand empowering any constable to enter (if need be by force) and search the premises, or to search the stall or vehicle[...][6] and to seize and remove any articles found therein or thereon which the constable has reason to believe to be obscene articles and to be kept for publication for gain. **15-003**

(2) A warrant under the foregoing subsection shall, if any obscene articles are seized under the warrant, also empower the seizure and removal of any documents found in the premises or, as the case may be, on the stall or vehicle which relate to a trade or business carried on at the premises or from the stall or vehicle.

(3) [Subject to subsection (3A) of this section][7] any articles seized under subsection (1) of this section shall be brought before a justice of the peace acting for the same petty sessions area as the justice who issued the warrant, and the justice before whom the articles are brought may thereupon issue a summons to the occupier of the premises or, as the case may be, the user of the stall or vehicle

1 Words substituted by Cinemas Act 1985 c.13 s 24 (1) Sch 2 para 6 (2)
2 Words substituted by Cinemas Act 1985 c.13 s 24 (1) Sch 2 para 6 (2)
3 Words substituted by Cinemas Act 1985 c.13 s 24 (1) Sch 2 para 6 (2)
4 Inserted by Criminal Law Act 1977 c.45 s 53 (3)
5 Inserted by Broadcasting Act 1990 c.42 s 162 (1) (b)
6 Words repealed by Broadcasting Act 1990 c.42 s 162 (1) (b)
7 Words inserted by Broadcasting Act 1990 c.42 s 162 (1) (b)

to appear on a day specified in the summons before a magistrates' court for that petty sessions area to show cause why the articles or any of them should not be forfeited; and if the court is satisfied, as respects any of the articles, that at the time when they were seized they were obscene articles kept for publication for gain, the court shall order those articles to be forfeited:

Provided that if the person summoned does not appear, the court shall not make an order unless service of the summons is proved. [Provided also that this subsection does not apply in relation to any article seized under subsection (1) of this section which is returned to the occupier of the premises or, as the case may be, to the user of the stall or vehicle in or on which it was found][1]

[(3A) Without prejudice to the duty of a court to make an order for the forfeiture of an article where section 1(4) of the Obscene Publications Act 1964 applies (orders made on conviction), in a case where by virtue of subsection (3A) of section 2 of this Act proceedings under the said section 2 for having an article for publication for gain could not be instituted except by or with the consent of the Director of Public Prosecutions, no order for the forfeiture of the article shall be made under this section unless the warrant under which the article was seized was issued on an information laid by or on behalf of the Director of Public Prosecutions][2]

(4) In addition to the person summoned, any other person being the owner, author or maker of any of the articles brought before the court, or any other person through whose hands they had passed before being seized, shall be entitled to appear before the court on the day specified in the summons to show cause why they should not be forfeited.

(5) Where an order is made under this section for the forfeiture of any articles, any person who appeared, or was entitled to appear, to show cause against the making of the order may appeal to [the Crown Court][3], and no such order shall take effect until the expiration of [the period within which notice of appeal to the Crown Court may be given against the order,][4] or, if before the expiration thereof notice of appeal is duly given or application is made for the statement of a case for the opinion of the High Court, until the final determination or abandonment of the proceedings on the appeal or case.

(6) If as respects any articles brought before it the court does not order forfeiture, the court may if it thinks fit order the person on whose information the warrant for the seizure of the articles was issued to pay such costs as the court thinks reasonable to any person who has appeared before the court to show cause why those articles should not be forfeited; and costs ordered to be paid under this subsection shall be enforceable as a civil debt.

(7) For the purposes of this section the question whether an article is obscene shall be determined on the assumption that copies of it would be published in any manner likely having regard to the circumstances in which it was found, but in no other manner.

Defence of public good

15-004 **4.**—(1) [Subject to subsection (1A) of this section][5] a person shall not be convicted of an offence against section two of this Act, and an order for forfeiture shall not be made under the foregoing section, if it is proved that publication of

[1] Words inserted by Broadcasting Act 1990 c.42 s 162 (1) (b)
[2] Inserted by Broadcasting Act 1990 c.42 s 162 (1) (b)
[3] Words substituted by Broadcasting Act 1990 c.42 s 162 (1) (b)
[4] Words substituted by Broadcasting Act 1990 c.42 s 162 (1) (b)
[5] Words inserted by Broadcasting Act 1990 c.42 s 162 (1) (b)

the article in question is justified as being for the public good on the ground that it is in the interests of science, literature, art or learning, or of other objects of general concern.

[(1A) Subsection (1) of this section shall not apply where the article in question is a moving picture film or soundtrack, but—

(a) a person shall not be convicted of an offence against section 2 of this Act in relation to any such film or soundtrack, and

(b) an order for forfeiture of any such film or soundtrack shall not be made under section 3 of this Act,

if it is proved that publication of the film or soundtrack is justified as being for the public good on the ground that it is in the interests of drama, opera, ballet or any other art, or of literature or learning.][1]

(2) It is hereby declared that the opinion of experts as to the literary, artistic, scientific or other merits of an article may be admitted in any proceedings under this Act either to establish or to negative the said ground.

[(3) In this section "moving picture soundtrack" means any sound record designed for playing with a moving picture film, whether incorporated with the film or not.][2]

Indecency with Children Act 1960

(8 AND 9 ELIZ. 2 C. 33)

Indecent conduct towards young child

1.—(1) Any person who commits an act of gross indecency with or towards a child under the age of [sixteen][3], or who incites a child under that age to such an act with him or another, shall be liable on conviction on indictment to imprisonment for a term not exceeding [ten years][4], or on summary conviction to imprisonment for a term not exceeding six months, to a fine not exceeding the prescribed sum, or to both. **16-001**

Suicide Act 1961

(9 AND 10 ELIZ. C. 60)

Suicide to cease to be a crime

1. The rule of law whereby it is a crime for a person to commit suicide is hereby abrogated. **17-001**

---

[1] Inserted by Broadcasting Act 1990 c.42 s 162 (1) (b)
[2] Inserted by Broadcasting Act 1990 c.42 s 162 (1) (b)
[3] Word substituted by Criminal Justice and Court Services Act 2000 c.43 Pt II s 39
[4] Words substituted by Crime (Sentences) Act 1997 c.43 Pt III s 52

Criminal liability for complicity in another's suicide

17-002 **2.**—(1) A person who aids, abets, counsels or procures the suicide of another, or an attempt by another to commit suicide, shall be liable on conviction on indictment to imprisonment for a term not exceeding fourteen years.

(2) If on the trial of an indictment for murder or manslaughter it is proved that the accused aided, abetted, counselled or procured the suicide of the person in question, the jury may find him guilty of that offence.

Obscene Publications Act 1964

CHAPTER 74

Obscene articles intended for publication for gain

18-001 **1.**—(2) For the purpose of any proceedings for an offence against the said section 2 a person shall be deemed to have an article for publication for gain if with a view to such publication he has the article in his ownership, possession or control.

(3) In proceedings brought against a person under the said section 2 for having an obscene article for publication for gain the following provisions shall apply in place of subsections (5) and (6) of that section, that is to say,—

(a) he shall not be convicted of that offence if he proves that he had not examined the article and had no reasonable cause to suspect that it was such that his having it would make him liable to be convicted of an offence against that section; and

(b) the question whether the article is obscene shall be determined by reference to such publication for gain of the article as in the circumstances it may reasonably be inferred he had in contemplation and to any further publication that could reasonably be expected to follow from it, but not to any other publication.

(4) Where articles are seized under section 3 of the Obscene Publications Act 1959 (which provides for the seizure and forfeiture of obscene articles kept for publication for gain), and a person is convicted under section 2 of that Act of having them for publication for gain, the court on his conviction shall order the forfeiture of those articles:

Provided that an order made by virtue of this subsection (including an order so made on appeal) shall not take effect until the expiration of the ordinary time within which an appeal in the matter of the proceedings in which the order was made may be instituted or, where such an appeal is duly instituted, until the appeal is finally decided or abandoned; and for this purpose—

(a) an application for a case to be stated or for leave to appeal shall be treated as the institution of an appeal; and

(b) where a decision on appeal is subject to a further appeal, the appeal shall not be deemed to be finally decided until the expiration of the ordinary time within which a further appeal may be instituted or, where a further appeal is duly instituted, until the further appeal is finally decided or abandoned.

(5) References in section 3 of the Obscene Publications Act 1959 and this section to publication for gain shall apply to any publication with a view to gain,

whether the gain is to accrue by way of consideration for the publication or in any other way.

Negatives, etc. for production of obscene articles

2.—(1) The Obscene Publications Act 1959 (as amended by this Act) shall apply in relation to anything which is intended to be used, either alone or as one of a set, for the reproduction or manufacture therefrom of articles containing or embodying matter to be read, looked at or listened to, as if it were an article containing or embodying that matter so far as that matter is to be derived from it or from the set. **18-002**

(2) For the purposes of the Obscene Publications Act 1959 (as so amended) an article shall be deemed to be had or kept for publication if it is had or kept for the reproduction or manufacture therefrom of articles for publication; and the question whether an article so had or kept is obscene shall—

(a) for purposes of section 2 of the Act be determined in accordance with section 1(3)(b) above as if any reference there to publication of the article were a reference to publication of articles reproduced or manufactured from it; and

(b) for purposes of section 3 of the Act be determined on the assumption that articles reproduced or manufactured from it would be published in any manner likely having regard to the circumstances in which it was found, but in no other manner.

Criminal Procedure (Insanity) Act 1964

CHAPTER 84

Acquittal on grounds of insanity

1. The special verdict required by section 2 of the Trial of Lunatics Act 1883 (hereinafter referred to as a "special verdict") shall be that the accused is not guilty by reason of insanity; and accordingly in subsection (1) of that section for the words from "a special verdict" to the end there shall be substituted the words "a special verdict that the accused is not guilty by reason of insanity". **19-001**

[Finding of unfitness to plead

4.—(1) This section applies where on the trial of a person the question arises (at the instance of the defence or otherwise) whether the accused is under a disability, that is to say, under any disability such that apart from this Act it would constitute a bar to his being tried. **19-002**

(2) If, having regard to the nature of the supposed disability, the court are of opinion that it is expedient to do so and in the interests of the accused, they may postpone consideration of the question of fitness to be tried until any time up to the opening of the case for the defence.

(3) If, before the question of fitness to be tried falls to be determined, the jury return a verdict of acquittal on the count or each of the counts on which the accused is being tried, that question shall not be determined.

(4) Subject to subsections (2) and (3) above, the question of fitness to be tried shall be determined as soon as it arises.

(5) The question of fitness to be tried shall be determined by a jury and—
(a) where it falls to be determined on the arraignment of the accused and the trial proceeds, the accused shall be tried by a jury other than that which determined that question;
(b) where it falls to be determined at any later time, it shall be determined by a separate jury or by the jury by whom the accused is being tried, as the court may direct.

(6) A jury shall not make a determination under subsection (5) above except on the written or oral evidence of two or more registered medical practitioners at least one of whom is duly approved.][1]

[Finding that the accused did the act or made the omission charged against him

19-003 **4A.**—(1) This section applies where in accordance with section 4(5) above it is determined by a jury that the accused is under a disability.

(2) The trial shall not proceed or further proceed but it shall be determined by a jury—
(a) on the evidence (if any) already given in the trial; and
(b) on such evidence as may be adduced or further adduced by the prosecution, or adduced by a person appointed by the court under this section to put the case for the defence,

whether they are satisfied, as respects the count or each of the counts on which the accused was to be or was being tried, that he did the act or made the omission charged against him as the offence.

(3) If as respects that count or any of those counts the jury are satisfied as mentioned in subsection (2) above, they shall make a finding that the accused did the act or made the omission charged against him.

(4) If as respects that count or any of those counts the jury are not so satisfied, they shall return a verdict of acquittal as if on the count in question the trial had proceeded to a conclusion.

(5) A determination under subsection (2) above shall be made—
(a) where the question of disability was determined on the arraignment of the accused, by a jury other than that which determined that question; and
(b) where that question was determined at any later time, by the jury by whom the accused was being tried.][2]

[Powers to deal with persons not guilty by reason of insanity or unfit to plead etc

19-004 **5.**—(1) This section applies where—
(a) a special verdict is returned that the accused is not guilty by reason of insanity; or
(b) findings are recorded that the accused is under a disability and that he did the act or made the omission charged against him.

(2) Subject to subsection (3) below, the court shall either—
(a) make an order that the accused be admitted, in accordance with the provisions of Schedule 1 to the Criminal Procedure (Insanity and Unfitness to Plead) Act 1991, to such hospital as may be specified by the Secretary of State; or

[1] Substituted by Criminal Procedure (Insanity and Unfitness to Plead) Act 1991 c.25 s 2
[2] Inserted by Criminal Procedure (Insanity and Unfitness to Plead) Act 1991 c.25 s 2

(b) where they have the power to do so by virtue of section 5 of that Act, make in respect of the accused such one of the following orders as they think most suitable in all the circumstances of the case, namely—

(i) a guardianship order within the meaning of the Mental Health Act 1983;

(ii) a supervision and treatment order within the meaning of Schedule 2 to the said Act of 1991; and

(iii) an order for his absolute discharge.

(3) Paragraph (b) of subsection (2) above shall not apply where the offence to which the special verdict or findings relate is an offence the sentence for which is fixed by law.][1]

Evidence by prosecution of insanity or diminished responsibility

6. Where on a trial for murder the accused contends— **19-005**

(a) that at the time of the alleged offence he was insane so as not to be responsible according to law for his actions; or

(b) that at that time he was suffering from such abnormality of mind as is specified in subsection (1) of section 2 of the Homicide Act 1957 (diminished responsibility),

the court shall allow the prosecution to adduce or elicit evidence tending to prove the other of those contentions, and may give directions as to the stage of the proceedings at which the prosecution may adduce such evidence.

Murder (Abolition of Death Penalty) Act 1965

CHAPTER 71

Abolition of death penalty for murder

1.—(1) No person shall suffer death for murder, and a person convicted of murder shall, [...][2] be sentenced to imprisonment for life. **20-001**

(2) On sentencing any person convicted of murder to imprisonment for life the Court may at the same time declare the period which it recommends to the Secretary of State as the minimum period which in its view should elapse before the Secretary of State orders the release of that person on licence under section [61 of the Criminal Justice Act 1967][3]

[1] Substituted by Criminal Procedure (Insanity and Unfitness to Plead) Act 1991 c.25 s 3

[2] Words repealed by Powers of Criminal Courts (Sentencing) Act 2000 c.6 Sch 12 (I) para 1

[3] Words substituted by Interpretation Act 1889 c.63 s 38 (1)

Criminal Law Act 1967

CHAPTER 58

PART I

FELONY AND MISDEMEANOUR

Abolition of distinction between felony and misdemeanour

21-001 **1.**—(1) All distinctions between felony and misdemeanour are hereby abolished.

(2) Subject to the provisions of this Act, on all matters on which a distinction has previously been made between felony and misdemeanour, including mode of trial, the law and practice in relation to all offences cognisable under the law of England and Wales (including piracy) shall be the law and practice applicable at the commencement of this Act in relation to misdemeanour.

Use of force in making arrest, etc

21-002 **3.**—(1) A person may use such force as is reasonable in the circumstances in the prevention of crime, or in effecting or assisting in the lawful arrest of offenders or suspected offenders or of persons unlawfully at large.

(2) Subsection (1) above shall replace the rules of the common law on the question when force used for a purpose mentioned in the subsection is justified by that purpose.

Penalties for assisting offenders

21-003 **4.**—(1) Where a person has committed an arrestable offence, any other person who, knowing or believing him to be guilty of the offence or of some other arrestable offence, does without lawful authority or reasonable excuse any act with intent to impede his apprehension or prosecution shall be guilty of an offence.

[(1A) In this section and section 5 below "arrestable offence" has the meaning assigned to it by section 24 of the Police and Criminal Evidence Act 1984.][1]

(2) If on the trial of an indictment for an arrestable offence the jury are satisfied that the offence charged (or some other offence of which the accused might on that charge be found guilty) was committed, but find the accused not guilty of it, they may find him guilty of any offence under subsection (1) above of which they are satisfied that he is guilty in relation to the offence charged (or that other offence).

(3) A person committing an offence under subsection (1) above with intent to impede another person's apprehension or prosecution shall on conviction on indictment be liable to imprisonment according to the gravity of the other person's offence, as follows:—

(a) if that offence is one for which the sentence is fixed by law, he shall be liable to imprisonment for not more than ten years;

[1] Inserted by Police and Criminal Evidence Act 1984 c.60 s 119 Sch 6 para 17

(b) if it is one for which a person (not previously convicted) may be sentenced to imprisonment for a term of fourteen years, he shall be liable to imprisonment for not more than seven years;

(c) if it is not one included above but is one for which a person (not previously convicted) may be sentenced to imprisonment for a term of ten years, he shall be liable to imprisonment for not more than five years;

(d) in any other case, he shall be liable to imprisonment for not more than three years.

(4) No proceedings shall be instituted for an offence under subsection (1) above except by or with the consent of the Director of Public Prosecutions:

Penalties for concealing offences or giving false information

5.—(1) Where a person has committed an arrestable offence, any other person who, knowing or believing that the offence, or some other arrestable offence has been committed, and that he has information which might be of material assistance in securing the prosecution or conviction of an offender for it, accepts or agrees to accept for not disclosing that information any consideration other than the making good of loss or injury caused by the offence, or the making of reasonable compensation for that loss or injury, shall be liable on conviction on indictment to imprisonment for not more than two years. **21-004**

(2) Where a person causes any wasteful employment of the police by knowingly making to any person a false report tending to show that an offence has been committed, or to give rise to apprehension for the safety of any persons or property, or tending to show that he has information material to any police inquiry, he shall be liable on summary conviction to imprisonment for not more than six months or to a fine of not more than level 4 on the standard scale or to both.

(3) No proceedings shall be instituted for an offence under this section except by or with the consent of the Director of Public Prosecutions.

(5) The compounding of an offence other than treason shall not be an offence otherwise than under this section.

Trial of offences

6.—(1) Where a person is arraigned on an indictment— **21-005**

(a) he shall in all cases be entitled to make a plea of not guilty in addition to any demurrer or special plea;

(b) he may plead not guilty of the offence specifically charged in the indictment but guilty of another offence of which he might be found guilty on that indictment;

(c) if he stands mute of malice or will not answer directly to the indictment, the court may order a plea of not guilty to be entered on his behalf, and he shall then be treated as having pleaded not guilty.

(2) On an indictment for murder a person found not guilty of murder may be found guilty—

(a) of manslaughter, or of causing grievous bodily harm with intent to do so; or

(b) of any offence of which he may be found guilty under an enactment specifically so providing, or under section 4(2) of this Act; or

(c) of an attempt to commit murder, or of an attempt to commit any other offence of which he might be found guilty;

but may not be found guilty of any offence not included above.

(3) Where, on a person's trial on indictment for any offence except treason or murder, the jury find him not guilty of the offence specifically charged in the indictment, but the allegations in the indictment amount to or include (expressly or by implication) an allegation of another offence falling within the jurisdiction of the court of trial, the jury may find him guilty of that other offence or of an offence of which he could be found guilty on an indictment specifically charging that other offence.

(4) For purposes of subsection (3) above any allegation of an offence shall be taken as including an allegation of attempting to commit that offence; and where a person is charged on indictment with attempting to commit an offence or with any assault or other act preliminary to an offence, but not with the completed offence, then (subject to the discretion of the court to discharge the jury with a view to the preferment of an indictment for the completed offence) he may be convicted of the offence charged notwithstanding that he is shown to be guilty of the completed offence.

(5) Where a person arraigned on an indictment pleads not guilty of an offence charged in the indictment but guilty of some other offence of which he might be found guilty on that charge, and he is convicted on that plea of guilty without trial for the offence of which he has pleaded not guilty, then (whether or not the two offences are separately charged in distinct counts) his conviction of the one offence shall be an acquittal of the other.

(6) Any power to bring proceedings for an offence by criminal information in the High Court is hereby abolished.

(7) Subsections (1) to (3) above shall apply to an indictment containing more than one count as if each count were a separate indictment.

Sexual Offences Act 1967

CHAPTER 60

Amendment of law relating to homosexual acts in private

22-001 **1.**—[(1) Notwithstanding any statutory or common law provision

(a) a homosexual act in private shall not be an offence provided that the parties consent thereto and have attained the age of [sixteen][1] years and;

(b) a homosexual act by any person shall not be an offence if he is under the age of sixteen years and the other party has attained that age.][2]

(2) An act which would otherwise be treated for the purposes of this act as being done in private shall not be so treated if done—

(a) when more than two persons take part or are present; or

(b) in a lavatory to which the public have or are permitted to have access, whether on payment or otherwise.

---

[1] Word substituted by Sexual Offences (Amendment) Act 2000 c.44 s 1 (2) (a)

[2] Existing text renumbered as (1)(a) and (b) by Sexual Offences (Amendment) Act 2000 c.44 s 2 (3)

(3) A man who is suffering from [severe mental handicap][1][...][2] cannot in law give any consent which, by virtue of subsection (1) of this section, would prevent a homosexual act from being an offence, but a person shall not be convicted, on account of the incapacity of such a man to consent, of an offence consisting of such an act if he proves that he did not know and had no reason to suspect that man to be suffering from [severe mental handicap][3].

[(3A) In subsection (3) of this section "severe mental handicap" means a state of arrested or incomplete development of mind which includes severe impairment of intelligence and social functioning.][4]

(4) Section 128 of the Mental Health Act 1959 (prohibition on men on the staff of a hospital, or otherwise having responsibility for mental patients, having sexual intercourse with women patients) shall have effect as if any reference therein to having unlawful sexual intercourse with a woman included a reference to committing buggery or an act of gross indecency with another man.

(6) It is hereby declared that where in any proceedings it is charged that a homosexual act is an offence the prosecutor shall have the burden of proving that the act was done otherwise than in private or otherwise than with the consent of the parties or that any of the parties had not attained the age of [sixteen][5] years.

(7) For the purposes of this section a man shall be treated as doing a homosexual act if, and only if, he commits buggery with another man or commits an act of gross indecency with another man or is a party to the commission by a man of such an act.

Procuring others to commit homosexual acts

4.—(1) A man who procures another man to commit with a third man an act of buggery which by reason of section 1 of this Act is not an offence shall be liable on conviction on indictment to imprisonment for a term not exceeding two years. **22-002**

(3) It shall not be an offence under section 13 of the Act of 1956 for a man to procure the commission by another man of an act of gross indecency with the first-mentioned man which by reason of section 1 of this Act is not an offence under the said section 13

Living on earnings of male prostitution

5.—(1) A man or woman who knowingly lives wholly or in part on the earnings of prostitution of another man shall be liable— **22-003**

(a) on summary conviction to imprisonment for a term not exceeding six months; or

(b) on conviction on indictment to imprisonment for a term not exceeding seven years.

(3) Anyone may arrest without a warrant a person found committing an offence under this section.

Premises resorted to for homosexual practices

6. Premises shall be treated for purposes of sections 33 to 35 of the Act of 1956 as a brothel if people resort to it for the purpose of lewd homosexual **22-004**

[1] Words substituted by Mental Health (Amendment) Act 1982 c.51 Sch 3 para 34 (a)
[2] Words repealed by Mental Health (Amendment) Act 1982 c.51 Sch 3 para 34 (a), Sch 4 Pt I
[3] Words substituted by Mental Health (Amendment) Act 1982 c.51 Sch 3 para 34 (a)
[4] Inserted by Mental Health (Amendment) Act 1982 c.51 Sch 3 para 34 (b)
[5] Word substituted by Sexual Offences (Amendment) Act 2000 c.44 s 1 (2) (a)

practices in circumstances in which resort thereto for lewd heterosexual practices would have led to it being treated as a brothel for the purposes of those sections.

Time limit on prosecutions

22-005 7.—(1) No proceedings for an offence to which this section applies shall be commenced after the expiration of twelve months from the date on which that offence was committed.

(2) This section applies to—

(a) any offence under section 13 of the Act of 1956 (gross indecency between men);

(c) any offence of buggery by a man with another man not amounting to an assault on that other man and not being an offence by a man with a boy under the age of sixteen.

Restriction on prosecutions

22-006 **8.** No proceedings shall be instituted except by or with the consent of the Director of Public Prosecutions against any man for the offence of buggery with, or gross indecency with, another man[...][1], or for aiding, abetting, counselling, procuring or commanding its commission where either of those men was at the time of its commission under the age of [sixteen][2]:[...][3]

Criminal Justice Act 1967

CHAPTER 80

Miscellaneous provisions as to evidence, procedure and trial

Proof of criminal intent

23-001 **8.** A court or jury, in determining whether a person has committed an offence,—

(a) shall not be bound in law to infer that he intended or foresaw a result of his actions by reasons only of its being a natural and probable consequence of those actions; but

(b) shall decide whether he did intend or foresee that result by reference to all the evidence, drawing such inferences from the evidence as appear proper in the circumstances.

---

[1] Words repealed by Criminal Attempts Act 1981 c.47 Sch Pt I
[2] Word substituted by Sexual Offences (Amendment) Act 2000 c.44 s 1 (2) (b)
[3] Words repealed by Criminal Jurisdiction Act 1975 c.59 Sch 6 Pt I

Abortion Act 1967

CHAPTER 87

Medical termination of pregnancy

1.—(1) Subject to the provisions of this section, a person shall not be guilty of an offence under the law relating to abortion when a pregnancy is terminated by a registered medical practitioner if two registered medical practitioners are of the opinion, formed in good faith— **24-001**

[(a) that the pregnancy has not exceeded its twenty-fourth week and that the continuance of the pregnancy would involve risk, greater than if the pregnancy were terminated, of injury to the physical or mental health of the pregnant woman or any existing children of her family; or

(b) that the termination is necessary to prevent grave permanent injury to the physical or mental health of the pregnant woman; or

(c) that the continuance of the pregnancy would involve risk to the life of the pregnant woman, greater than if the pregnancy were terminated; or

(d) that there is a substantial risk that if the child were born it would suffer from such physical or mental abnormalities as to be seriously handicapped.][1]

(2) In determining whether the continuance of a pregnancy would involve such risk of injury to health as is mentioned in paragraph (a) [or (b)][2] of subsection (1) of this section, account may be taken of the pregnant woman's actual or reasonably foreseeable environment.

(3) Except as provided by subsection (4) of this section, any treatment for the termination of pregnancy must be carried out in a hospital vested in [the Secretary of State for the purposes of his functions under the National Health Service Act 1977 or the National Health Service (Scotland) Act 1978 [or in a hospital vested in [a Primary Care Trust or][3] a National Health Service trust][4] or in a place approved for the purposes of this section by the Secretary of State][5].

[(3A) The power under subsection (3) of this section to approve a place includes power, in relation to treatment consisting primarily in the use of such medicines as may be specified in the approval and carried out in such manner as may be so specified, to approve a class of places.][6]

(4) Subsection (3) of this section, and so much of subsection (1) as relates to the opinion of two registered medical practitioners, shall not apply to the termination of a pregnancy by a registered medical practitioner in a case where he is of the opinion, formed in good faith, that the termination is immediately necessary to save the life or to prevent grave permanent injury to the physical or mental health of the pregnant woman.

---

[1] Substituted by Human Fertilisation and Embryology Act 1990 c.37 s 37 (1) (with savings in ss 39 (3) and 43 (2))

[2] Words inserted by Human Fertilisation and Embryology Act 1990 c.37 s 37 (2) (with savings in ss 39 (3) and 43 (2))

[3] Words inserted by SI 2000/90 Sch 1 para 6

[4] Words inserted by National Health Service and Community Care Act 1990 c.19 s 66 (1) Sch 9 para 8

[5] Words substituted by Health Services Act 1980 c.53 ss 1, 2, Sch 1 para 17 (1)

[6] Inserted by Human Fertilisation and Embryology Act 1990 c.37 s 37 (3) (with savings in ss 39 (3) and 43 (2))

Conscientious objection to participation in treatment

24-002 **4.**—(1) Subject to subsection (2) of this section, no person shall be under any duty, whether by contract or by any statutory or other legal requirement, to participate in any treatment authorised by this Act to which he has a conscientious objection:

Provided that in any legal proceedings the burden of proof of conscientious objection shall rest on the person claiming to rely on it.

(2) Nothing in subsection (1) of this section shall affect any duty to participate in treatment which is necessary to save the life or to prevent grave permanent injury to the physical or mental health of a pregnant woman.

(3) In any proceedings before a court in Scotland, a statement on oath by any person to the effect that he has a conscientious objection to participating in any treatment authorised by this Act shall be sufficient evidence for the purpose of discharging the burden of proof imposed upon him by subsection (1) of this section.

Supplementary provisions

24-003 **5.**—[(1) No offence under the Infant Life (Preservation) Act 1929 shall be committed by a registered medical practitioner who terminates a pregnancy in accordance with the provisions of this Act.][1]

(2) For the purposes of the law relating to abortion, anything done with intent to procure [a woman's miscarriage (or, in the case of a woman carrying more than one foetus, her miscarriage of any foetus) is unlawfully done unless authorised by section 1 of this Act and, in the case of a woman carrying more than one foetus, anything done with intent to procure her miscarriage of any foetus is authorised by that section if—][2]

[(a) the ground for termination of the pregnancy specified in subsection (1)(d) of that section applies in relation to any foetus and the thing is done for the purposes of procuring the miscarriage of that foetus, or

(b) any of the other grounds for termination of the pregnancy specified in that section applies.][3]

Interpretation

24-004 **6.** In this Act, the following expressions have meanings hereby assigned to them:—

"the law relating to abortion" means sections 58 and 59 of the Offences against the Person Act 1861, and any rule of law relating to the procurement of abortion;

[...][4]

[1] Substituted by Human Fertilisation and Embryology Act 1990 c.37 s 37 (4) (with savings in ss 39 (3) and 43 (2))

[2] Words inserted by Human Fertilisation and Embryology Act 1990 c.37 s 37 (2) (with savings in ss 39 (3) and 43 (2))

[3] Words inserted by Human Fertilisation and Embryology Act 1990 c.37 s 37 (2) (with savings in ss 39 (3) and 43 (2))

[4] Words inserted by Human Fertilisation and Embryology Act 1990 c.37 s 37 (2) (with savings in ss 39 (3) and 43 (2))

Criminal Appeal Act 1968

CHAPTER 19

PART I

APPEAL TO COURT OF APPEAL IN CRIMINAL CASES

Appeal against conviction on indictment

Right of appeal

1.—(1) [Subject to subsection (3) below][1] a person convicted of an offence on indictment may appeal to the Court of Appeal against his conviction. **25-001**

[[(2) An appeal under this section lies only—

(a) with the leave of the Court of Appeal; or

(b) if the judge of the court of trial grants a certificate that the case is fit for appeal.][2]

(3) Where a person is convicted before the Crown Court of a scheduled offence it shall not be open to him to appeal to the Court of Appeal against the conviction on the ground that the decision of the court which committed him for trial as to the value involved was mistaken.

(4) In subsection (3) above "scheduled offence" and "the value involved" have the same meanings as they have in section 22 of the Magistrates' Courts Act 1980 (certain offences against property to be tried summarily if value of property or damage is small).][3]

Grounds for allowing appeal under s. 1

2.—[(1) Subject to the provisions of this Act, the Court of Appeal— **25-002**

(a) shall allow an appeal against conviction if they think that the conviction is unsafe; and

(b) shall dismiss such an appeal in any other case.][4]

(2) In the case of an appeal against conviction the Court shall, if they allow the appeal, quash the conviction.

(3) An order of the Court of Appeal quashing a conviction shall, except when under section 7 below the appellant is ordered to be retried, operate as a direction to the court of trial to enter, instead of the record of conviction, a judgment and verdict of acquittal.

Power to substitute conviction of alternative offence

3.—(1) This section applies on an appeal against conviction, where the appellant has been convicted of an offence and the jury could on the indictment have found him guilty of some other offence, and on the finding of the jury it appears to the Court of Appeal that the jury must have been satisfied of facts which proved him guilty of the other offence. **25-003**

[1] Words inserted by Magistrates' Courts Act 1980 c.43 Sch 7 para 71 (a)
[2] Substituted by Criminal Appeal Act 1995 c.35 Pt I s 1 (1)
[3] Inserted by Magistrates' Courts Act 1980 c.43 Sch 7 para 71 (b)
[4] Substituted by Criminal Appeal Act 1995 c.35 Pt I s 2 (1)

(2) The Court may, instead of allowing or dismissing the appeal, substitute for the verdict found by the jury a verdict of guilty of the other offence, and pass such sentence in substitution for the sentence passed at the trial as may be authorised by law for the other offence, not being a sentence of greater severity.

Sentence when appeal allowed on part of an indictment

25-004 **4.**—(1) This section applies where, on an appeal against conviction on an indictment containing two or more counts, the Court of Appeal allow the appeal in respect of part of the indictment.

(2) Except as provided by subsection (3) below, the Court may in respect of any count on which the appellant remains convicted pass such sentence, in substitution for any sentence passed thereon at the trial, as they think proper and is authorised by law.for the offence of which he remains convicted on that count.

(3) The Court shall not under this section pass any sentence such that the appellant's sentence on the indictment as a whole will, in consequence of the appeal, be of greater severity than the sentence (taken as a whole) which was passed at the trial for all offences of which he was convicted on the indictment.

Disposal of appeal against conviction on special verdict

25-005 **5.**—(1) This section applies on an appeal against conviction [in a case where][1] the jury have found a special verdict.

(2) If the Court of Appeal consider that a wrong conclusion has been arrived at by the court of trial on the effect of the jury's verdict they may, instead of allowing the appeal, order such conclusion to be recorded as appears to them to be in law required by the verdict, and pass such sentence in substitution for the sentence passed at the trial as may be authorised by law.

[Substitution of finding of insanity or findings of unfitness to plead etc

25-006 **6.**—(1) This section applies where, on an appeal against conviction, the Court of Appeal, on the written or oral evidence of two or more registered medical practitioners at least one of whom is duly approved, are of opinion—

(a) that the proper verdict would have been one of not guilty by reason of insanity; or

(b) that the case is not one where there should have been a verdict of acquittal, but there should have been findings that the accused was under a disability and that he did the act or made the omission charged against him.

(2) Subject to subsection (3) below, the Court of Appeal shall either—

(a) make an order that the appellant be admitted, in accordance with the provisions of Schedule 1 to the Criminal Procedure (Insanity and Unfitness to Plead) Act 1991, to such hospital as may be specified by the Secretary of State; or

(b) where they have the power to do so by virtue of section 5 of that Act, make in respect of the appellant such one of the following orders as they think most suitable in all the circumstances of the case, namely—

(i) a guardianship order within the meaning of the Mental Health Act 1983;

(ii) a supervision and treatment order within the meaning of Schedule 2 to the said Act of 1991; and

(iii) an order for his absolute discharge.

[1] Words substituted by Criminal Appeal Act 1995 c.35 Sch 2 para 4 (2)

(3) Paragraph (b) of subsection (2) above shall not apply where the offence to which the appeal relates is an offence the sentence for which is fixed by law.][1]

Retrial

Power to order retrial

7.—(1) Where the Court of Appeal allow an appeal against conviction [...][2] and it appears to the Court that the interests of justice so require, they may order the appellant to be retried. **25-007**

(2) A person shall not under this section be ordered to be retried for any offence other than—

(a) the offence of which he was convicted at the original trial and in respect of which his appeal is allowed as mentioned in subsection (1) above;

(b) an offence of which he could have been convicted at the original trial on an indictment for the first-mentioned offence; or

(c) an offence charged in an alternative count of the indictment in respect of which the jury were discharged from giving a verdict in consequence of convicting him of the first-mentioned offence.

Supplementary provisions as to retrial

8.—(1) A person who is to be retried for an offence in pursuance of an order under section 7 of this Act shall be tried on a fresh indictment preferred by direction of the Court of Appeal, [...][3] but after the end of two months from the date of the order for his retrial he may not be arraigned on an indictment preferred in pursuance of such a direction unless the Court of Appeal give leave.[4] **25-008**

[(1A) Where a person has been ordered to be retried but may not be arraigned without leave, he may apply to the Court of Appeal to set aside the order for retrial and to direct the court of trial to enter a judgment and verdict of acquittal of the offence for which he was ordered to be retried.

(1B) On an application under subsection (1) or (1A) above the Court of Appeal shall have power—

(a) to grant leave to arraign; or

(b) to [set aside the order for retrial and][5] direct the entry of a judgment and verdict of acquittal, but shall not give leave to arraign unless they are satisfied—

(i) that the prosecution has acted with all due expedition; and

(ii) that there is a good and sufficient cause for a retrial in spite of the lapse of time since the order under section 7 of this Act was made.][6]

(2) The Court of Appeal may, on ordering a retrial, make such orders as appear to them to be necessary or expedient—

[1] Substituted by Criminal Procedure (Insanity and Unfitness to Plead) Act 1991 c.25 s 4 (1)
[2] Words repealed by Criminal Justice Act 1988 c.33 ss 43 (1) (5), 170 Sch 8 para 16, Sch 16
[3] Words repealed by Courts Act 1971 c.23 Sch 11 Pt IV
[4] Inserted by Criminal Justice Act 1988 c.33 s 43 (3) (5)
[5] Words added by Access to Justice Act 1999 c.22 Pt IV s 58 (2)
[6] Inserted by Criminal Justice Act 1988 c.33 s 43 (4) (5) Sch 8 para 16

(a) for the custody or [[, subject to section 25 of the Criminal Justice and Public Order Act 1994,][1] release on][2] bail of the person ordered to be retried pending his retrial; or

(b) for the retention pending the retrial of any property or money forfeited, restored or paid by virtue of the original conviction or any order made on that conviction.

(3) If the person ordered to be retried was, immediately before the determination of his appeal, liable to be detained in pursuance of an order or direction under Part V of the Mental Health Act 1959[or under Part III of the Mental Health Act 1983 (other than under section 35, 36 or 38 of that Act)][3],—

(a) that order or direction shall continue in force pending the retrial as if the appeal had not been allowed; and

(b) any order made by the Court of Appeal under this section for his custody or [release on][4] bail shall have effect subject to the said order or direction.

[(3A) If the person ordered to be retried was, immediately before the determination of his appeal, liable to be detained in pursuance of a remand under [section 36 of the Mental Health Act 1983][5] or an interim hospital order under [section 38 of that Act][6], the Court of Appeal may, if they think fit, order that he shall continue to be detained in a hospital or mental nursing home, and in that event [Part III of that Act][7] shall apply as if he had been ordered under this section to be kept in custody pending his retrial and were detained in pursuance of a transfer direction together with a restriction direction.][8]

(4) Schedule 2 to this Act has effect with respect to the procedure in the case of a person ordered to be retried, the sentence which may be passed if the retrial results in his conviction and the order for costs which may be made if he is acquitted.

Appeal in cases of insanity

Appeal against verdict of not guilty by reason of insanity

25-009 **12.** A person in whose case there is returned a verdict of not guilty by reason of insanity may appeal to the Court of Appeal [against the verdict—][9]

[(a) with the leave of the Court of Appeal; or

(b) if the judge of the court of trial grants a certificate that the case is fit for appeal.]

Disposal of appeal under s. 12

25-010 **13.**—[(1) Subject to the provisions of this section, the Court of Appeal—

(a) shall allow an appeal under section 12 of this Act if they think that the verdict is unsafe; and

(b) shall dismiss such an appeal in any other case.][10]

(3) Where apart from this subsection—

---

[1] Words inserted by Criminal Justice and Public Order Act 1994 c.33 Sch 10 para 19
[2] Words substituted by Bail Act 1976 c.63 Sch 2 para 38
[3] Words inserted by Mental Health Act 1983 c.20 Sch 4 para 23 (b)
[4] Words substituted by Bail Act 1976 c.63 Sch 2 para 38
[5] Words substituted by Mental Health Act 1983 c.20 Sch 4 para 23 (c)
[6] Words substituted by Mental Health Act 1983 c.20 Sch 4 para 23 (c)
[7] Words substituted by Mental Health Act 1983 c.20 Sch 4 para 23 (c)
[8] Inserted by Mental Health (Amendment) Act1982 c.51 Sch 3 para 36
[9] Words substituted by Criminal Appeal Act 1995 c.35 Pt I s 1 (3)
[10] Substituted by Criminal Appeal Act 1995 c.35 Pt I s 2 (3)

(a) an appeal under section 12 of this Act would fall to be allowed; and

(b) none of the grounds for allowing it relates to the question of the insanity of the accused,

the Court of Appeal may dismiss the appeal if they are of opinion that, but for the insanity of the accused, the proper verdict would have been that he was guilty of an offence other than the offence charged.

(4) Where an appeal under section 12 of this Act is allowed, the following provisions apply:—

(a) if the ground, or one of the grounds, for allowing the appeal is that the finding of the jury as to the insanity of the accused ought not to stand and the Court of Appeal are of opinion that the proper verdict would have been that he was guilty of an offence (whether the offence charged or any other offence of which the jury could have found him guilty), the Court—

(i) shall substitute for the verdict of not guilty by reason of insanity a verdict of guilty of that offence; and

(ii) shall, subject to subsection (5) below, have the like powers of punishing or otherwise dealing with the appellant, and other powers, as the court of trial would have had if the jury had come to the substituted verdict; and

(b) in any other case, the Court of Appeal shall substitute for the verdict of the jury a verdict of acquittal.

(5) The Court of Appeal shall not by virtue of subsection (4)(a) above sentence any person to death; but where under that paragraph they substitute a verdict of guilty of an offence for which apart from this subsection they would be required to sentence the appellant to death, their sentence shall (whatever the circumstances) be one of imprisonment for life.

(6) An order of the Court of Appeal allowing an appeal in accordance with this section shall operate as a direction to the court of trial to amend the record to conform with the order.

[Substitution of findings of unfitness to plead etc

14.—(1) This section applies where, on an appeal under section 12 of this Act, the Court of Appeal, on the written or oral evidence of two or more registered medical practitioners at least one of whom is duly approved, are of opinion that— **25-011**

(a) the case is not one where there should have been a verdict of acquittal; but

(b) there should have been findings that t[the accused was under a disability and][1] that he did the act or made the omission charged against him.

(2) Subject to subsection (3) below, the Court of Appeal shall either—

(a) make an order that the appellant be admitted, in accordance with the provisions of Schedule 1 to the Criminal Procedure (Insanity and Unfitness to Plead) Act 1991, to such hospital as may be specified by the Secretary of State; or

(b) where they have the power to do so by virtue of section 5 of that Act, make in respect of the appellant such one of the following orders as they think most suitable in all the circumstances of the case, namely—

(i) a guardianship order within the meaning of the Mental Health Act 1983;

[1] Words substituted by Criminal Cases Review (Insanity) Act 1999 c.25 s 2 (2) (b)

(ii) a supervision and treatment order within the meaning of Schedule 2 to the said Act of 1991; and

(iii) an order for his absolute discharge.

(3) Paragraph (b) of subsection (2) above shall not apply where the offence to which the appeal relates is an offence the sentence for which is fixed by law.][1]

[Substitution of verdict of acquittal

25-012 **14A.**—(1) This section applies where, in accordance with section 13(4)(b) of this Act, the Court of Appeal substitute a verdict of acquittal and the Court, on the written or oral evidence of two or more registered medical practitioners at least one of whom is duly approved, are of opinion—

(a) that the appellant is suffering from mental disorder of a nature or degree which warrants his detention in a hospital for assessment (or for assessment followed by medical treatment) for at least a limited period; and

(b) that he ought to be so detained in the interests of his own health or safety or with a view to the protection of other persons.

(2) The Court of Appeal shall make an order that the appellant be admitted for assessment, in accordance with the provisions of Schedule 1 to the Criminal Procedure (Insanity and Unfitness to Plead) Act 1991, to such hospital as may be specified by the Secretary of State.][2]

Unfitness to stand trial

Right of appeal against finding of disability

25-013 **15.**—(1) Where there has been a determination under section 4 of the Criminal Procedure (Insanity) Act 1964 of the question of a person's fitness to be tried, and the jury has returned [findings that he is under a disability and that he did the act or made the omission charged against him, the person may appeal to the Court of Appeal against either or both of those findings][3].

[(2) An appeal under this section lies only—

(a) with the leave of the Court of Appeal; or

(b) if the judge of the court of trial grants a certificate that the case is fit for appeal.][4]

Disposal of appeal under s. 15

25-014 **16.**—[(1) The Court of Appeal—

(a) shall allow an appeal under section 15 of this Act against a finding if they think that the finding is unsafe; and

(b) shall dismiss such an appeal in any other case.][5]

[(3) Where the Court of Appeal allow an appeal under section 15 of this Act against a finding that the appellant is under a disability—

(a) the appellant may be tried accordingly for the offence with which he was charged; and

[1] Substituted by Criminal Procedure (Insanity and Unfitness to Plead) Act 1991 c.25 s 4 (2)

[2] Substituted by Criminal Procedure (Insanity and Unfitness to Plead) Act 1991 c.25 s 4 (2)

[3] Words substituted by Criminal Procedure (Insanity and Unfitness to Plead) Act 1991 c.25 Sch 3 para 2

[4] Substituted by Criminal Appeal Act 1995 c.35 Pt I s 1 (5)

[5] Substituted by Criminal Appeal Act 1995 c.35 Pt I s 2 (5)

(b) the Court may [, subject to section 25 of the Criminal Justice and Public Order Act 1994][1] make such orders as appear to them necessary or expedient pending any such trial for his custody, release on bail or continued detention under the Mental Health Act 1983;

and Schedule 3 to this Act has effect for applying provisions in Part III of that Act to persons in whose case an order is made by the Court under this subsection.

(4) Where, otherwise than in a case falling within subsection (3) above, the Court of Appeal allow an appeal under section 15 of this Act against a finding that the appellant did the act or made the omission charged against him, the Court shall, in addition to quashing the finding, direct a verdict of acquittal to be recorded (but not a verdict of not guilty by reason of insanity).][2]

The hearing

[Power to order investigations

23A.—(1) On an appeal against conviction the Court of Appeal may direct the Criminal Cases Review Commission to investigate and report to the Court on any matter if it appears to the Court that— **25-015**

(a) the matter is relevant to the determination of the case and ought, if possible, to be resolved before the case is determined;
(b) an investigation of the matter by the Commission is likely to result in the Court being able to resolve it; and
(c) the matter cannot be resolved by the Court without an investigation by the Commission.

(2) A direction by the Court of Appeal under subsection (1) above shall be given in writing and shall specify the matter to be investigated.

(3) Copies of such a direction shall be made available to the appellant and the respondent.

(4) Where the Commission have reported to the Court of Appeal on any matter which they have been directed under subsection (1) above to investigate, the Court—

(a) shall notify the appellant and the respondent that the Commission have reported; and
(b) may make available to the appellant and the respondent the report of the Commission and any statements, opinions and reports which accompanied it.][3]

[1] Words inserted by Criminal Justice and Public Order Act 1994 c.33 Sch 10 para 21
[2] Substituted by Criminal Procedure (Insanity and Unfitness to Plead) Act 1991 c.25 Sch 3 para 3 (3)
[3] Added by Criminal Appeal Act 1995 c.35 Pt I s 5 (1)

Firearms Act 1968

CHAPTER 27

Prevention of crime and preservation of public safety

Possession of firearm with intent to injure

26-001 **16.** It is an offence for a person to have in his possession any firearm or ammunition with intent by means thereof to endanger life or cause serious injury to property, or to enable another person by means thereof to endanger life or cause serious injury to property, whether any injury to person or property has been caused or not.

[Possession of firearm with intent to cause fear of violence

26-002 **16A.** It is an offence for a person to have in his possession any firearm or imitation firearm with intent—

(a) by means thereof to cause, or

(b) to enable another person by means thereof to cause,

any person to believe that unlawful violence will be used against him or another person.][1]

Use of firearm to resist arrest

26-003 **17.**—(1) It is an offence for a person to make or attempt to make any use whatsoever of a firearm or imitation firearm with intent to resist or prevent the lawful arrest or detention of himself or another person.

(2) If a person, at the time of his committing or being arrested for an offence specified in Schedule 1 to this Act, has in his possession a firearm or imitation firearm, he shall be guilty of an offence under this subsection unless he shows that he had it in his possession for a lawful object.

(4) For purposes of this section, the definition of "firearm" in section 57(1) of this Act shall apply without paragraphs (b) and (c) of that subsection, and "imitation firearm" shall be construed accordingly.

Carrying firearm with criminal intent

26-004 **18.**—(1) It is an offence for a person to have with him a firearm or imitation firearm with intent to commit an indictable offence, or to resist arrest or prevent the arrest of another, in either case while he has the firearm or imitation firearm with him.

(2) In proceedings for an offence under this section proof that the accused had a firearm or imitation firearm with him and intended to commit an offence, or to resist or prevent arrest, is evidence that he intended to have it with him while doing so.

Carrying firearm in a public place

26-005 **19.** A person commits an offence if, without lawful authority or reasonable excuse (the proof whereof lies on him) he has with him in a public place a loaded shot gun or loaded air weapon, or any other firearm (whether loaded or not) together with ammunition suitable for use in that firearm.

---

[1] Added by Firearms (Amendment) Act 1994 c.31 s 1 (1)

Trespassing with firearm

20.—(1) A person commits an offence if, while he has a firearm [or imitation firearm][1] with him, he enters or is in any building or part of a building as a trespasser and without reasonable excuse (the proof whereof lies on him). **26-006**

(2) A person commits an offence if, while he has a firearm [or imitation firearm][2] with him, he enters or is on any land as a trespasser and without reasonable excuse (the proof whereof lies on him).

(3) In subsection (2) of this section the expression "land" includes land covered with water.

Possession of firearms by persons previously convicted of crime

21.—(1) A person who has been sentenced to custody for life or to imprisonment for a term of three years or more, or to youth custody or detention in a young offender institution for such a term, shall not at any time have a firearm or ammunition in his possession. **26-007**

(2) A person who has been sentenced [...][3] to imprisonment for a term of three months or more but less than three years or to youth custody or detention in a young offender institution [for such a term][4], or who has been sentenced to be detained for such a term in a detention centre or in a young offenders institution in Scotland [or who has been subject to a secure training order][5] [or a detention and training order][6], shall not at any time before the expiration of the period of five years from the date of his release have a firearm or ammunition in his possession.

[(2A) For the purposes of subsection (2) above, "the date of his release" means—

(a) in the case of a person sentenced to imprisonment with an order under section 47(1) of the Criminal Law Act 1977 (prison sentence partly served and partly suspended), the date on which he completes service of so much of the sentence as was by that order required to be served in prison;

(b) in the case of a person who has been subject to a secure training order—

(i) the date on which he is released from detention under the order;

(ii) the date on which he is released from detention ordered under section 4 of the Criminal Justice and Public Order Act 1994; or

(iii) the date halfway through the total period specified by the court in making the order,

whichever is the later.

[(c) in the case of a person who has been subject to a detention and training order—

(i) the date on which he is released from detention under the order;

(ii) the date on which he is released from detention ordered under [section 104 of the Powers of Criminal Courts (Sentencing) Act 2000][7]; or

[1] Words added by Firearms (Amendment) Act 1994 c.31 s 2 (1)
[2] Words added by Firearms (Amendment) Act 1994 c.31 s 2 (1)
[3] Words repealed by CriminalJustice Act 1988 c.33 ss 123 (6), 170 (2) Sch 8 para 16, Sch 16
[4] Words inserted by Criminal Justice Act 1982 c.48 s 77 Sch 14 para 24 (b)
[5] Words inserted by Criminal Justice and Public Order Act 1994 c.33 Sch 10 para 24 (2) (a)
[6] Words inserted by Crime and Disorder Act 1998 c.37 Sch 8 para 14 (1)
[7] Words substituted by Powers of Criminal Courts (Sentencing) Act 2000 c.6 Sch 9 para 31

(iii) the date of the half-way point of the term of the order, whichever is the later.][1]][2]

(3) A person who—

(a) is the holder of a licence issued under section 53 of the Children and Young Persons Act 1933 (which section provides for the detention of children and young persons convicted of serious crime, but enables them to be discharged on licence by the Secretary of State); or

(b) is subject to a recognizance to keep the peace or to be of good behaviour, a condition of which is that he shall not possess, use or carry a firearm, or is subject to a probation order containing a requirement that he shall not possess, use or carry a firearm; or

(c) has, in Scotland, been ordained to find caution a condition of which is that he shall not possess, use or carry a firearm;

shall not, at any time during which he holds the licence or is so subject or has been so ordained, have a firearm or ammunition in his possession.

[(3A) Where by section 19 of the Firearms Act (Northern Ireland) 1969, or by any other enactment for the time being in force in Northern Ireland and corresponding to this section, a person is prohibited in Northern Ireland from having a firearm or ammunition in his possession, he shall also be so prohibited in Great Britain at any time when to have it in his possession in Northern Ireland would be a contravention of the said section 19 or corresponding enactment;][3]

(4) It is an offence for a person to contravene any of the foregoing provisions of this section.

(5) It is an offence for a person to sell or transfer a firearm or ammunition to, or to repair, test or prove a firearm or ammunition for, a person whom he knows or has reasonable ground for believing to be prohibited by this section from having a firearm or ammunition in his possession.

(6) A person prohibited under subsection (1), (2) [(3) or (3A)][4] of this section from having in his possession a firearm or ammunition may apply to [the Crown Court][5] or, in Scotland, in accordance with Act of Sederunt to the sheriff for a removal of the prohibition; and if the application is granted that prohibition shall not then apply to him.

(7) Schedule 3 to this Act shall have effect with respect to the courts with jurisdiction to entertain an application under this section and to the procedure appertaining thereto.

Acquisition and possession of firearms by minors

26-008 **22.**—(1) It is an offence for a person under the age of seventeen to purchase or hire any firearm or ammunition.

[(1A) Where a person under the age of eighteen is entitled, as the holder of a certificate under this Act, to have a firearm in his possession, it is an offence for that person to use that firearm for a purpose not authorised by the European weapons directive.][6]

(2) It is an offence for a person under the age of fourteen to have in his possession any firearm or ammunition to which section 1 of this Act applies, except in circumstances where under section 11(1), (3) or (4) of this Act or section

[1] Added by Crime and Disorder Act 1998 c.37 Sch 8 para 14 (2)
[2] Substituted by Criminal Justice and Public Order Act 1994 c.33 Sch 10 para 24 (2) (b)
[3] Inserted by Criminal Justice Act 1972 c.71 ss 29, 66 (7) (a)
[4] Words substituted by Criminal Justice Act 1972 c.71 ss 29, 66 (7) (a)
[5] Words substituted by Courts Act 1971 c.23 s 56 (2) Sch 9 Pt II
[6] Added by SI 1992/2823 Reg 4 (1)

15 of the Firearms (Amendment) Act 1988 he is entitled to have possession of it without holding a firearm certificate.

(3) It is an offence for a person under the age of fifteen to have with him an assembled shot gun except while under the supervision of a person of or over the age of twenty-one, or while the shot gun is so covered with a securely fastened gun cover that it cannot be fired.

(4) Subject to section 23 below, it is an offence for a person under the age of fourteen to have with him an air weapon or ammunition for an air weapon.

(5) Subject to section 23 below, it is an offence for a person under the age of seventeen to have an air weapon with him in a public place, except an air gun or air rifle which is so covered with a securely fastened gun cover that it cannot be fired.

Exceptions from s. 22(4) and (5)

23.—(1) It is not an offence under section 22(4) of this Act for a person to **26-009** have with him an air weapon or ammunition while he is under the supervision of a person of or over the age of twenty-one; but where a person has with him an air weapon on any premises in circumstances where he would be prohibited from having it with him but for this subsection, it is an offence—

(a) for him to use it for firing any missile beyond those premises; or

(b) for the person under whose supervision he is to allow him so to use it.

(2) It is not an offence under section 22(4) or (5) of this Act for a person to have with him an air weapon or ammunition at a time when—

(a) being a member of a rifle club or miniature rifle club for the time being approved by the Secretary of State for the purposes of this section or [section 15 of the Firearms (Amendment) Act 1988][1], he is engaged as such a member [...][2]in connection with [target shooting][3]; or

(b) he is using the weapon or ammunition at a shooting gallery where the only firearms used are either air weapons or miniature rifles not exceeding .23 inch calibre.

Supplying firearms to minors

24.—(1) It is an offence to sell or let on hire any firearm or ammunition to a **26-010** person under the age of seventeen.

(2) It is an offence—

(a) to make a gift of or lend any firearm or ammunition to which section 1 of this Act applies to a person under the age of fourteen; or

(b) to part with the possession of any such firearm or ammunition to a person under that age, except in circumstances where that person is entitled under section 11(1), (3) or (4) of this Act [or section 15 of the Firearms (Amendment) Act 1988][4] to have possession thereof without holding a firearm certificate.

(3) It is an offence to make a gift of a shot gun or ammunition for a shot gun to a person under the age of fifteen.

(4) It is an offence—

(a) to make a gift of an air weapon or ammunition for an air weapon to a person under the age of fourteen; or

[1] Words substituted by Firearms (Amendment) Act 1988 c.45 s 23 (4)
[2] Words repealed by Firearms (Amendment) Act 1997 c.5 Sch 3 para 1
[3] Words substituted by Firearms (Amendment) Act 1997 c.5 Sch 2 para 3
[4] Words inserted by Firearms (Amendment) Act 1988 c.45 s 23 (4)

(b) to part with the possession of an air weapon or ammunition for an air weapon to a person under that age except where by virtue of section 23 of this Act the person is not prohibited from having it with him.

(5) In proceedings for an offence under any provision of this section it is a defence to prove that the person charged with the offence believed the other person to be of or over the age mentioned in that provision and had reasonable ground for the belief.

Supplying firearm to person drunk or insane

26-011 **25.** It is an offence for a person to sell or transfer any firearm or ammunition to, or to repair, prove or test any firearm or ammunition for, another person whom he knows or has reasonable cause for believing to be drunk or of unsound mind.

Theft Act 1968

CHAPTER 60

Definition of "theft"

Basic definition of theft

27-001 **1.**—(1) A person is guilty of theft if he dishonestly appropriates property belonging to another with the intention of permanently depriving the other of it; and "thief" and "steal" shall be construed accordingly.

(2) It is immaterial whether the appropriation is made with a view to gain, or is made for the thief's own benefit.

(3) The five following sections of this Act shall have effect as regards the interpretation and operation of this section (and, except as otherwise provided by this Act, shall apply only for purposes of this section).

"Dishonestly"

27-002 **2.**—(1) A person's appropriation of property belonging to another is not to be regarded as dishonest—

(a) if he appropriates the property in the belief that he has in law the right to deprive the other of it, on behalf of himself or of a third person; or

(b) if he appropriates the property in the belief that he would have the other's consent if the other knew of the appropriation and the circumstances of it; or

(c) (except where the property came to him as trustee or personal representative) if he appropriates the property in the belief that the person to whom the property belongs cannot be discovered by taking reasonable steps.

(2) A person's appropriation of property belonging to another may be dishonest notwithstanding that he is willing to pay for the property.

"Appropriates"

27-003 **3.**—(1) Any assumption by a person of the rights of an owner amounts to an appropriation, and this includes, where he has come by the property (innocently or not) without stealing it, any later assumption of a right to it by keeping or dealing with it as owner.

(2) Where property or a right or interest in property is or purports to be transferred for value to a person acting in good faith, no later assumption by him of rights which he believed himself to be acquiring shall, by reason of any defect in the transferor's title, amount to theft of the property.

"Property"

4.—(1) "Property" includes money and all other property, real or personal, including things in action and other intangible property. **27-004**

(2) A person cannot steal land, or things forming part of land and severed from it by him or by his directions, except in the following cases, that is to say—

(a) when he is a trustee or personal representative, or is authorised by power of attorney, or as liquidator of a company, or otherwise, to sell or dispose of land belonging to another, and he appropriates the land or anything forming part of it by dealing with it in breach of the confidence reposed in him; or

(b) when he is not in possession of the land and appropriates anything forming part of the land by severing it or causing it to be severed, or after it has been severed; or

(c) when, being in possession of the land under a tenancy, he appropriates the whole or part of any fixture or structure let to be used with the land.

For purposes of this subsection "land" does not include incorporeal hereditaments; "tenancy" means a tenancy for years or any less period and includes an agreement for such a tenancy, but a person who after the end of a tenancy remains in possession as statutory tenant or otherwise is to be treated as having possession under the tenancy, and "let" shall be construed accordingly.

(3) A person who picks mushrooms growing wild on any land, or who picks flowers, fruit or foliage from a plant growing wild on any land, does not (although not in possession of the land) steal what he picks, unless he does it for reward or for sale or other commercial purpose.

For purposes of this subsection "mushroom" includes any fungus, and "plant" includes any shrub or tree.

(4) Wild creatures, tamed or untamed, shall be regarded as property; but a person cannot steal a wild creature not tamed nor ordinarily kept in captivity, or the carcase of any such creature, unless either it has been reduced into possession by or on behalf of another person and possession of it has not since been lost or abandoned, or another person is in course of reducing it into possession.

"Belonging to another"

5.—(1) Property shall be regarded as belonging to any person having possession or control of it, or having in it any proprietary right or interest (not being an equitable interest arising only from an agreement to transfer or grant an interest). **27-005**

(2) Where property is subject to a trust, the persons to whom it belongs shall be regarded as including any person having a right to enforce the trust, and an intention to defeat the trust shall be regarded accordingly as an intention to deprive of the property any person having that right.

(3) Where a person receives property from or on account of another, and is under an obligation to the other to retain and deal with that property or its

proceeds in a particular way, the property or proceeds shall be regarded (as against him) as belonging to the other.

(4) Where a person gets property by another's mistake, and is under an obligation to make restoration (in whole or in part) of the property or its proceeds or of the value thereof, then to the extent of that obligation the property or proceeds shall be regarded (as against him) as belonging to the person entitled to restoration, and an intention not to make restoration shall be regarded accordingly as an intention to deprive that person of the property or proceeds.

(5) Property of a corporation sole shall be regarded as belonging to the corporation notwithstanding a vacancy in the corporation.

"With the intention of permanently depriving the other of it"

27-006 **6.**—(1) A person appropriating property belonging to another without meaning the other permanently to lose the thing itself is nevertheless to be regarded as having the intention of permanently depriving the other of it if his intention is to treat the thing as his own to dispose of regardless of the other's rights; and a borrowing or lending of it may amount to so treating it if, but only if, the borrowing or lending is for a period and in circumstances making it equivalent to an outright taking or disposal.

(2) Without prejudice to the generality of subsection (1) above, where a person, having possession or control (lawfully or not) of property belonging to another, parts with the property under a condition as to its return which he may not be able to perform, this (if done for purposes of his own and without the other's authority) amounts to treating the property as his own to dispose of regardless of the other's rights.

Theft, robbery, burglary, etc

Theft

27-007 **7.** A person guilty of theft shall on conviction on indictment be liable to imprisonment for a term not exceeding [seven years][1].

Robbery

27-008 **8.**—(1) A person is guilty of robbery if he steals, and immediately before or at the time of doing so, and in order to do so, he uses force on any person or puts or seeks to put any person in fear of being then and there subjected to force.

(2) A person guilty of robbery, or of an assault with intent to rob, shall on conviction on indictment be liable to imprisonment for life.

Burglary

27-009 **9.**—(1) A person is guilty of burglary if—

(a) he enters any building or part of a building as a trespasser and with intent to commit any such offence as is mentioned in subsection (2) below; or

(b) having entered any building or part of a building as a trespasser he steals or attempts to steal anything in the building or that part of it or inflicts or attempts to inflict on any person therein any grievous bodily harm.

(2) The offences referred to in subsection (1)(a) above are offences of stealing anything in the building or part of a building in question, of inflicting on any

[1] Words substituted by Criminal Justice Act 1991 c.53 Pt I s 26 (1)

person therein any grievous bodily harm or [raping any person][1] therein, and of doing unlawful damage to the building or anything therein.

[(3) A person guilty of burglary shall on conviction on indictment be liable to imprisonment for a term not exceeding—

(a) where the offence was committed in respect of a building or part of a building which is a dwelling, fourteen years;

(b) in any other case, ten years.

(4) References in subsections (1) and (2) above to a building, and the reference in subsection (3) above to a building which is a dwelling, shall apply also to an inhabited vehicle or vessel, and shall apply to any such vehicle or vessel at times when the person having a habitation in it is not there as well as at times when he is.][2]

Aggravated burglary

10.—(1) A person is guilty of aggravated burglary if he commits any burglary and at the time has with him any firearm or imitation firearm, any weapon of offence, or any explosive; and for this purpose— **27-010**

(a) "firearm" includes an airgun or air pistol, and "imitation firearm" means anything which has the appearance of being a firearm, whether capable of being discharged or not; and

(b) "weapon of offence" means any article made or adapted for use for causing injury to or incapacitating a person, or intended by the person having it with him for such use; and

(c) "explosive" means any article manufactured for the purpose of producing a practical effect by explosion, or intended by the person having it with him for that purpose.

(2) A person guilty of aggravated burglary shall on conviction on indictment be liable to imprisonment for life.

Removal of articles from places open to the public

11.—(1) Subject to subsections (2) and (3) below, where the public have access to a building in order to view the building or part of it, or a collection or part of a collection housed in it, any person who without lawful authority removes from the building or its grounds the whole or part of any article displayed or kept for display to the public in the building or that part of it or in its grounds shall be guilty of an offence. **27-011**

For this purpose "collection" includes a collection got together for a temporary purpose, but references in this section to a collection do not apply to a collection made or exhibited for the purpose of effecting sales or other commercial dealings.

(2) It is immaterial for purposes of subsection (1) above, that the public's access to a building is limited to a particular period or particular occasion; but where anything removed from a building or its grounds is there otherwise than as forming part of, or being on loan for exhibition with, a collection intended for permanent exhibition to the public, the person removing it does not thereby commit an offence under this section unless he removes it on a day when the public have access to the building as mentioned in subsection (1) above.

(3) A person does not commit an offence under this section if he believes that he has lawful authority for the removal of the thing in question or that he

[1] Words substituted by Criminal Justice and Public Order Act 1994 c.33 Sch 10 para 26
[2] Substituted by Criminal Justice Act 1991 c.53 Pt I s 26 (2)

would have it if the person entitled to give it knew of the removal and the circumstances of it.

(4) A person guilty of an offence under this section shall, on conviction on indictment, be liable to imprisonment for a term not exceeding five years.

Taking motor vehicle or other conveyance without authority

27-012 **12.**—(1) Subject to subsections (5) and (6) below, a person shall be guilty of an offence if, without having the consent of the owner or other lawful authority, he takes any conveyance for his own or another's use or, knowing that any conveyance has been taken without such authority, drives it or allows himself to be carried in or on it.

(2) A person guilty of an offence under subsection (1) above shall [be liable on summary conviction to a fine not exceeding level 5 on the standard scale, to imprisonment for a term not exceeding six months, or to both.][1].

(4) If on the trial of an indictment for theft the jury are not satisfied that the accused committed theft, but it is proved that the accused committed an offence under subsection (1) above, the jury may find him guilty of the offence under subsection (1) [and if he is found guilty of it, he shall be liable as he would have been liable under subsection (2) above on summary conviction.][2]

[(4A) Proceedings for an offence under subsection (1) above (but not proceedings of a kind falling within subsection (4) above) in relation to a mechanically propelled vehicle–

(a) shall not be commenced after the end of the period of three years beginning with the day on which the offence was committed; but

(b) subject to that, may be commenced at any time within the period of six months beginning with the relevant day.

(4B) In subsection (4A)(b) above "the relevant day" means–

(a) in the case of a prosecution for an offence under subsection (1) above by a public prosecutor, the day on which sufficient evidence to justify the proceedings came to the knowledge of any person responsible for deciding whether to commence any such prosecution;

(b) in the case of a prosecution for an offence under subsection (1) above which is commenced by a person other than a public prosecutor after the discontinuance of a prosecution falling within paragraph (a) above which relates to the same facts, the day on which sufficient evidence to justify the proceedings came to the knowledge of the person who has decided to commence the prosecution or (if later) the discontinuance of the other prosecution;

(c) in the case of any other prosecution for an offence under subsection (1) above, the day on which sufficient evidence to justify the proceedings came to the knowledge of the person who has decided to commence the prosecution.

(4C) For the purposes of subsection (4A)(b) above a certificate of a person responsible for deciding whether to commence a prosecution of a kind mentioned in subsection (4B)(a) above as to the date on which such evidence as is mentioned in the certificate came to the knowledge of any person responsible for deciding whether to commence any such prosecution shall be conclusive evidence of that fact.][3]

---

[1] Words substituted by Criminal Justice Act 1988 c.33 s 37 (1) (a) Sch 8 para 16
[2] Words inserted by Criminal Justice Act 1988 c.33 s 37 (1) (6) Sch 8 para 16
[3] Added by Vehicles (Crime) Act 2001 c.3 Pt 3 s 37 (1)

(5) Subsection (1) above shall not apply in relation to pedal cycles; but, subject to subsection (6) below, a person who, without having the consent of the owner or other lawful authority, takes a pedal cycle for his own or another's use, or rides a pedal cycle knowing it to have been taken without such authority, shall on summary conviction be liable to a fine not exceeding [level 3 on the standard scale][1]

(6) A person does not commit an offence under this section by anything done in the belief that he has lawful authority to do it or that he would have the owner's consent if the owner knew of his doing it and the circumstances of it.

(7) For purposes of this section—

(a) "conveyance" means any conveyance constructed or adapted for the carriage of a person or persons whether by land, water or air, except that it does not include a conveyance constructed or adapted for use only under the control of a person not carried in or on it, and "drive" shall be construed accordingly; and

(b) "owner", in relation to a conveyance which is the subject of a hiring agreement or hire-purchase agreement, means the person in possession of the conveyance under that agreement.

[Aggravated vehicle-taking

12A.—(1) Subject to subsection (3) below, a person is guilty of aggravated taking of a vehicle if— **27-013**

(a) he commits an offence under section 12(1) above (in this section referred to as a "basic offence") in relation to a mechanically propelled vehicle; and

(b) it is proved that, at any time after the vehicle was unlawfully taken (whether by him or another) and before it was recovered, the vehicle was driven, or injury or damage was caused, in one or more of the circumstances set out in paragraphs (a) to (d) of subsection (2) below.

(2) The circumstances referred to in subsection (1)(b) above are—

(a) that the vehicle was driven dangerously on a road or other public place;

(b) that, owing to the driving of the vehicle, an accident occurred by which injury was caused to any person;

(c) that, owing to the driving of the vehicle, an accident occurred by which damage was caused to any property, other than the vehicle;

(d) that damage was caused to the vehicle.

(3) A person is not guilty of an offence under this section if he proves that, as regards any such proven driving, injury or damage as is referred to in subsection (1)(b) above, either—

(a) the driving, accident or damage referred to in subsection (2) above occurred before he committed the basic offence; or

(b) he was neither in nor on nor in the immediate vicinity of the vehicle when that driving, accident or damage occurred.

(4) A person guilty of an offence under this section shall be liable on conviction on indictment to imprisonment for a term not exceeding two years or, if it is proved that, in circumstances falling within subsection (2)(b) above, the accident caused the death of the person concerned, five years.

(5) If a person who is charged with an offence under this section is found not guilty of that offence but it is proved that he committed a basic offence, he may be convicted of the basic offence.

[1] Words substituted by virtue of Criminal Justice Act 1982 c.48 ss 38, 46

(6) If by virtue of subsection (5) above a person is convicted of a basic offence before the Crown Court, that court shall have the same powers and duties as a magistrates' court would have had on convicting him of such an offence.

(7) For the purposes of this section a vehicle is driven dangerously if—

(a) it is driven in a way which falls far below what would be expected of a competent and careful driver; and

(b) it would be obvious to a competent and careful driver that driving the vehicle in that way would be dangerous.

(8) For the purposes of this section a vehicle is recovered when it is restored to its owner or to other lawful possession or custody; and in this subsection "owner" has the same meaning as in section 12 above.][1]

Abstracting of electricity

27-014 **13.** A person who dishonestly uses without due authority, or dishonestly causes to be wasted or diverted, any electricity shall on conviction on indictment be liable to imprisonment for a term not exceeding five years.

Extension to thefts from mails outside England and Wales, and robbery etc. on such a theft

27-015 **14.**—(1) Where a person—

(a) steals or attempts to steal any mail bag or postal packet in the course of transmission as such between places in different jurisdictions in the British postal area, or any of the contents of such a mail bag or postal packet; or

(b) in stealing or with intent to steal any such mail bag or postal packet or any of its contents, commits any robbery, attempted robbery or assault with intent to rob;

then, notwithstanding that he does so outside England and Wales, he shall be guilty of committing or attempting to commit the offence against this Act as if he had done so in England or Wales, and he shall accordingly be liable to be prosecuted, tried and punished in England and Wales without proof that the offence was committed there.

(2) In subsection (1) above the reference to different jurisdictions in the British postal area is to be construed as referring to the several jurisdictions of England and Wales, of Scotland, of Northern Ireland, of the Isle of Man and of the Channel Islands.

(3) For purposes of this section "mail bag" includes any article serving the purpose of a mail bag.

Fraud and blackmail

Obtaining property by deception

27-016 **15.**—(1) A person who by any deception dishonestly obtains property belonging to another, with the intention of permanently depriving the other of it, shall on conviction on indictment be liable to imprisonment for a term not exceeding ten years.

(2) For purposes of this section a person is to be treated as obtaining property if he obtains ownership, possession or control of it, and "obtain" includes obtaining for another or enabling another to obtain or to retain.

[1] Added by Aggravated Vehicle-Taking Act 1992 c.11 s 1 (1)

(3) Section 6 above shall apply for purposes of this section, with the necessary adaptation of the reference to appropriating, as it applies for purposes of section 1.

(4) For purposes of this section "deception" means any deception (whether deliberate or reckless) by words or conduct as to fact or as to law, including a deception as to the present intentions of the person using the deception or any other person.

[Obtaining a money transfer by deception

15A.—(1) A person is guilty of an offence if by any deception he dishonestly obtains a money transfer for himself or another. **27-017**

(2) A money transfer occurs when—

(a) a debit is made to one account,

(b) a credit is made to another, and

(c) the credit results from the debit or the debit results from the credit.

(3) References to a credit and to a debit are to a credit of an amount of money and to a debit of an amount of money.

(4) It is immaterial (in particular)—

(a) whether the amount credited is the same as the amount debited;

(b) whether the money transfer is effected on presentment of a cheque or by another method;

(c) whether any delay occurs in the process by which the money transfer is effected;

(d) whether any intermediate credits or debits are made in the course of the money transfer;

(e) whether either of the accounts is overdrawn before or after the money transfer is effected.

(5) A person guilty of an offence under this section shall be liable on conviction on indictment to imprisonment for a term not exceeding ten years.][1]

[Section 15A: supplementary

15B.—(1) The following provisions have effect for the interpretation of section 15A of this Act. **27-018**

(2) "Deception" has the same meaning as in section 15 of this Act.

(3) "Account" means an account kept with—

(a) a bank; or

(b) a person carrying on a business which falls within subsection (4) below.

(4) A business falls within this subsection if—

(a) in the course of the business money received by way of deposit is lent to others; or

(b) any other activity of the business is financed, wholly or to any material extent, out of the capital of or the interest on money received by way of deposit;[...][2]

[(4A) References in subsection (4) to a deposit must be read with—

(a) section 22 of the Financial Services and Markets Act 2000;

(b) any relevant order under that section; and

(c) Schedule 2 to that Act,

[1] Added by Theft (Amendment) Act 1996 c.62 s 1 (1)

[2] Words repealed by SI 2001/3649 Pt 8 art 278 (2)

but any restriction on the meaning of deposit which arises from the identity of the person making it is to be disregarded.][1]

(5) For the purposes of subsection (4) above—

(a) all the activities which a person carries on by way of business shall be regarded as a single business carried on by him; and

(b) "money" includes money expressed in a currency other than sterling or in the European currency unit (as defined in Council Regulation No. 3320/94/EC or any Community instrument replacing it).][2]

Obtaining pecuniary advantage by deception

27-019 **16.**—(1) A person who by any deception dishonestly obtains for himself or another any pecuniary advantage shall on conviction on indictment be liable to imprisonment for a term not exceeding five years.

(2) The cases in which a pecuniary advantage within the meaning of this section is to be regarded as obtained for a person are cases where—

(b) he is allowed to borrow by way of overdraft, or to take out any policy of insurance or annuity contract, or obtains an improvement of the terms on which he is allowed to do so; or

(c) he is given the opportunity to earn remuneration or greater remuneration in an office or employment, or to win money by betting.

(3) For purposes of this section "deception" has the same meaning as in section 15 of this Act.

False accounting

27-020 **17.**—(1) Where a person dishonestly, with a view to gain for himself or another or with intent to cause loss to another,—

(a) destroys, defaces, conceals or falsifies any account or any record or document made or required for any accounting purpose; or

(b) in furnishing information for any purpose produces or makes use of any account, or any such record or document as aforesaid, which to his knowledge is or may be misleading, false or deceptive in a material particular;

he shall, on conviction on indictment, be liable to imprisonment for a term not exceeding seven years.

(2) For purposes of this section a person who makes or concurs in making in an account or other document an entry which is or may be misleading, false or deceptive in a material particular, or who omits or concurs in omitting a material particular from an account or other document, is to be treated as falsifying the account or document.

Liability of company officers for certain offences by company

27-021 **18.**—(1) Where an offence committed by a body corporate under section 15, 16 or 17 of this Act is proved to have been committed with the consent or connivance of any director, manager, secretary or other similar officer of the body corporate, or any person who was purporting to act in any such capacity, he as well as the body corporate shall be guilty of that offence, and shall be liable to be proceeded against and punished accordingly

(2) Where the affairs of a body corporate are managed by its members, this section shall apply in relation to the acts and defaults of a member in connection with his functions of management as if he were a director of the body corporate.

[1] Added by SI 2001/3649 Pt 8 art 278 (3)
[2] Added by Theft (Amendment) Act 1996 c.62 s 1 (1)

False statements by company directors, etc

19.—(1) Where an officer of a body corporate or unincorporated association (or person purporting to act as such), with intent to deceive members or creditors of the body corporate or association about its affairs, publishes or concurs in publishing a written statement or account which to his knowledge is or may be misleading, false or deceptive in a material particular, he shall on conviction on indictment be liable to imprisonment for a term not exceeding seven years. **27-022**

(2) For purposes of this section a person who has entered into a security for the benefit of a body corporate or association is to be treated as a creditor of it.

(3) Where the affairs of a body corporate or association are managed by its members, this section shall apply to any statement which a member publishes or concurs in publishing in connection with his functions of management as if he were an officer of the body corporate or association.

Suppression, etc. of documents

20.—(1) A person who dishonestly, with a view to gain for himself or another or with intent to cause loss to another, destroys, defaces or conceals any valuable security, any will or other testamentary document or any original document of or belonging to, or filed or deposited in, any court of justice or any government department shall on conviction on indictment be liable to imprisonment for a term not exceeding seven years. **27-023**

(2) A person who dishonestly, with a view to gain for himself or another or with intent to cause loss to another, by any deception procures the execution of a valuable security shall on conviction on indictment be liable to imprisonment for a term not exceeding seven years; and this subsection shall apply in relation to the making, acceptance, indorsement, alteration, cancellation or destruction in whole or in part of a valuable security, and in relation to the signing or sealing of any paper or other material in order that it may be made or converted into, or used or dealt with as, a valuable security, as if that were the execution of a valuable security.

(3) For purposes of this section "deception" has the same meaning as in section 15 of this Act, and "valuable security" means any document creating, transferring, surrendering or releasing any right to, in or over property, or authorising the payment of money or delivery of any property, or evidencing the creation, transfer, surrender or release of any such right, or the payment of money or delivery of any property, or the satisfaction of any obligation.

Blackmail

21.—(1) A person is guilty of blackmail if, with a view to gain for himself or another or with intent to cause loss to another, he makes any unwarranted demand with menaces; and for this purpose a demand with menaces is unwarranted unless the person making it does so in the belief— **27-024**

(a) that he has reasonable grounds for making the demand; and
(b) that the use of the menaces is a proper means of reinforcing the demand.

(2) The nature of the act or omission demanded is immaterial, and it is also immaterial whether the menaces relate to action to be taken by the person making the demand.

(3) A person guilty of blackmail shall on conviction on indictment be liable to imprisonment for a term not exceeding fourteen years.

Offences relating to goods stolen etc

Handling stolen goods

27-025 **22.**—(1) A person handles stolen goods if (otherwise than in the course of the stealing) knowing or believing them to be stolen goods he dishonestly receives the goods, or dishonestly undertakes or assists in their retention, removal, disposal or realisation by or for the benefit of another person, or if he arranges to do so.

(2) A person guilty of handling stolen goods shall on conviction on indictment be liable to imprisonment for a term not exceeding fourteen years.

Advertising rewards for return of goods stolen or lost

27-026 **23.** Where any public advertisement of a reward for the return of any goods which have been stolen or lost uses any words to the effect that no questions will be asked, or that the person producing the goods will be safe from apprehension or inquiry, or that any money paid for the purchase of the goods or advanced by way of loan on them will be repaid, the person advertising the reward and any person who prints or publishes the advertisement shall on summary conviction be liable to a fine not exceeding [level 3 on the standard scale][1].

Scope of offences relating to stolen goods

27-027 **24.**—(1) The provisions of this Act relating to goods which have been stolen shall apply whether the stealing occurred in England or Wales or elsewhere, and whether it occurred before or after the commencement of this Act, provided that the stealing (if not an offence under this Act) amounted to an offence where and at the time when the goods were stolen; and references to stolen goods shall be construed accordingly.

(2) For purposes of those provisions references to stolen goods shall include, in addition to the goods originally stolen and parts of them (whether in their original state or not),—

(a) any other goods which directly or indirectly represent or have at any time represented the stolen goods in the hands of the thief as being the proceeds of any disposal or realisation of the whole or part of the goods stolen or of goods so representing the stolen goods; and

(b) any other goods which directly or indirectly represent or have at any time represented the stolen goods in the hands of a handler of the stolen goods or any part of them as being the proceeds of any disposal or realisation of the whole or part of the stolen goods handled by him or of goods so representing them.

(3) But no goods shall be regarded as having continued to be stolen goods after they have been restored to the person from whom they were stolen or to other lawful possession or custody, or after that person and any other person claiming through him have otherwise ceased as regards those goods to have any right to restitution in respect of the theft.

(4) For purposes of the provisions of this Act relating to goods which have been stolen (including subsections (1) to (3) above) goods obtained in England or Wales or elsewhere either by blackmail or in the circumstances described in section 15(1) of this Act shall be regarded as stolen; and "steal", "theft" and "thief" shall be construed accordingly.

---

[1] Words substituted by virtue of Criminal Justice Act 1982 c.48 ss 38, 46

[Dishonestly retaining a wrongful credit

24A.—(1) A person is guilty of an offence if— 27-028

(a) a wrongful credit has been made to an account kept by him or in respect of which he has any right or interest;

(b) he knows or believes that the credit is wrongful; and

(c) he dishonestly fails to take such steps as are reasonable in the circumstances to secure that the credit is cancelled.

(2) References to a credit are to a credit of an amount of money.

(3) A credit to an account is wrongful if it is the credit side of a money transfer obtained contrary to section 15A of this Act.

(4) A credit to an account is also wrongful to the extent that it derives from—

(a) theft;

(b) an offence under section 15A of this Act;

(c) blackmail; or

(d) stolen goods.

(5) In determining whether a credit to an account is wrongful, it is immaterial (in particular) whether the account is overdrawn before or after the credit is made.

(6) A person guilty of an offence under this section shall be liable on conviction on indictment to imprisonment for a term not exceeding ten years.

(7) Subsection (8) below applies for purposes of provisions of this Act relating to stolen goods (including subsection (4) above).

(8) References to stolen goods include money which is dishonestly withdrawn from an account to which a wrongful credit has been made, but only to the extent that the money derives from the credit.

(9) In this section "account" and "money" shall be construed in accordance with section 15B of this Act.][1]

Possession of housebreaking implements, etc

Going equipped for stealing, etc

25.—(1) A person shall be guilty of an offence if, when not at his place of abode, he has with him any article for use in the course of or in connection with any burglary, theft or cheat. 27-029

(2) A person guilty of an offence under this section shall on conviction on indictment be liable to imprisonment for a term not exceeding three years.

(3) Where a person is charged with an offence under this section, proof that he had with him any article made or adapted for use in committing a burglary, theft or cheat shall be evidence that he had it with him for such use.

(4) Any person may arrest without warrant anyone who is, or whom he, with reasonable cause, suspects to be, committing an offence under this section.

(5) For purposes of this section an offence under section 12(1) of this Act of taking a conveyance shall be treated as theft, and "cheat" means an offence under section 15 of this Act.

---

[1] Added by Theft (Amendment) Act 1996 c.62 s 2 (1)

Supplementary

Interpretation

27-030 **34.**—(1) Sections 4(1) and 5(1) of this Act shall apply generally for purposes of this Act as they apply for purposes of section 1.

(2) For purposes of this Act—

(a) "gain" and "loss" are to be construed as extending only to gain or loss in money or other property, but as extending to any such gain or loss whether temporary or permanent; and—

(i) "gain" includes a gain by keeping what one has, as well as a gain by getting what one has not; and

(ii) "loss" includes a loss by not getting what one might get, as well as a loss by parting with what one has;

(b) "goods", except in so far as the context otherwise requires, includes money and every other description of property except land, and includes things severed from the land by stealing.

Misuse of Drugs Act 1971

CHAPTER 38

Restrictions relating to controlled drugs etc

Restriction of production and supply of controlled drugs

28-001 **4.**—(1) Subject to any regulations under section 7 of this Act for the time being in force, it shall not be lawful for a person—

(a) to produce a controlled drug; or

(b) to supply or offer to supply a controlled drug to another.

(2) Subject to section 28 of this Act, it is an offence for a person—

(a) to produce a controlled drug in contravention of subsection (1) above; or

(b) to be concerned in the production of such a drug in contravention of that subsection by another.

(3) Subject to section 28 of this Act, it is an offence for a person—

(a) to supply or offer to supply a controlled drug to another in contravention of subsection (1) above; or

(b) to be concerned in the supplying of such a drug to another in contravention of that subsection; or

(c) to be concerned in the making to another in contravention of that subsection of an offer to supply such a drug.

Restriction of possession of controlled drugs

28-002 **5.**—(1) Subject to any regulations under section 7 of this Act for the time being in force, it shall not be lawful for a person to have a controlled drug in his possession.

(2) Subject to section 28 of this Act and to subsection (4) below, it is an offence for a person to have a controlled drug in his possession in contravention of subsection (1) above.

(3) Subject to section 28 of this Act, it is an offence for a person to have a controlled drug in his possession, whether lawfully or not, with intent to supply it to another in contravention of section 4(1) of this Act.

(4) In any proceedings for an offence under subsection (2) above in which it is proved that the accused had a controlled drug in his possession, it shall be a defence for him to prove—

(a) that, knowing or suspecting it to be a controlled drug, he took possession of it for the purpose of preventing another from committing or continuing to commit an offence in connection with that drug and that as soon as possible after taking possession of it he took all such steps as were reasonably open to him to destroy the drug or to deliver it into the custody of a person lawfully entitled to take custody of it; or

(b) that, knowing or suspecting it to be a controlled drug, he took possession of it for the purpose of delivering it into the custody of a person lawfully entitled to take custody of it and that as soon as possible after taking possession of it he took all such steps as were reasonably open to him to deliver it into the custody of such a person.

(6) Nothing in subsection (4) above shall prejudice any defence which it is open to a person charged with an offence under this section to raise apart from that subsection.

Restriction of cultivation of cannabis plant

6.—(1) Subject to any regulations under section 7 of this Act for the time being in force, it shall not be lawful for a person to cultivate any plant of the genus Cannabis. **28-003**

(2) Subject to section 28 of this Act, it is an offence to cultivate any such plant in contravention of subsection (1) above.

Miscellaneous offences involving controlled drugs etc

Occupiers etc. of premises to be punishable for permitting certain activities to take place there

8. A person commits an offence if, being the occupier or concerned in the management of any premises, he knowingly permits or suffers any of the following activities to take place on those premises, that is to say— **28-004**

(a) producing or attempting to produce a controlled drug in contravention of section 4(1) of this Act;

(b) supplying or attempting to supply a controlled drug to another in contravention of section 4(1) of this Act, or offering to supply a controlled drug to another in contravention of section 4(1);

(c) preparing opium for smoking;

(d) smoking cannabis, cannabis resin or prepared opium.

Prohibition of certain activities etc. relating to opium

9. Subject to section 28 of this Act, it is an offence for a person— **28-005**

(a) to smoke or otherwise use prepared opium; or

(b) to frequent a place used for the purpose of opium smoking; or

(c) to have in his possession—

(i) any pipes or other utensils made or adapted for use in connection with the smoking of opium, being pipes or utensils which have been used by him or with his knowledge and permission in that connection, or which he intends to use or permit others to use in that connection; or

(ii) any utensils which have been used by him or with his knowledge and permission in connection with the preparation of opium for smoking.

[Prohibition of supply etc. of articles for administering or preparing controlled drugs

28-006 **9A.**—(1) A person who supplies or offers to supply any article which may be used or adapted to be used (whether by itself or in combination with another article or other articles) in the administration by any person of a controlled drug to himself or another, believing that the article (or the article as adapted) is to be so used in circumstances where the administration is unlawful, is guilty of an offence.

(2) It is not an offence under subsection (1) above to supply or offer to supply a hypodermic syringe, or any part of one.

(3) A person who supplies or offers to supply any article which may be used to prepare a controlled drug for administration by any person to himself or another believing that the article is to be so used in circumstances where the administration is unlawful is guilty of an offence.

(4) For the purposes of this section, any administration of a controlled drug is unlawful except—

(a) the administration by any person of a controlled drug to another in circumstances where the administration of the drug is not unlawful under section 4(1) of this Act, or

(b) the administration by any person of a controlled drug to himself in circumstances where having the controlled drug in his possession is not unlawful under section 5(1) of this Act.

(5) In this section, references to administration by any person of a controlled drug to himself include a reference to his administering it to himself with the assistance of another][1]

Miscellaneous offences and powers

Attempts etc. to commit offences

28-007 **19.** It is an offence for a person to attempt to commit an offence under any other provision of this Act or to incite or attempt to incite another to commit such an offence.

Miscellaneous and supplementary provisions

Proof of lack of knowledge etc. to be a defence in proceedings for certain offences

28-008 **28.**—(1) This section applies to offences under any of the following provisions of this Act, that is to say section 4(2) and (3), section 5(2) and (3), section 6(2) and section 9.

[1] Inserted by Drug Trafficking Offences Act1986 c.32 s 34 (1)

(2) Subject to subsection (3) below, in any proceedings for an offence to which this section applies it shall be a defence for the accused to prove that he neither knew of nor suspected nor had reason to suspect the existence of some fact alleged by the prosecution which it is necessary for the prosecution to prove if he is to be convicted of the offence charged.

(3) Where in any proceedings for an offence to which this section applies it is necessary, if the accused is to be convicted of the offence charged, for the prosecution to prove that some substance or product involved in the alleged offence was the controlled drug which the prosecution alleges it to have been, and it is proved that the substance or product in question was that controlled drug, the accused—

(a) shall not be acquitted of the offence charged by reason only of proving that he neither knew nor suspected nor had reason to suspect that the substance or product in question was the particular controlled drug alleged; but

(b) shall be acquitted thereof—

(i) if he proves that he neither believed nor suspected nor had reasons to suspect that the substance or product in question was a controlled drug; or

(ii) if he proves that he believed the substance or product in question to be a controlled drug, or a controlled drug of a description, such that, if it had in fact been that controlled drug or a controlled drug of that description, he would not at the material time have been committing any offence to which this section applies.

(4) Nothing in this section shall prejudice any defence which it is open to a person charged with an offence to which this section applies to raise apart from this section.

Criminal Damage Act 1971

CHAPTER 48

Destroying or damaging property

1.—(1) A person who without lawful excuse destroys or damages any property belonging to another intending to destroy or damage any such property or being reckless as to whether any such property would be destroyed or damaged shall be guilty of an offence. **29-001**

(2) A person who without lawful excuse destroys or damages any property, whether belonging to himself or another—

(a) intending to destroy or damage any property or being reckless as to whether any property would be destroyed or damaged; and

(b) intending by the destruction or damage to endanger the life of another or being reckless as to whether the life of another would be thereby endangered;

shall be guilty of an offence.

(3) An offence committed under this section by destroying or damaging property by fire shall be charged as arson.

Threats to destroy or damage property

29-002 **2.** A person who without lawful excuse makes to another a threat, intending that that other would fear it would be carried out,—

(a) to destroy or damage any property belonging to that other or a third person; or

(b) to destroy or damage his own property in a way which he knows is likely to endanger the life of that other or third person;

shall be guilty of an offence.

Possessing anything with intent to destroy or damage property

29-003 **3.** A person who has anything in his custody or under his control intending without lawful excuse to use it or cause or permit another to use it—

(a) to destroy or damage any property belonging to some other person; or

(b) to destroy or damage his own or the user's property in a way which he knows is likely to endanger the life of some other person;

shall be guilty of an offence.

Punishment of offences

29-004 **4.**—(1) A person guilty of arson under section 1 above or of an offence under section 1(2) above (whether arson or not) shall on conviction on indictment be liable to imprisonment for life.

(2) A person guilty of any other offence under this Act shall on conviction on indictment be liable to imprisonment for a term not exceeding ten years.

"Without lawful excuse."

29-005 **5.**—(1) This section applies to any offence under section 1(1) above and any offence under section 2 or 3 above other than one involving a threat by the person charged to destroy or damage property in a way which he knows is likely to endanger the life of another or involving an intent by the person charged to use or cause or permit the use of something in his custody or under his control so to destroy or damage property.

(2) A person charged with an offence to which this section applies, shall, whether or not he would be treated for the purposes of this Act as having a lawful excuse apart from this subsection, be treated for those purposes as having a lawful excuse—

(a) if at the time of the act or acts alleged to constitute the offence he believed that the person or persons whom he believed to be entitled to consent to the destruction of or damage to the property in question had so consented, or would have so consented to it if he or they had known of the destruction or damage and its circumstances; or

(b) if he destroyed or damaged or threatened to destroy or damage the property in question or, in the case of a charge of an offence under section 3 above, intended to use or cause or permit the use of something to destroy or damage it, in order to protect property belonging to himself or another or a right or interest in property which was or which he believed to be vested in himself or another, and at the time of the act or acts alleged to constitute the offence he believed—

(i) that the property, right or interest was in immediate need of protection; and

(ii) that the means of protection adopted or proposed to be adopted were or would be reasonable having regard to all the circumstances.

(3) For the purposes of this section it is immaterial whether a belief is justified or not if it is honestly held.

(4) For the purposes of subsection (2) above a right or interest in property includes any right or privilege in or over land, whether created by grant, licence or otherwise.

(5) This section shall not be construed as casting doubt on any defence recognised by law as a defence to criminal charges.

Interpretation

10.—(1) In this Act "property" means property of a tangible nature, whether real or personal, including money and— **29-006**

(a) including wild creatures which have been tamed or are ordinarily kept in captivity, and any other wild creatures or their carcasses if, but only if, they have been reduced into possession which has not been lost or abandoned or are in the course of being reduced into possession; but

(b) not including mushrooms growing wild on any land or flowers, fruit or foliage of a plant growing wild on any land.

For the purposes of this subsection "mushroom" includes any fungus and "plant" includes any shrub or tree.

(2) Property shall be treated for the purposes of this Act as belonging to any person—

(a) having the custody or control of it;

(b) having in it any proprietary right or interest (not being an equitable interest arising only from an agreement to transfer or grant an interest); or

(c) having a charge on it.

(3) Where property is subject to a trust, the persons to whom it belongs shall be so treated as including any person having a right to enforce the trust.

(4) Property of a corporation sole shall be so treated as belonging to the corporation notwithstanding a vacancy in the corporation.

Sexual Offences (Amendment) Act 1976

CHAPTER 82

Meaning of "rape" etc

1.—(2) It is hereby declared that if at a trial for a rape offence the jury has to consider whether a man believed that a woman [or man][1] was consenting to sexual intercourse, the presence or absence of reasonable grounds for such a belief is a matter to which the jury is to have regard, in conjunction with any other relevant matters, in considering whether he so believed. **30-001**

[1] Words inserted by Criminal Justice and Public Order Act 1994 c.33 Sch 10 para 35 (2)

Citation, interpretation, commencement and extent

30-002 7.—(1) This Act may be cited as the Sexual Offences (Amendment) Act 1976, and this Act and the Sexual Offences Acts 1956 and 1967 may be cited together as the Sexual Offences Acts 1956 to 1976.

(2) In this Act—

"a rape offence" means any of the following, namely, rape, attempted rape, aiding, abetting, counselling and procuring rape or attempted rape, [incitement to rape, conspiracy to rape and burglary with intent to rape][1];and[...][2]

[section 46 of the Sexual Offences Act 1956][3] (which relates to the meaning of "man"and "woman" in that Act) shall have effect as if the reference to that Act included a reference to this Act.

Criminal Law Act 1977

CHAPTER 45

PART I

CONSPIRACY

The offence of conspiracy

31-001 1.—[(1) Subject to the following provisions of this Part of this Act, if a person agrees with any other person or persons that a course of conduct shall be pursued which, if the agreement is carried out in accordance with their intentions, either—

(a) will necessarily amount to or involve the commission of any offence or offences by one or more of the parties to the agreement, or

(b) would do so but for the existence of facts which render the commission of the offence or any of the offences impossible,

he is guilty of conspiracy to commit the offence or offences in question.][4]

(2) Where liability for any offence may be incurred without knowledge on the part of the person committing it of any particular fact or circumstance necessary for the commission of the offence, a person shall nevertheless not be guilty of conspiracy to commit that offence by virtue of subsection (1) above unless he and at least one other party to the agreement intend or know that that fact or circumstance shall or will exist at the time when the conduct constituting the offence is to take place.

(4) In this Part of this Act "offence" means an offence triable in England and Wales [...][5].

[1] S 4 (1)-(1A) substituted for s 4 (1) by Criminal Justice Act 1988 c.33 s 158 Sch 8 para 16
[2] Words repealed by Criminal Justice and Public Order Act 1994 c.33 Sch 11 para 1
[3] Words substituted by Criminal Justice and Public Order Act 1994 c.33 Sch 10 para 35 (4) (b)
[4] Substituted (with saving) by Criminal Attempts Act 1981 c.47 s 5 (1)
[5] Words repealed by Criminal Justice (Terrorism and Conspiracy) Act 1998 c.40 Sch 2 (II) para 1

[Conspiracy to commit offences outside the United Kingdom

1A.—(1) Where each of the following conditions is satisfied in the case of an agreement, this Part of this Act has effect in relation to the agreement as it has effect in relation to an agreement falling within section 1(1) above. **31-002**

(2) The first condition is that the pursuit of the agreed course of conduct would at some stage involve—

(a) an act by one or more of the parties, or

(b) the happening of some other event,

intended to take place in a country or territory outside the United Kingdom.

(3) The second condition is that that act or other event constitutes an offence under the law in force in that country or territory.

(4) The third condition is that the agreement would fall within section 1(1) above as an agreement relating to the commission of an offence but for the fact that the offence would not be an offence triable in England and Wales if committed in accordance with the parties' intentions.

(5) The fourth condition is that—

(a) a party to the agreement, or a party's agent, did anything in England and Wales in relation to the agreement before its formation, or

(b) a party to the agreement became a party in England and Wales (by joining it either in person or through an agent), or

(c) a party to the agreement, or a party's agent, did or omitted anything in England and Wales in pursuance of the agreement.

(6) In the application of this Part of this Act to an agreement in the case of which each of the above conditions is satisfied, a reference to an offence is to be read as a reference to what would be the offence in question but for the fact that it is not an offence triable in England and Wales.

(7) Conduct punishable under the law in force in any country or territory is an offence under that law for the purposes of this section, however it is described in that law.

(8) Subject to subsection (9) below, the second condition is to be taken to be satisfied unless, not later than rules of court may provide, the defence serve on the prosecution a notice—

(a) stating that, on the facts as alleged with respect to the agreed course of conduct, the condition is not in their opinion satisfied,

(b) showing their grounds for that opinion, and

(c) requiring the prosecution to show that it is satisfied.

(9) The court may permit the defence to require the prosecution to show that the second condition is satisfied without the prior service of a notice under subsection (8) above.

(10) In the Crown Court the question whether the second condition is satisfied shall be decided by the judge alone, and shall be treated as a question of law for the purposes of—

(a) section 9(3) of the Criminal Justice Act 1987 (preparatory hearing in fraud cases), and

(b) section 31(3) of the Criminal Procedure and Investigations Act 1996 (preparatory hearing in other cases).

(11) Any act done by means of a message (however communicated) is to be treated for the purposes of the fourth condition as done in England and Wales if the message is sent or received in England and Wales.

(12) In any proceedings in respect of an offence triable by virtue of this section, it is immaterial to guilt whether or not the accused was a British citizen

at the time of any act or other event proof of which is required for conviction of the offence.

(13) Reference in any enactment, instrument or document (except those in this Part of this Act) to an offence of conspiracy to commit an offence include an offence triable in England and Wales as such a conspiracy by virtue of this section (without prejudice to subsection (6) above).

(14) Nothing in this section—

(a) applies to an agreement entered into before the day on which the Criminal Justice (Terrorism and Conspiracy) Act 1998 was passed, or

(b) imposes criminal liability on any person acting on behalf of, or holding office under, the Crown.][1]

Exemptions from liability for conspiracy

31-003 **2.**—(1) A person shall not by virtue of section 1 above be guilty of conspiracy to commit any offence if he is an intended victim of that offence.

(2) A person shall not by virtue of section 1 above be guilty of conspiracy to commit any offence or offences if the only other person or persons with whom he agrees are (both initially and at all times during the currency of the agreement) persons of any one or more of the following descriptions, that is to say—

(a) his spouse;

(b) a person under the age of criminal responsibility; and

(c) an intended victim of that offence or of each of those offences.

(3) A person is under the age of criminal responsibility for the purposes of subsection (2)(b) above so long as it is conclusively presumed, by virtue of section 50 of the Children and Young Persons Act 1933, that he cannot be guilty of any offence.

Penalties for conspiracy

31-004 **3.**—(1) A person guilty by virtue of section 1 above of conspiracy to commit any offence or offences shall be liable on conviction on indictment—

(a) in a case falling within subsection (2) or (3) below, to imprisonment for a term related in accordance with that subsection to the gravity of the offence or offences in question (referred to below in this section as the relevant offence or offences); and

(b) in any other case, to a fine.

Paragraph (b) above shall not be taken as prejudicing the application of [section 127 of the Powers of Criminal Courts (Sentencing) Act 2000][2] (general power of court to fine offender convicted on indictment) in a case falling within subsection (2) or (3) below.

(2) Where the relevant offence or any of the relevant offences is an offence of any of the following descriptions, that is to say—

(a) murder, or any other offence the sentence for which is fixed by law;

(b) an offence for which a sentence extending to imprisonment for life is provided; or

(c) an indictable offence punishable with imprisonment for which no maximum term of imprisonment is provided,

the person convicted shall be liable to imprisonment for life.

(3) Where in a case other than one to which subsection (2) above applies the relevant offence or any of the relevant offences is punishable with imprisonment, the person convicted shall be liable to imprisonment for a term not exceeding the

---

[1] Added by Criminal Justice (Terrorism and Conspiracy) Act 1998 c.40 s 5 (1)

[2] Words substituted by Powers of Criminal Courts (Sentencing) Act 2000 c.6 Sch 9 para 55

maximum term provided for that offence or (where more than one such offence is in question) for any one of those offences (taking the longer or the longest term as the limit for the purposes of this section where the terms provided differ).

In the case of an offence triable either way the references above in this subsection to the maximum term provided for that offence are references to the maximum term so provided on conviction on indictment.

Restrictions on the institution of proceedings for conspiracy

4.—(1) Subject to subsection (2) below proceedings under section 1 above for conspiracy to commit any offence or offences shall not be instituted against any person except by or with the consent of the Director of Public Prosecutions if the offence or (as the case may be) each of the offences in question is a summary offence. **31-005**

(2) In relation to the institution of proceedings under section 1 above for conspiracy to commit—

(a) an offence which is subject to a prohibition by or under any enactment on the institution of proceedings otherwise than by, or on behalf or with the consent of, the Attorney General, or

(b) two or more offences of which at least one is subject to such a prohibition,

subsection (1) above shall have effect with the substitution of a reference to the Attorney General for the reference to the Director of Public Prosecutions.

(3) Any prohibition by or under any enactment on the institution of proceedings for any offence which is not a summary offence otherwise than by, or on behalf or with the consent of, the Director of Public Prosecutions or any other person shall apply also in relation to proceedings under section 1 above for conspiracy to commit that offence.

(4) Where—

(a) an offence has been committed in pursuance of any agreement; and

(b) proceedings may not be instituted for that offence because any time limit applicable to the institution of any such proceedings has expired,

proceedings under section 1 above for conspiracy to commit that offence shall not be instituted against any person on the basis of that agreement.

[(5) Subject to subsection (6) below, no proceedings for an offence triable by virtue of section 1A above may be instituted except by or with the consent of the Attorney General.

(6) The Secretary of State may by order provide that subsection (5) above shall not apply, or shall not apply to any case of a description specified in the order.][1]

Abolitions, savings, transitional provisions, consequential amendment and repeals

5.—(1) Subject to the following provisions of this section, the offence of conspiracy at common law is hereby abolished. **31-006**

(2) Subsection (1) above shall not affect the offence of conspiracy at common law so far as relates to conspiracy to defraud,

(3) Subsection (1) above shall not affect the offence of conspiracy at common law if and in so far as it may be committed by entering into an agreement to engage in conduct which—

(a) tends to corrupt public morals or outrages public decency; but

[1] Added by Criminal Justice (Terrorism and Conspiracy) Act 1998 c.40 s 5 (2)

(b) would not amount to or involve the commission of an offence if carried out by a single person otherwise than in pursuance of an agreement.

(6) The rules laid down by sections 1 and 2 above shall apply for determining whether a person is guilty of an offence of conspiracy under any enactment other than section 1 above, but conduct which is an offence under any such other enactment shall not also be an offence under section 1 above.

(7) Incitement [...][1] to commit the offence of conspiracy (whether the conspiracy incited [...][2] would be an offence at common law or under section 1 above or any other enactment) shall cease to be offences.

(8) The fact that the person or persons who, so far as appears from the indictment on which any person has been convicted of conspiracy, were the only other parties to the agreement on which his conviction was based have been acquitted of conspiracy by reference to that agreement (whether after being tried with the person convicted or separately) shall not be a ground for quashing his conviction unless under all the circumstances of the case his conviction is inconsistent with the acquittal of the other person or persons in question.

(9) Any rule of law or practice inconsistent with the provisions of subsection (8) above is hereby abolished.

PART II

OFFENCES RELATING TO ENTERING AND REMAINING ON PROPERTY

Violence for securing entry

31-007 **6.**—(1) Subject to the following provisions of this section, any person who, without lawful authority, uses or threatens violence for the purpose of securing entry into any premises for himself or for any other person is guilty of an offence, provided that—

(a) there is someone present on those premises at the time who is opposed to the entry which the violence is intended to secure; and

(b) the person using or threatening the violence knows that that is the case.

[(1A) Subsection (1) above does not apply to a person who is a displaced residential occupier or a protected intending occupier of the premises in question or who is acting on behalf of such an occupier; and if the accused adduces sufficient evidence that he was, or was acting on behalf of, such an occupier he shall be presumed to be, or to be acting on behalf of, such an occupier unless the contrary is proved by the prosecution.][3]

(2) [Subject to subsection (1A) above,][4]The fact that a person has any interest in or right to possession or occupation of any premises shall not for the purposes of subsection (1) above constitute lawful authority for the use or threat of violence by him or anyone else for the purpose of securing his entry into those premises.

(4) It is immaterial for the purposes of this section—

(a) whether the violence in question is directed against the person or against property; and

---

[1] Words repealed by Criminal Attempts Act 1981 c.47 Sch Pt I
[2] Words repealed by Criminal Attempts Act 1981 c.47 Sch Pt I
[3] Added by Criminal Justice and Public Order Act 1994 c.33 Pt V s 72 (2)
[4] Words inserted by Criminal Justice and Public Order Act 1994 c.33 Pt V s 72 (3)

(b) whether the entry which the violence is intended to secure is for the purpose of acquiring possession of the premises in question or for any other purpose.

(5) A person guilty of an offence under this section shall be liable on summary conviction to imprisonment for a term not exceeding six months or to a fine not exceeding [level 5 on the standard scale][1] or to both.

(6) A constable in uniform may arrest without warrant anyone who is, or whom he, with reasonable cause, suspects to be, guilty of an offence under this section.

(7) Section 12 below contains provisions which apply for determining when any person is to be regarded for the purposes of this Part of this Act as a displaced residential occupier of any premises or of any access to any premises[and section 12A below contains provisions which apply for determining when any person is to be regarded for the purposes of this Part of this Act as a protected intending occupier of any premises or of any access to any premises][2].

[Adverse occupation of residential premises

7.—(1) Subject to the following provisions of this section and to section 12A(9) below, any person who is on any premises as a trespasser after having entered as such is guilty of an offence if he fails to leave those premises on being required to do so by or on behalf of— **31-008**

(a) a displaced residential occupier of the premises; or

(b) an individual who is a protected intending occupier of the premises.

(2) In any proceedings for an offence under this section it shall be a defence for the accused to prove that he believed that the person requiring him to leave the premises was not a displaced residential occupier or protected intending occupier of the premises or a person acting on behalf of a displaced residential occupier or protected intending occupier.

(3) In any proceedings for an offence under this section it shall be a defence for the accused to prove—

(a) that the premises in question are or form part of premises used mainly for non-residential purposes; and

(b) that he was not on any part of the premises used wholly or mainly for residential purposes.

(4) Any reference in the preceding provisions of this section to any premises includes a reference to any access to them, whether or not any such access itself constitutes premises, within the meaning of this Part of this Act.

(5) A person guilty of an offence under this section shall be liable on summary conviction to imprisonment for a term not exceeding six months or to a fine not exceeding level 5 on the standard scale or to both.

(6) A constable in uniform may arrest without warrant anyone who is, or whom he, with reasonable cause, suspects to be, guilty of an offence under this section.

(7) Section 12 below contains provisions which apply for determining when any person is to be regarded for the purposes of this Part of this Act as a displaced residential occupier of any premises or of any access to any premises and section 12A below contains provisions which apply for determining when any person is to be regarded for the purposes of this Part of this Act as a protected intending occupier of any premises or of any access to any premises.][3]

[1] Words substituted by Criminal Justice Act 1982 c.48 s 46
[2] Words inserted by Criminal Justice and Public Order Act 1994 c.33 Pt V s 72 (5)
[3] Substituted by Criminal Justice and Public Order Act 1994 c.33 Pt V s 73

Trespassing with a weapon of offence

31-009 **8.**—(1) A person who is on any premises as a trespasser, after having entered as such, is guilty of an offence if, without lawful authority or reasonable excuse, he has with him on the premises any weapon of offence.

(2) In subsection (1) above "weapon of offence" means any article made or adapted for use for causing injury to or incapacitating a person, or intended by the person having it with him for such use.

(3) A person guilty of an offence under this section shall be liable on summary conviction to imprisonment for a term not exceeding three months or to a fine not exceeding [level 5 on the standard scale][1] or to both.

(4) A constable in uniform may arrest without warrant anyone who is, or whom he, with reasonable cause, suspects to be, in the act of committing an offence under this section.

PART IV

MISCELLANEOUS PROVISIONS

Inciting girl under sixteen to have incestuous sexual intercourse

31-010 **54.**—(1) It is an offence for a man to incite to have sexual intercourse with him a girl under the age of sixteen whom he knows to be his grand-daughter, daughter or sister.

(2) In the preceding subsection "man" includes boy, "sister" includes half-sister, and for the purposes of that subsection any expression importing a relationship between two people shall be taken to apply notwithstanding that the relationship is not traced through lawful wedlock.

(3) The following provisions of section 1 of the Indecency with Children Act 1960, namely—

subsection (3) (references in Children and Young Persons Act 1933 to the offences mentioned in Schedule 1 to that Act to include offences under that section);

subsection (4) (offences under that section to be deemed offences against the person for the purpose of section 3 of the Visiting Forces Act 1952),

shall apply in relation to offences under this section.

(4) A person guilty of an offence under this section shall be liable -

(a) on summary conviction, to imprisonment for a term not exceeding six months or to a fine not exceeding the prescribed sum, or both;

(b) on conviction on indictment, to imprisonment for a term not exceeding two years.

[1] Words substituted by Criminal Justice Act 1982 c.48 s 46

Theft Act 1978

CHAPTER 31

Obtaining services by deception

1.—(1) A person who by any deception dishonestly obtains services from another shall be guilty of an offence. **32-001**

(2) It is an obtaining of services where the other is induced to confer a benefit by doing some act, or causing or permitting some act to be done, on the understanding that the benefit has been or will be paid for.

[(3) Without prejudice to the generality of subsection (2) above, it is an obtaining of services where the other is induced to make a loan, or to cause or permit a loan to be made, on the understanding that any payment (whether by way of interest or otherwise) will be or has been made in respect of the loan.][1]

Evasion of liability by deception

2.—(1) Subject to subsection (2) below, where a person by any deception— **32-002**

(a) dishonestly secures the remission of the whole or part of any existing liability to make a payment, whether his own liability or another's; or

(b) with intent to make permanent default in whole or in part on any existing liability to make a payment, or with intent to let another do so, dishonestly induces the creditor or any person claiming payment on behalf of the creditor to wait for payment (whether or not the due date for payment is deferred) or to forgo payment; or

(c) dishonestly obtains any exemption from or abatement of liability to make a payment.

he shall be guilty of an offence.

(2) For purposes of this section "liability" means legally enforceable liability; and subsection (1) shall not apply in relation to a liability that has not been accepted or established to pay compensation for a wrongful act or omission.

(3) For purposes of subsection (1)(b) a person induced to take in payment a cheque or other security for money by way of conditional satisfaction of a pre-existing liability is to be treated not as being paid but as being induced to wait for payment.

(4) For purposes of subsection (1)(c) "obtains" includes obtaining for another or enabling another to obtain.

Making off without payment

3.—(1) Subject to subsection (3) below, a person who, knowing that payment on the spot for any goods supplied or service done is required or expected from him, dishonestly makes off without having paid as required or expected and with intent to avoid payment of the amount due shall be guilty of an offence. **32-003**

(2) For purposes of this section "payment on the spot" includes payment at the time of collecting goods on which work has been done or in respect of which service has been provided.

(3) Subsection (1) above shall not apply where the supply of the goods or the doing of the service is contrary to law, or where the service done is such that payment is not legally enforceable.

[1] Added by Theft (Amendment) Act 1996 c.62 s 4 (1)

(4) Any person may arrest without warrant anyone who is, or whom he, with reasonable cause, suspects to be, committing or attempting to commit an offence under this section.

Punishments

32-004 **4.**—(1) Offences under this Act shall be punishable either on conviction on indictment or on summary conviction.

(2) A person convicted on indictment shall be liable—

(a) for an offence under section 1 or section 2 of this Act, to imprisonment for a term not exceeding five years; and

(b) for an offence under section 3 of this Act, to imprisonment for a term not exceeding two years.

(3) A person convicted summarily of any offence under this Act shall be liable—

(a) to imprisonment for a term not exceeding six months; or

(b) to a fine not exceeding the prescribed sum for the purposes of [section 32 of the Magistrates' Courts Act 1980][1] (punishment on summary conviction of offences triable either way: £5,000 or other sum substituted by order under that Act),

or to both.

Supplementary

32-005 **5.**—(1) For purposes of sections 1 and 2 above "deception" has the same meaning as in section 15 of the Theft Act 1968, that is to say, it means any deception (whether deliberate or reckless) by words or conduct as to fact or as to law, including a deception as to the present intentions of the person using the deception or any other person; and section 18 of that Act (liability of company officers for offences by the company) shall apply in relation to sections 1 and 2 above as it applies in relation to section 15 of that Act.

(2) Sections 30(1) (husband and wife), 31(1) (effect on civil proceedings) and 34 (interpretation) of the Theft Act 1968, so far as they are applicable in relation to this Act, shall apply as they apply in relation to that Act.

Magistrates' Courts Act 1980

CHAPTER 43

PART I

CRIMINAL JURISDICTION AND PROCEDURE

Miscellaneous

Aiders and abettors

33-001 **44.**—(1) A person who aids, abets, counsels or procures the commission by another person of a summary offence shall be guilty of the like offence and may

[1] Words substituted by Magistrates' Courts Act 1980 c.43 Sch 7 para 170

be tried (whether or not he is charged as a principal) either by a court having jurisdiction to try that other person or by a court having by virtue of his own offence jurisdiction to try him.

(2) Any offence consisting in aiding, abetting, counselling or procuring the commission of an offence triable either way (other than an offence listed in Schedule 1 to this Act) shall by virtue of this subsection be triable either way.

Incitement

45.—(1) Any offence consisting in the incitement to commit a summary offence shall be triable only summarily. **33-002**

(2) Subsection (1) above is without prejudice to any other enactment by virtue of which any offence is triable only summarily.

(3) On conviction of an offence consisting in the incitement to commit a summary offence a person shall be liable to the same penalties as he would be liable to on conviction of the last-mentioned offence.

Forgery and Counterfeiting Act 1981

CHAPTER 45

PART I

FORGERY AND KINDRED OFFENCES

Offences

The offence of forgery

1. A person is guilty of forgery if he makes a false instrument, with the intention that he or another shall use it to induce somebody to accept it as genuine, and by reason of so accepting it to do or not to do some act to his own or any other person's prejudice. **34-001**

The offence of copying a false instrument

2. It is an offence for a person to make a copy of an instrument which is, and which he knows or believes to be, a false instrument, with the intention that he or another shall use it to induce somebody to accept it as a copy of a genuine instrument, and by reason of so accepting it to do or not to do some act to his own or any other person's prejudice. **34-002**

The offence of using a false instrument

3. It is an offence for a person to use an instrument which is, and which he knows or believes to be, false, with the intention of inducing somebody to accept it as genuine, and by reason of so accepting it to do or not to do some act to his own or any other person's prejudice. **34-003**

The offence of using a copy of a false instrument

34-004 **4.** It is an offence for a person to use a copy of an instrument which is, and which he knows or believes to be, a false instrument, with the intention of inducing somebody to accept it as a copy of a genuine instrument, and by reason of so accepting it to do or not to do some act to his own or any other person's prejudice.

Offences relating to money orders, share certificates, passports, etc

34-005 **5.**—(1) It is an offence for a person to have in his custody or under his control an instrument to which this section applies which is, and which he knows or believes to be, false, with the intention that he or another shall use it to induce somebody to accept it as genuine, and by reason of so accepting it to do or not to do some act to his own or any other person's prejudice.

(2) It is an offence for a person to have in his custody or under his control, without lawful authority or excuse, an instrument to which this section applies which is, and which he knows or believes to be, false.

(3) It is an offence for a person to make or to have in his custody or under his control a machine or implement, or paper or any other material, which to his knowledge is or has been specially designed or adapted for the making of an instrument to which this section applies, with the intention that he or another shall make an instrument to which this section applies which is false and that he or another shall use the instrument to induce somebody to accept it as genuine, and by reason of so accepting it to do or not to do some act to his own or any other person's prejudice.

(4) It is an offence for a person to make or to have in his custody or under his control any such machine, implement, paper or material, without lawful authority or excuse.

(5) The instruments to which this section applies are—

(a) money orders;
(b) postal orders;
(c) United Kingdom postage stamps;
(d) Inland Revenue stamps;
(e) share certificates;
(f) passports and documents which can be used instead of passports;
(g) cheques;
(h) travellers' cheques;
(j) cheque cards;
(k) credit cards;
(l) certified copies relating to an entry in a register of births, adoptions, marriages or deaths and issued by the Registrar General, the Registrar General for Northern Ireland, a registration officer or a person lawfully authorised to register marriages; and
(m) certificates relating to entries in such registers.

(6) In subsection (5)(e) above "share certificate" means an instrument entitling or evidencing the title of a person to a share or interest—

(a) in any public stock, annuity, fund or debt of any government or state, including a state which forms part of another state; or
(b) in any stock, fund or debt of a body (whether corporate or unincorporated) established in the United Kingdom or elsewhere.

Penalties etc

Penalties for offences under Part I

6.—(1) A person guilty of an offence under this Part of this Act shall be liable on summary conviction— **34-006**

(a) to a fine not exceeding the statutory maximum; or
(b) to imprisonment for a term not exceeding six months; or
(c) to both.

(2) A person guilty of an offence to which this subsection applies shall be liable on conviction on indictment to imprisonment for a term not exceeding ten years.

(3) The offences to which subsection (2) above applies are offences under the following provisions of this Part of this Act—

(a) section 1;
(b) section 2;
(c) section 3;
(d) section 4;
(e) section 5(1); and
(f) section 5(3).

(4) A person guilty of an offence under section 5(2) or (4) above shall be liable on conviction on indictment to imprisonment for a term not exceeding two years.

Interpretation of Part I

Meaning of "instrument"

8.—(1) Subject to subsection (2) below, in this Part of this Act "instrument" means— **34-007**

(a) any document, whether of a formal or informal character;
(b) any stamp issued or sold by [a postal operator][1];
(c) any Inland Revenue stamp; and
(d) any disc, tape, sound track or other device on or in which information is recorded or stored by mechanical, electronic or other means.

(2) A currency note within the meaning of Part II of this Act is not an instrument for the purposes of this Part of this Act.

(3) A mark denoting payment of postage which [a postal operator authorises][2] to be used instead of an adhesive stamp is to be treated for the purposes of this Part of this Act as if it were a stamp issued by the [the postal operator concerned][3].

[(3A) In this section "postal operator" has the same meaning as in the Postal Services Act 2000.][4]

(4) In this Part of this Act "Inland Revenue stamp" means a stamp as defined in section 27 of the Stamp Duties Management Act 1891.

Meaning of "false" and "making"

9.—(1) An instrument is false for the purposes of this Part of this Act— **34-008**

[1] Words substituted by SI 2001/1149 Sch 1 (1) para 50 (2)
[2] Words substituted by SI 2001/1149 Sch 1 (1) para 50 (3) (b)
[3] Words substituted by SI 2001/1149 Sch 1 (1) para 50 (3) (b)
[4] Added by SI 2001/1149 Sch 1 (1) para 50 (4)

(a) if it purports to have been made in the form in which it is made by a person who did not in fact make it in that form; or

(b) if it purports to have been made in the form in which it is made on the authority of a person who did not in fact authorise its making in that form; or

(c) if it purports to have been made in the terms in which it is made by a person who did not in fact make it in those terms; or

(d) if it purports to have been made in the terms in which it is made on the authority of a person who did not in fact authorise its making in those terms; or

(e) if it purports to have been altered in any respect by a person who did not in fact alter it in that respect; or

(f) if it purports to have been altered in any respect on the authority of a person who did not in fact authorise the alteration in that respect; or

(g) if it purports to have been made or altered on a date on which, or at a place at which, or otherwise in circumstances in which, it was not in fact made or altered; or

(h) if it purports to have been made or altered by an existing person but he did not in fact exist.

(2) A person is to be treated for the purposes of this Part of this Act as making a false instrument if he alters an instrument so as to make it false in any respect (whether or not it is false in some other respect apart from that alteration).

Meaning of "prejudice" and "induce"

34-009 **10.**—(1) Subject to subsections (2) and (4) below, for the purposes of this Part of this Act an act or omission intended to be induced is to a person's prejudice if, and only if, it is one which, if it occurs—

(a) will result—

(i) in his temporary or permanent loss of property; or

(ii) in his being deprived of an opportunity to earn remuneration or greater remuneration; or

(iii) in his being deprived of an opportunity to gain a financial advantage otherwise than by way of remuneration; or

(b) will result in somebody being given an opportunity—

(i) to earn remuneration or greater remuneration from him; or

(ii) to gain a financial advantage from him otherwise than by way of remuneration; or

(c) will be the result of his having accepted a false instrument as genuine, or a copy of a false instrument as a copy of a genuine one, in connection with his performance of any duty.

(2) An act which a person has an enforceable duty to do and an omission to do an act which a person is not entitled to do shall be disregarded for the purposes of this Part of this Act.

(3) In this Part of this Act references to inducing somebody to accept a false instrument as genuine, or a copy of a false instrument as a copy of a genuine one, include references to inducing a machine to respond to the instrument or copy as if it were a genuine instrument or, as the case may be, a copy of a genuine one.

(4) Where subsection (3) above applies, the act or omission intended to be induced by the machine responding to the instrument or copy shall be treated as an act or omission to a person's prejudice.

(5) In this section "loss" includes not getting what one might get as well as parting with what one has.

Miscellaneous

Abolition of offence of forgery at common law

13. The offence of forgery at common law is hereby abolished for all purposes not relating to offences committed before the commencement of this Act. **34-010**

PART II

COUNTERFEITING AND KINDRED OFFENCES

Offences

Offences of counterfeiting notes and coins

14.—(1) It is an offence for a person to make a counterfeit of a currency note or of a protected coin, intending that he or another shall pass or tender it as genuine. **34-011**

(2) It is an offence for a person to make a counterfeit of a currency note or of a protected coin without lawful authority or excuse.

Offences of passing etc. counterfeit notes and coins

15.—(1) It is an offence for a person— **34-012**

(a) to pass or tender as genuine any thing which is, and which he knows or believes to be, a counterfeit of a currency note or of a protected coin; or

(b) to deliver to another any thing which is, and which he knows or believes to be, such a counterfeit, intending that the person to whom it is delivered or another shall pass or tender it as genuine.

(2) It is an offence for a person to deliver to another, without lawful authority or excuse, any thing which is, and which he knows or believes to be, a counterfeit of a currency note or of a protected coin.

Offences involving the custody or control of counterfeit notes and coins

16.—(1) It is an offence for a person to have in his custody or under his control any thing which is, and which he knows or believes to be, a counterfeit of a currency note or of a protected coin, intending either to pass or tender it as genuine or to deliver it to another with the intention that he or another shall pass or tender it as genuine. **34-013**

(2) It is an offence for a person to have in his custody or under his control, without lawful authority or excuse, any thing which is, and which he knows or believes to be, a counterfeit of a currency note or of a protected coin.

(3) It is immaterial for the purposes of subsections (1) and (2) above that a coin or note is not in a fit state to be passed or tendered or that the making or counterfeiting of a coin or note has not been finished or perfected.

Offences involving the making or custody or control of counterfeiting materials and implements

34-014 **17.**—(1) It is an offence for a person to make, or to have in his custody or under his control, any thing which he intends to use, or to permit any other person to use, for the purpose of making a counterfeit of a currency note or of a protected coin with the intention that it be passed or tendered as genuine.

(2) It is an offence for a person without lawful authority or excuse—

(a) to make; or

(b) to have in his custody or under his control,

any thing which, to his knowledge, is or has been specially designed or adapted for the making of a counterfeit of a currency note.

(3) Subject to subsection (4) below, it is an offence for a person to make, or to have in his custody or under his control, any implement which, to his knowledge, is capable of imparting to any thing a resemblance—

(a) to the whole or part of either side of a protected coin; or

(b) to the whole or part of the reverse of the image on either side of a protected coin.

(4) It shall be a defence for a person charged with an offence under subsection (3) above to show—

(a) that he made the implement or, as the case may be, had it in his custody or under his control, with the written consent of the Treasury; or

(b) that he had lawful authority otherwise than by virtue of paragraph (a) above, or a lawful excuse, for making it or having it in his custody or under his control.

The offence of reproducing British currency notes

34-015 **18.**—(1) It is an offence for any person, unless the relevant authority has previously consented in writing, to reproduce on any substance whatsoever, and whether or not on the correct scale, any British currency note or any part of a British currency note.

(2) In this section—

"British currency note" means any note which—

(a) has been lawfully issued in England and Wales, Scotland or Northern Ireland; and

(b) is or has been customarily used as money in the country where it was issued; and

(c) is payable on demand;

and "the relevant authority", in relation to a British currency note of any particular description, means the authority empowered by law to issue notes of that description.

Offences of making etc. imitation British coins

34-016 **19.**—(1) It is an offence for a person—

(a) to make an imitation British coin in connection with a scheme intended to promote the sale of any product or the making of contracts for the supply of any service; or

(b) to sell or distribute imitation British coins in connection with any such scheme, or to have imitation British coins in his custody or under his control with a view to such sale or distribution, unless the Treasury have previously consented in writing to the sale or distribution of such imitation British coins in connection with that scheme.

(2) In this section—

"British coin" means any coin which is legal tender in any part of the United Kingdom; and

"imitation British coin" means any thing which resembles a British coin in shape, size and the substance of which it is made.

Prohibition of importation and exportation of counterfeits

Prohibition of importation of counterfeit notes and coins

20. The importation, landing or unloading of a counterfeit of a currency note or of a protected coin without the consent of the Treasury is hereby prohibited. **34-017**

Prohibition of exportation of counterfeit notes and coins

21.—(1) The exportation of a counterfeit of a currency note or of a protected coin without the consent of the Treasury is hereby prohibited. **34-018**

Penalties etc

Penalties for offences under PART II

22.—(1) A person guilty of an offence to which this subsection applies shall be liable— **34-019**

(a) on summary conviction—
  (i) to a fine not exceeding the statutory maximum; or
  (ii) to imprisonment for a term not exceeding six months; or
  (iii) to both; and
(b) on conviction on indictment—
  (i) to a fine; or
  (ii) to imprisonment for a term not exceeding ten years; or
  (iii) to both.

(2) The offences to which subsection (1) above applies are offences under the following provisions of this Part of this Act—

(a) section 14(1);
(b) section 15(1);
(c) section 16(1); and
(d) section 17(1).

(3) A person guilty of an offence to which this subsection applies shall be liable—

(a) on summary conviction—
  (i) to a fine not exceeding the statutory maximum; or
  (ii) to imprisonment for a term not exceeding six months; or
  (iii) to both; and
(b) on conviction on indictment—
  (i) to a fine; or
  (ii) to imprisonment for a term not exceeding two years; or
  (iii) to both.

(4) The offences to which subsection (3) above applies are offences under the following provisions of this Part of this Act—

(a) section 14(2);
(b) section 15(2);

(c) section 16(2);
(d) section 17(2); and
(e) section 17(3).

(5) A person guilty of an offence under section 18 or 19 above shall be liable—
(a) on summary conviction, to a fine not exceeding the statutory maximum; and
(b) on conviction on indictment, to a fine.

Interpretation of Part II

Meaning of "currency note" and "protected coin"

34-020 **27.**—(1) In this Part of this Act—
"currency note" means—
(a) any note which—
(i) has been lawfully issued in England and Wales, Scotland, Northern Ireland, any of the Channel Islands, the Isle of Man or the Republic of Ireland; and
(ii) is or has been customarily used as money in the country where it was issued; and
(iii) is payable on demand; or
(b) any note which—
(i) has been lawfully issued in some country other than those mentioned in paragraph (a)(i) above; and
(ii) is customarily used as money in that country;
and "protected coin" means any coin which—
(a) is customarily used as money in any country; or
(b) is specified in an order made by the Treasury for the purposes of this Part of this Act.

(2) The power to make an order conferred on the Treasury by subsection (1) above shall be exercisable by statutory instrument.

(3) A statutory instrument containing such an order shall be laid before Parliament after being made.

Meaning of "counterfeit"

34-021 **28.**—(1) For the purposes of this Part of this Act a thing is a counterfeit of a currency note or of a protected coin—
(a) if it is not a currency note or a protected coin but resembles a currency note or protected coin (whether on one side only or on both) to such an extent that it is reasonably capable of passing for a currency note or protected coin of that description; or
(b) if it is a currency note or protected coin which has been so altered that it is reasonably capable of passing for a currency note or protected coin of some other description.

(2) For the purposes of this Part of this Act—
(a) a thing consisting of one side only of a currency note, with or without the addition of other material, is a counterfeit of such a note;
(b) a thing consisting—
(i) of parts of two or more currency notes; or
(ii) of parts of a currency note, or of parts of two or more currency notes, with the addition of other material,

is capable of being a counterfeit of a currency note.

(3) References in this Part of this Act to passing or tendering a counterfeit of a currency note or a protected coin are not to be construed as confined to passing or tendering it as legal tender.

Criminal Attempts Act 1981

CHAPTER 47

PART I

ATTEMPTS ETC

Attempt

Attempting to commit an offence

1.—(1) If, with intent to commit an offence to which this section applies, a person does an act which is more than merely preparatory to the commission of the offence, he is guilty of attempting to commit the offence. **35-001**

[(1A) Subject to section 8 of the Computer Misuse Act 1990 (relevance of external law), if this subsection applies to an act, what the person doing it had in view shall be treated as an offence to which this section applies.

(1B) Subsection (1A) above applies to an act if—

(a) it is done in England and Wales; and

(b) it would fall within subsection (1) above as more than merely preparatory to the commission of an offence under section 3 of the Computer Misuse Act 1990 but for the fact that the offence, if completed, would not be an offence triable in England and Wales.][1]

(2) A person may be guilty of attempting to commit an offence to which this section applies even though the facts are such that the commission of the offence is impossible.

(3) In any case where—

(a) apart from this subsection a person's intention would not be regarded as having amounted to an intent to commit an offence; but

(b) if the facts of the case had been as he believed them to be, his intention would be so regarded,

then, for the purposes of subsection (1) above, he shall be regarded as having had an intent to commit that offence.

(4) This section applies to any offence which, if it were completed, would be triable in England and Wales as an indictable offence, other than—

(a) conspiracy (at common law or under section 1 of the Criminal Law Act 1977 or any other enactment);

(b) aiding, abetting, counselling, procuring or suborning the commission of an offence;

[1] Added by Computer Misuse Act 1990 c.18 s 7 (3)

(c) offences under section 4(1) (assisting offenders) or 5(1) (accepting or agreeing to accept consideration for not disclosing information about an arrestable offence) of the Criminal Law Act 1967.

[Extended jurisdiction in relation to certain attempts

35-002 **1A.**—(1) If this section applies to an act, what the person doing the act had in view shall be treated as an offence to which section 1(1) above applies.

(2) This section applies to an act if—

(a) it is done in England and Wales, and

(b) it would fall within section 1(1) above as more than merely preparatory to the commission of a Group A offence but for the fact that that offence, if completed, would not be an offence triable in England and Wales.

(3) In this section "Group A offence" has the same meaning as in Part 1 of the Criminal Justice Act 1993.

(4) Subsection (1) above is subject to the provisions of section 6 of the Act of 1993 (relevance of external law).

(5) Where a person does any act to which this section applies, the offence which he commits shall for all purposes be treated as the offence of attempting to commit the relevant Group A offence.][1]

Application of procedural and other provisions to offences under s. 1

35-003 **2.**—(1) Any provision to which this section applies shall have effect with respect to an offence under section 1 above of attempting to commit an offence as it has effect with respect to the offence attempted.

(2) This section applies to provisions of any of the following descriptions made by or under any enactment (whenever passed)—

(a) provisions whereby proceedings may not be instituted or carried on otherwise than by, or on behalf or with the consent of, any person (including any provisions which also make other exceptions to the prohibition);

(b) provisions conferring power to institute proceedings;

(c) provisions as to the venue of proceedings;

(d) provisions whereby proceedings may not be instituted after the expiration of a time limit;

(e) provisions conferring a power of arrest or search;

(f) provisions conferring a power of seizure and detention of property;

(g) provisions whereby a person may not be convicted [or committed for trial][2][...][3] on the uncorroborated evidence of one witness (including any provision requiring the evidence of not less than two credible witnesses);

(h) provisions conferring a power of forfeiture, including any power to deal with anything liable to be forfeited;

(i) provisions whereby, if an offence committed by a body corporate is proved to have been committed with the consent or connivance of another person, that person also is guilty of the offence.

1 Added by Criminal Justice Act 1993 c.36 Pt I s 5 (2)

2 Words restored by Criminal Procedure and Investigations Act 1996 c.25 Pt V s 44 (5) (i)

3 Words repealed by Criminal Justice and Public Order Act 1994 c.33 Sch 11 para 1

Specific offences of attempt

Offences of attempt under other enactments

3.—(1) Subsections (2) to (5) below shall have effect, subject to subsection (6) below and to any inconsistent provision in any other enactment, for the purpose of determining whether a person is guilty of an attempt under a special statutory provision. **35-004**

(2) For the purposes of this Act an attempt under a special statutory provision is an offence which—

(a) is created by an enactment other than section 1 above, including an enactment passed after this Act; and

(b) is expressed as an offence of attempting to commit another offence (in this section referred to as "the relevant full offence").

(3) A person is guilty of an attempt under a special statutory provision if, with intent to commit the relevant full offence, he does an act which is more than merely preparatory to the commission of that offence.

(4) A person may be guilty of an attempt under a special statutory provision even though the facts are such that the commission of the relevant full offence is impossible.

(5) In any case where—

(a) apart from this subsection a person's intention would not be regarded as having amounted to an intent to commit the relevant full offence; but

(b) if the facts of the case had been as he believed them to be, his intention would be so regarded,

then, for the purposes of subsection (3) above, he shall be regarded as having had an intent to commit that offence.

Trial etc. of offences of attempt

Trial and penalties

4.—(1) A person guilty by virtue of section 1 above of attempting to commit an offence shall— **35-005**

(a) if the offence attempted is murder or any other offence the sentence for which is fixed by law, be liable on conviction on indictment to imprisonment for life; and

(b) if the offence attempted is indictable but does not fall within paragraph (a) above, be liable on conviction on indictment to any penalty to which he would have been liable on conviction on indictment of that offence; and

(c) if the offence attempted is triable either way, be liable on summary conviction to any penalty to which he would have been liable on summary conviction of that offence.

(2) In any case in which a court may proceed to summary trial of an information charging a person with an offence and an information charging him with an offence under section 1 above of attempting to commit it or an attempt under a special statutory provision, the court may, without his consent, try the informations together.

(3) Where, in proceedings against a person for an offence under section 1 above, there is evidence sufficient in law to support a finding that he did an act

falling within subsection (1) of that section, the question whether or not his act fell within that subsection is a question of fact.

(4) Where, in proceedings against a person for an attempt under a special statutory provision, there is evidence sufficient in law to support a finding that he did an act falling within subsection (3) of section 3 above, the question whether or not his act fell within that subsection is a question of fact.

(5) Subsection (1) above shall have effect—

(a) subject to section 37 of and Schedule 2 to the Sexual Offences Act 1956 (mode of trial of and penalties for attempts to commit certain offences under that Act); and

(b) notwithstanding anything—

(i) in section 32(1) (no limit to fine on conviction on indictment) of the Criminal Law Act 1977; or

(ii) in [section 78(1) and (2)][1] (maximum of six months' imprisonment on summary conviction unless express provision made to the contrary) of the[Powers of Criminal Courts (Sentencing) Act 2000][2].

Supplementary

Effect of Part I on common law

35-006 **6.**—(1) The offence of attempt at common law and any offence at common law of procuring materials for crime are hereby abolished for all purposes not relating to acts done before the commencement of this Act.

(2) Except as regards offences committed before the commencement of this Act, references in any enactment passed before this Act which fall to be construed as references to the offence of attempt at common law shall be construed as references to the offence under section 1 above.

PART II

SUSPECTED PERSONS ETC

Interference with vehicles

35-007 **9.**—(1) A person is guilty of the offence of vehicle interference if he interferes with a motor vehicle or trailer or with anything carried in or on a motor vehicle or trailer with the intention that an offence specified in subsection (2) below shall be committed by himself or some other person.

(2) The offences mentioned in subsection (1) above are—

(a) theft of the motor vehicle or trailer or part of it;

(b) theft of anything carried in or on the motor vehicle or trailer; and

(c) an offence under section 12(1) of the Theft Act 1968 (taking and driving away without consent);

and, if it is shown that a person accused of an offence under this section intended that one of those offences should be committed, it is immaterial that it cannot be shown which it was.

[1] Words substituted by Powers of Criminal Courts (Sentencing) Act 2000 c.6 Sch 9 para 82
[2] Words substituted by Powers of Criminal Courts (Sentencing) Act 2000 c.6 Sch 9 para 82

(3) A person guilty of an offence under this section shall be liable on summary conviction to imprisonment for a term not exceeding three months or to a fine not exceeding [level 4 on the standard scale][1] or to both.

(5) In this section "motor vehicle" and "trailer" have the meanings assigned to them by [section 185(1) of the Road Traffic Act 1988][2].

Contempt of Court Act 1981

CHAPTER 49

Strict liability

The strict liability rule

1. In this Act "the strict liability rule" means the rule of law whereby conduct may be treated as a contempt of court as tending to interfere with the course of justice in particular legal proceedings regardless of intent to do so. **36-001**

Limitation of scope of strict liability

2.—(1) The strict liability rule applies only in relation to publications, and for this purpose "publication" includes any speech, writing, [programme included in a programme service][3] or other communication in whatever form, which is addressed to the public at large or any section of the public. **36-002**

(2) The strict liability rule applies only to a publication which creates a substantial risk that the course of justice in the proceedings in question will be seriously impeded or prejudiced.

(3) The strict liability rule applies to a publication only if the proceedings in question are active within the meaning of this section at the time of the publication.

(4) Schedule 1 applies for determining the times at which proceedings are to be treated as active within the meaning of this section.

[(5) In this section "programme service" has the same meaning as in the Broadcasting Act 1990.][4]

Defence of innocent publication or distribution

3.—(1) A person is not guilty of contempt of court under the strict liability rule as the publisher of any matter to which that rule applies if at the time of publication (having taken all reasonable care) he does not know and has no reason to suspect that relevant proceedings are active. **36-003**

(2) A person is not guilty of contempt of court under the strict liability rule as the distributor of a publication containing any such matter if at the time of distribution (having taken all reasonable care) he does not know that it contains such matter and has no reason to suspect that it is likely to do so.

(3) The burden of proof of any fact tending to establish a defence afforded by this section to any person lies upon that person.

[1] Words substituted by Criminal Justice Act 1982 c.48 s 46
[2] Words substituted by Road Traffic (Consequential Provisions) Act 1988 c.54 s 4 Sch 3 para 23
[3] Words substituted by Broadcasting Act 1990 c.42 s 203 (1) Sch 20 para 31 (1) (a)
[4] Inserted by Broadcasting Act 1990 c.42 s 203 (1) Sch 20 para 31 (1) (b)

Contemporary reports of proceedings

36-004 **4.**—(1) Subject to this section a person is not guilty of contempt of court under the strict liability rule in respect of a fair and accurate report of legal proceedings held in public, published contemporaneously and in good faith.

(2) In any such proceedings the court may, where it appears to be necessary for avoiding a substantial risk of prejudice to the administration of justice in those proceedings, or in any other proceedings pending or imminent, order that the publication of any report of the proceedings, or any part of the proceedings, be postponed for such period as the court thinks necessary for that purpose.

(2A) Where in proceedings for any offence which is an administration of justice offence for the purposes of section 54 of the Criminal Procedure and Investigations Act 1996 (acquittal tainted by an administration of justice offence) it appears to the court that there is a possibility that (by virtue of that section) proceedings may be taken against a person for an offence of which he has been acquitted, subsection (2) of this section shall apply as if those proceedings were pending or imminent.

(3) For the purposes of subsection (1) of this section [...][1] a report of proceedings shall be treated as published contemporaneously—

(a) in the case of a report of which publication is postponed pursuant to an order under subsection (2) of this section, if published as soon as practicable after that order expires;

(b) in the case of a report of committal proceedings of which publication is permitted by virtue only of subsection (3) of section 8 of the Magistrates' Courts Act 1980, if published as soon as practicable after publication is so permitted.

Discussion of public affairs

36-005 **5.** A publication made as or as part of a discussion in good faith of public affairs or other matters of general public interest is not to be treated as a contempt of court under the strict liability rule if the risk of impediment or prejudice to particular legal proceedings is merely incidental to the discussion.

Savings

36-006 **6.** Nothing in the foregoing provisions of this Act—

(a) prejudices any defence available at common law to a charge of contempt of court under the strict liability rule;

(b) implies that any publication is punishable as contempt of court under that rule which would not be so punishable apart from those provisions;

(c) restricts liability for contempt of court in respect of conduct intended to impede or prejudice the administration of justice.

Consent required for institution of proceedings

36-007 **7.** Proceedings for a contempt of court under the strict liability rule (other than Scottish proceedings) shall not be instituted except by or with the consent of the Attorney General or on the motion of a court having jurisdiction to deal with it.

[1] Words repealed by Defamation Act 1996 c.31 Sch 2 para 1

Other aspects of law and procedure

Confidentiality of jury's deliberations

8.—(1) Subject to subsection (2) below, it is a contempt of court to obtain, disclose or solicit any particulars of statements made, opinions expressed, arguments advanced or votes cast by members of a jury in the course of their deliberations in any legal proceedings. **36-008**

(2) This section does not apply to any disclosure of any particulars—

(a) in the proceedings in question for the purpose of enabling the jury to arrive at their verdict, or in connection with the delivery of that verdict, or

(b) in evidence in any subsequent proceedings for an offence alleged to have been committed in relation to the jury in the first mentioned proceedings,

or to the publication of any particulars so disclosed.

(3) Proceedings for a contempt of court under this section (other than Scottish proceedings) shall not be instituted except by or with the consent of the Attorney General or on the motion of a court having jurisdiction to deal with it.

Use of tape recorders

9.—(1) Subject to subsection (4) below, it is a contempt of court— **36-009**

(a) to use in court, or bring into court for use, any tape recorder or other instrument for recording sound, except with the leave of the court;

(b) to publish a recording of legal proceedings made by means of any such instrument, or any recording derived directly or indirectly from it, by playing it in the hearing of the public or any section of the public, or to dispose of it or any recording so derived, with a view to such publication;

(c) to use any such recording in contravention of any conditions of leave granted under paragraph (a).

(2) Leave under paragraph (a) of subsection (1) may be granted or refused at the discretion of the court, and if granted may be granted subject to such conditions as the court thinks proper with respect to the use of any recording made pursuant to the leave; and where leave has been granted the court may at the like discretion withdraw or amend it either generally or in relation to any particular part of the proceedings.

(3) Without prejudice to any other power to deal with an act of contempt under paragraph (a) of subsection (1), the court may order the instrument, or any recording made with it, or both, to be forfeited; and any object so forfeited shall (unless the court otherwise determines on application by a person appearing to be the owner) be sold or otherwise disposed of in such manner as the court may direct.

(4) This section does not apply to the making or use of sound recordings for purposes of official transcripts of proceedings.

Sources of information

10. No court may require a person to disclose, nor is any person guilty of contempt of court for refusing to disclose, the source of information contained in a publication for which he is responsible, unless it be established to the satisfaction of the court that disclosure is necessary in the interests of justice or national security or for the prevention of disorder or crime. **36-010**

Publication of matters exempted from disclosure in court

36-011 **11.** In any case where a court (having power to do so) allows a name or other matter to be withheld from the public in proceedings before the court, the court may give such directions prohibiting the publication of that name or matter in connection with the proceedings as appear to the court to be necessary for the purpose for which it was so withheld.

Offences of contempt of magistrates' courts

36-012 **12.**—(1) A magistrates' court has jurisdiction under this section to deal with any person who—

(a) wilfully insults the justice or justices, any witness before or officer of the court or any solicitor or counsel having business in the court, during his or their sitting or attendance in court or in going to or returning from the court; or

(b) wilfully interrupts the proceedings of the court or otherwise misbehaves in court.

(2) In any such case the court may order any officer of the court, or any constable, to take the offender into custody and detain him until the rising of the court; and the court may, if it thinks fit, commit the offender to custody for a specified period not exceeding one month or impose on him a fine not exceeding [£2,500][1], or both.

[(2A) A fine imposed under subsection (2) above shall be deemed, for the purposes of any enactment, to be a sum adjudged to be paid by a conviction.][2]

(4) A magistrates' court may at any time revoke an order of committal made under subsection (2) and, if the offender is in custody, order his discharge.

(5) Section 135 of the Powers of Criminal Courts (Sentencing) Act 2000 (limit on fines in respect of young persons) and the following provisions of the Magistrates' Courts Act 1980 apply in relation to an order under this section as they apply in relation to a sentence on conviction or finding of guilty of an offence[; and those provisions of the Magistrates' Court Act 1980 are sections 75 to 91 (enforcement); section 108 (appeal to Crown Court); section 136 (overnight detention in default of payment); and section 142(1)(power to rectify mistakes)][3].

Penalties for contempt and kindred offences

Proceedings in England and Wales

36-013 **14.**—(1) In any case where a court has power to commit a person to prison for contempt of court and (apart from this provision) no limitation applies to the period of committal, the committal shall (without prejudice to the power of the court to order his earlier discharge) be for a fixed term, and that term shall not on any occasion exceed two years in the case of committal by a superior court, or one month in the case of committal by an inferior court.

(2) In any case where an inferior court has power to fine a person for contempt of court and (apart from this provision) no limit applies to the amount of the fine, the fine shall not on any occasion exceed [£2,500][4].

(2A) In the exercise of jurisdiction to commit for contempt of court or any kindred offence the court shall not deal with the offender by making an order

[1] Amount substituted by Criminal Justice Act 1991 c.53 Sch 4 (I) para 1
[2] Substituted by Criminal Justice Act 1993 c.36 Sch 3 para 6 (4)
[3] Words substituted by Powers of Criminal Courts (Sentencing) Act 2000 c.6 Sch 9 para 83 (b)
[4] Amount substituted by Criminal Justice Act 1991 c.53 Sch 4 (I) para 1

under section 60 of the Powers of Criminal Courts (Sentencing) Act 2000 (an attendance centre order) if it appears to the court, after considering any available evidence, that he is under 17 years of age.

(2A) A fine imposed under subsection (2) above shall be deemed, for the purposes of any enactment, to be a sum adjudged to be paid by a conviction.

(4) Each of the superior courts shall have the like power to make a hospital order or guardianship order under [section 37 of the Mental Health Act 1983 or an interim hospital order under section 38 of that Act][1] in the case of a person suffering from mental illness or [severe mental impairment][2] who could otherwise be committed to prison for contempt of court as the Crown Court has under that section in the case of a person convicted of an offence.

(4A) Each of the superior courts shall have the like power to make an order under section 35 of the said Act of 1983 (remand for report on accused's mental condition) where there is reason to suspect that a person who could be committed to prison for contempt of court is suffering from mental illness or severe mental impairment as the Crown Court has under that section in the case of an accused person within the meaning of that section.

(4A) For the purposes of the preceding provisions of this section a county court shall be treated as a superior court and not as an inferior court.

Child Abduction Act 1984

CHAPTER 37

PART I

OFFENCES UNDER LAW OF ENGLAND AND WALES

Offence of abduction of child by parent, etc

1.—(1) Subject to subsections (5) and (8) below, a person connected with a child under the age of sixteen commits an offence if he takes or sends the child out of the United Kingdom without the appropriate consent. **37-001**

(2) A person is connected with a child for the purposes of this section if—

(a) he is a parent of the child; or

(b) in the case of a child whose parents were not married to each other at the time of his birth, there are reasonable grounds for believing that he is the father of the child; or

(c) he is a guardian of the child; or

(ca) he is a special guardian of the child; or

(d) he is a person in whose favour a residence order is in force with respect to the child; or

(e) he has custody of the child.

(3) In this section 'the appropriate consent', in relation to a child, means —

(a) the consent of each of the following—

(i) the child's mother;

(ii) the child's father, if he has parental responsibility for him;

---

[1] Words substituted by Mental Health Act 1983 c.20 Sch 4 para 57 (a)

[2] Words substituted by Mental Health Act 1983 c.20 Sch 4 para 57 (a)

(iii) any guardian of the child;
(iiia) any special guardian of the child;
(iv) any person in whose favour a residence order is in force with respect to the child;
(v) any person who has custody of the child; or

(b) the leave of the court granted under or by virtue of any provision of Part II of the Children Act 1989; or

(c) if any person has custody of the child, the leave of the court which awarded custody to him'

(4) A person does not commit an offence under this section by taking or sending a child out of the United Kingdom without obtaining the appropriate consent if—

(a) he is a person in whose favour there is a residence order in force with respect to the child, and he takes or sends the child out of the United Kingdom for a period of less than one month; or

(b) he is a special guardian of the child and he takes or sends the child out of the United Kingdom for a period of less than three months.

(4A) Subsection (4) above does not apply if the person taking or sending the child out of the United Kingdom does so in breach of an order under Part II of the Children Act 1989.

(5) A person does not commit an offence under this section by doing anything without the consent of another person whose consent is required under the foregoing provisions if—

(a) he does it in the belief that the other person—
(i) has consented; or
(ii) would consent if he was aware of all the relevant circumstances; or

(b) he has taken all reasonable steps to communicate with the other person but has been unable to communicate with him; or

(c) the other person has unreasonably refused to consent,

(5A) Subsection (5)(c) above does not apply if—

(a) the person who refused to consent is a person—
(i) in whose favour there is a residence order in force with respect to the child;
(ia) who is a special guardian of the child; or
(ii) who has custody of the child; or

(b) the person taking or sending the child out of the United Kingdom is, by so acting, in breach of an order made by a court in the United Kingdom.

(6) Where, in proceedings for an offence under this section, there is sufficient evidence to raise an issue as to the application of subsection (5) above, it shall be for the prosecution to prove that that subsection does not apply.

(7) For the purposes of this section—

(a) 'guardian of a child', 'special guardian''residence order' and 'parental responsibility' have the same meaning as in the Children Act 1989; and

(b) a person shall be treated as having custody of a child if there is in force an order of a court in the United Kingdom awarding him (whether solely or jointly with another person) custody, legal custody or care and control of the child.

(8) This section shall have effect subject to the provisions of the Schedule to this Act in relation to a child who is in the care of a local authority [detained in a

place of safety, remanded to a local authority accommodation or the subject of] proceedings or an order relating to adoption.

Offence of abduction of child by other persons

2.—(1) [Subject to subsection (3) below, a person, other than one mentioned in subsection (2) below][1] commits an offence if, without lawful authority or reasonable excuse, he takes or detains a child under the age of sixteen— **37-002**

(a) so as to remove him from the lawful control of any person having lawful control of the child; or

(b) so as to keep him out of the lawful control of any person entitled to lawful control of the child.

(2) The persons are—

(a) where the father and mother of the child in question were married to each other at the time of his birth, the child's father and mother;

(b) where the father and mother of the child in question were not married to each other at the time of his birth, the child's mother; and

(c) any other person mentioned in section 1(2)(c) to (e) above.

(3) In proceedings against any person for an offence under this section, it shall be a defence for that person to prove—

(a) where the father and mother of the child in question were not married to each other at the time of his birth—

(i) that he is the child's father; or

(ii) that, at the time of the alleged offence, he believed, on reasonable grounds, that he was the child's father; or

(b) that, at the time of the alleged offence, he believed that the child had attained the age of sixteen.

Construction of references to taking, sending and detaining

3. For the purposes of this Part of this Act— **37-003**

(a) a person shall be regarded as taking a child if he causes or induces the child to accompany him or any other person or causes the child to be taken;

(b) a person shall be regarded as sending a child if he causes the child to be sent;

(c) a person shall be regarded as detaining a child if he causes the child to be detained or induces the child to remain with him or any other person; and

(d) references to a child's parents and to a child whose parents were (or were not) married to each other at the time of his birth shall be construed in accordance with section 1 of the Family Law Reform Act 1987 (which extends their meaning).

Penalties and prosecutions

4.—(1) A person guilty of an offence under this Part of this Act shall be liable— **37-004**

(a) on summary conviction, to imprisonment for a term not exceeding six months or to a fine not exceeding the statutory maximum, or to both such imprisonment and fine;

(b) on conviction on indictment, to imprisonment for a term not exceeding seven years.

[1] Words substituted by Children Act 1989 c.41 Sch 12 para 38 (1)

(2) No prosecution for an offence under section 1 above shall be instituted except by or with the consent of the Director of Public Prosecutions.

Restriction on prosecutions for offence of kidnapping

37-005 **5.** Except by or with the consent of the Director of Public Prosecutions no prosecution shall be instituted for an offence of kidnapping if it was committed—

(a) against a child under the age of sixteen; and

(b) by a person connected with the child, within the meaning of section 1 above.

Police and Criminal Evidence Act 1984

CHAPTER 60

PART III

ARREST

Arrest without warrant for arrestable offences

38-001 **24.**—(1) The powers of summary arrest conferred by the following subsections shall apply—

(a) to offences for which the sentence is fixed by law;

(b) to offences for which a person of 18 years of age or over (not previously convicted) may be sentenced to imprisonment for a term of five years (or might be so sentenced but for the restrictions imposed by section 33 of the Magistrates' Courts Act 1980); and

(c) to the offences [listed in Schedule 1A][1],

and in this Act "arrestable offence" means any such offence.

(2) Schedule 1A (which lists the offences referred to in subsection (1)(c)) shall have effect.

(3) Without prejudice to section 2 of the Criminal Attempts Act 1981, the powers of summary arrest conferred by the following subsections shall also apply to the offences of—

(a) conspiring to commit any of the offences listed in Schedule 1A;

(b) attempting to commit any such offence other than one which is a summary offence;

(c) inciting, aiding, abetting, counselling or procuring the commission of any such offence;

and such offences are also arrestable offences for the purposes of this Act.

(4) Any person may arrest without a warrant—

(a) anyone who is in the act of committing an arrestable offence;

(b) anyone whom he has reasonable grounds for suspecting to be committing such an offence.

(5) Where an arrestable offence has been committed, any person may arrest without a warrant—

(a) anyone who is guilty of the offence;

---

[1] Words substituted by Police Reform Act 2002 c.30 Pt 4 c 2 s 48 (2)

(b) anyone whom he has reasonable grounds for suspecting to be guilty of it.

(6) Where a constable has reasonable grounds for suspecting that an arrestable offence has been committed, he may arrest without a warrant anyone whom he has reasonable grounds for suspecting to be guilty of the offence.

(7) A constable may arrest without a warrant—

(a) anyone who is about to commit an arrestable offence;

(b) anyone whom he has reasonable grounds for suspecting to be about to commit an arrestable offence.

General arrest conditions

25.—(1) Where a constable has reasonable grounds for suspecting that any offence which is not an arrestable offence has been committed or attempted, or is being committed or attempted, he may arrest the relevant person if it appears to him that service of a summons is impracticable or inappropriate because any of the general arrest conditions is satisfied. **38-002**

(2) In this section "the relevant person" means any person whom the constable has reasonable grounds to suspect of having committed or having attempted to commit the offence or of being in the course of committing or attempting to commit it.

(3) The general arrest conditions are—

(a) that the name of the relevant person is unknown to, and cannot be readily ascertained by, the constable;

(b) that the constable has reasonable grounds for doubting whether a name furnished by the relevant person as his name is his real name;

(c) that—

(i) the relevant person has failed to furnish a satisfactory address for service; or

(ii) the constable has reasonable grounds for doubting whether an address furnished by the relevant person is a satisfactory address for service;

(d) that the constable has reasonable grounds for believing that arrest is necessary to prevent the relevant person—

(i) causing physical injury to himself or any other person;

(ii) suffering physical injury;

(iii) causing loss of or damage to property;

(iv) committing an offence against public decency; or

(v) causing an unlawful obstruction of the highway;

(e) that the constable has reasonable grounds for believing that arrest is necessary to protect a child or other vulnerable person from the relevant person.

(4) For the purposes of subsection (3) above an address is a satisfactory address for service if it appears to the constable—

(a) that the relevant person will be at it for a sufficiently long period for it to be possible to serve him with a summons; or

(b) that some other person specified by the relevant person will accept service of a summons for the relevant person at it.

(5) Nothing in subsection (3)(d) above authorises the arrest of a person under sub-paragraph (iv) of that paragraph except where members of the public going about their normal business cannot reasonably be expected to avoid the person to be arrested.

(6) This section shall not prejudice any power of arrest conferred apart from this section.

Information to be given on arrest

38-003 **28.**—(1) Subject to subsection (5) below, where a person is arrested, otherwise than by being informed that he is under arrest, the arrest is not lawful unless the person arrested is informed that he is under arrest as soon as is practicable after his arrest.

(2) Where a person is arrested by a constable, subsection (1) above applies regardless of whether the fact of the arrest is obvious.

(3) Subject to subsection (5) below, no arrest is lawful unless the person arrested is informed of the ground for the arrest at the time of, or as soon as is practicable after, the arrest.

(4) Where a person is arrested by a constable, subsection (3) above applies regardless of whether the ground for the arrest is obvious.

(5) Nothing in this section is to be taken to require a person to be informed—

(a) that he is under arrest; or

(b) of the ground for the arrest,

if it was not reasonably practicable for him to be so informed by reason of his having escaped from arrest before the information could be given.

Power of constable to use reasonable force

38-004 **117.** Where any provision of this Act—

(a) confers a power on a constable; and

(b) does not provide that the power may only be exercised with the consent of some person, other than a police officer,

the officer may use reasonable force, if necessary, in the exercise of the power.

Schedule 1A

SPECIFIC OFFENCES WHICH ARE ARRESTABLE OFFENCES

Customs and Excise Acts

38-005 [**1.** An offence for which a person may be arrested under the customs and excise Acts (within the meaning of the Customs and Excise Management Act 1979 c.2)).][1]

Official Secrets Act 1920

38-006 [**2.** An offence under the Official Secrets Act 1920 c.75) which is not an arrestable offence by virtue of the term of imprisonment for which a person may be sentenced in respect of them.][2]

Prevention of Crime Act 1953

38-007 [**3.** An offence under section 1(1) of the Prevention of Crime Act 1953 c.14) (prohibition of carrying offensive weapons without lawful authority or excuse).][3]

Sexual Offences Act 1956

38-008 [**4.** An offence under—

[1] Added by Police Reform Act 2002 c.30 Sch 6 para 1
[2] Added by Police Reform Act 2002 c.30 Sch 6 para 1
[3] Added by Police Reform Act 2002 c.30 Sch 6 para 1

(a) section 22 of the Sexual Offences Act 1956 c.69) (causing prostitution of women; or
(b) section 23 of that Act (procuration of girl under 21).][1]

Obscene Publications Act 1959

[5. An offence under section 2 of the Obscene Publications Act 1959 c.66) (publication of obscene matter).][2] **38-009**

Theft Act 1968

[6. An offence under— **38-010**
(a) section 12(1) of the Theft Act 1968 c.60) (taking motor vehicle or other conveyance without authority etc.); or
(b) section 25(1) of that Act (going equipped for stealing etc.).][3]

Theft Act 1978

[7. An offence under section 3 of the Theft Act 1978 c.31) (making off without payment).][4] **38-011**

Protection of Children Act 1978

[8. An offence under section 1 of the Protection of Children Act 1978 c.37) (indecent photographs and pseudo-photographs of children).][5] **38-012**

Wildlife and Countryside Act 1981

[9. An offence under section 1(1) or (2) or 6 of the Wildlife and Countryside Act 1981 c.69) (taking, possessing, selling etc. of wild birds) in respect of a bird included in Schedule 1 to that Act or any part of, or anything derived from, such a bird.][6] **38-013**

38-014

[10. An offence under—
(a) section 1(5) of the Wildlife and Countryside Act 1981 (disturbance of wild birds);
(b) section 9 or 13(1)(a) or (2) of that Act (taking, possessing, selling etc. of wild animals or plants); or
(c) section 14 of that Act (introduction of new species etc.).][7]

Civil Aviation Act 1982

[11. An offence under section 39(1) of the Civil Aviation Act 1982 c.16) (trespass on aerodrome).][8] **38-015**

Aviation Security Act 1982

[12. An offence under section 21C(1) or 21D(1) of the Aviation Security Act 1982 c.36) (unauthorised presence in a restricted zone or on an aircraft).][9] **38-016**

[1] Added by Police Reform Act 2002 c.30 Sch 6 para 1
[2] Added by Police Reform Act 2002 c.30 Sch 6 para 1
[3] Added by Police Reform Act 2002 c.30 Sch 6 para 1
[4] Added by Police Reform Act 2002 c.30 Sch 6 para 1
[5] Added by Police Reform Act 2002 c.30 Sch 6 para 1
[6] Added by Police Reform Act 2002 c.30 Sch 6 para 1
[7] Added by Police Reform Act 2002 c.30 Sch 6 para 1
[8] Added by Police Reform Act 2002 c.30 Sch 6 para 1
[9] Added by Police Reform Act 2002 c.30 Sch 6 para 1

Sexual Offences Act 1985

38-017 [**13.** An offence under section 1 of the Sexual Offences Act 1985 c.44) (kerb-crawling).][1]

Public Order Act 1986

38-018 [**14.** An offence under section 19 of the Public Order Act 1986 c.64) (publishing etc. material likely to stir up racial or religious hatred).][2]

Criminal Justice Act 1988

38-019 [**15.** An offence under—

(a) section 139(1) of the Criminal Justice Act 1988 c.33) (offence of having article with a blade or point in public place); or

(b) section 139A(1) or (2) of that Act (offence of having article with a blade or point or offensive weapon on school premises).][3]

Road Traffic Act 1988

38-020 [**16.** An offence under section 103(1)(b) of the Road Traffic Act 1988 c.52) (driving while disqualified).][4]

38-021 [**17.** An offence under subsection (4) of section 170 of the Road Traffic Act 1988 (failure to stop and report an accident) in respect of an accident to which that section applies by virtue of subsection (1)(a) of that section (accidents causing personal injury).][5]

Official Secrets Act 1989

38-022 [**18.** An offence under any provision of the Official Secrets Act 1989 c.6) other than subsection (1), (4) or (5) of section 8 of that Act.][6]

Football Spectators Act 1989

38-023 [**19.** An offence under section 14J or 21C of the Football Spectators Act 1989 c.37) (failing to comply with requirements imposed by or under a banning order or a notice under section 21B).][7]

Football (Offences) Act 1991

38-024 [**20.** An offence under any provision of the Football (Offences) Act 1991 c.19).][8]

Criminal Justice and Public Order Act 1994

38-025 [**21.** An offence under—

(a) section 60AA(7) of the Criminal Justice and Public Order Act 1994 c.33) (failing to comply with requirement to remove disguise);

(b) section 166 of that Act (sale of tickets by unauthorised persons); or

(c) section 167 of that Act (touting for car hire services).][9]

1 Added by Police Reform Act 2002 c.30 Sch 6 para 1
2 Added by Police Reform Act 2002 c.30 Sch 6 para 1
3 Added by Police Reform Act 2002 c.30 Sch 6 para 1
4 Added by Police Reform Act 2002 c.30 Sch 6 para 1
5 Added by Police Reform Act 2002 c.30 Sch 6 para 1
6 Added by Police Reform Act 2002 c.30 Sch 6 para 1
7 Added by Police Reform Act 2002 c.30 Sch 6 para 1
8 Added by Police Reform Act 2002 c.30 Sch 6 para 1
9 Added by Police Reform Act 2002 c.30 Sch 6 para 1

Police Act 1996

[**22.** An offence under section 89(1) of the Police Act 1996 c.16) (assaulting a police officer in the execution of his duty or a person assisting such an officer).][1] **38-026**

Protection from Harassment Act 1997

[**23.** An offence under section 2 of the Protection from Harassment Act 1997 c.40) (harassment).][2] **38-027**

Crime and Disorder Act 1998

[**24.** An offence falling within section 32(1)(a) of the Crime and Disorder Act 1998 c.37) (racially or religiously aggravated harassment).][3] **38-028**

Criminal Justice and Police Act 2001

[**25.** An offence under— **38-029**

(a) section 12(4) of the Criminal Justice and Police Act 2001 c.16) (failure to comply with requirements imposed by constable in relation to consumption of alcohol in public place); or

(b) section 46 of that Act (placing of advertisements in relation to prostitution).][4]

Prosecution of Offences Act 1985

CHAPTER 23

PART I

THE CROWN PROSECUTION SERVICE

Guidelines

Guidelines for Crown Prosecutors

10.—(1) The Director shall issue a Code for Crown Prosecutors[5] giving guidance on general principles to be applied by them— **39-001**

(a) in determining, in any case—

(i) whether proceedings for an offence should be instituted or, where proceedings have been instituted, whether they should be discontinued; or

(ii) what charges should be preferred; and

(b) in considering, in any case, representations to be made by them to any magistrates' court about the mode of trial suitable for that case.

(2) The Director may from time to time make alterations in the Code.

---

[1] Added by Police Reform Act 2002 c.30 Sch 6 para 1
[2] Added by Police Reform Act 2002 c.30 Sch 6 para 1
[3] Added by Police Reform Act 2002 c.30 Sch 6 para 1
[4] Added by Police Reform Act 2002 c.30 Sch 6 para 1
[5] See Code for Crown Prosecutors, Para A-001, p.219

(3) The provisions of the Code shall be set out in the Director's report under section 9 of this Act for the year in which the Code is issued; and any alteration in the Code shall be set out in his report under that section for the year in which the alteration is made.

Intoxicating Substances (Supply) Act 1985

CHAPTER 26

Offence of supply of intoxicating substance

40-001 **1.**—(1) It is an offence for a person to supply or offer to supply a substance other than a controlled drug—

(a) to a person under the age of eighteen whom he knows, or has reasonable cause to believe, to be under that age; or

(b) to a person—

(i) who is acting on behalf of a person under that age; and

(ii) whom he knows, or has reasonable cause to believe, to be so acting,

if he knows or has reasonable cause to believe that the substance is, or its fumes are, likely to be inhaled by the person under the age of eighteen for the purpose of causing intoxication.

(2) In proceedings against any person for an offence under subsection (1) above it is a defence for him to show that at the time he made the supply or offer he was under the age of eighteen and was acting otherwise than in the course or furtherance of a business.

(3) A person guilty of an offence under this section shall be liable on summary conviction to imprisonment for a term not exceeding six months or to a fine not exceeding level 5 on the standard scale [...][1], or to both.

(4) In this section "controlled drug" has the same meaning as in the Misuse of Drugs Act 1971.

Prohibition of Female Circumcision Act 1985

CHAPTER 38

Prohibition of female circumcision

41-001 **1.**—(1) Subject to section 2 below, it shall be an offence for any person—

(a) to excise, infibulate or otherwise mutilate the whole or any part of the labia majora or labia minora or clitoris of another person; or

(b) to aid, abet, counsel or procure the performance by another person of any of those acts on that other person's own body.

(2) A person guilty of an offence under this section shall be liable—

[1] Words repealed by Statute Law (Repeals) Act 1993 c.50 Sch 1 (XIV) para 1

(a) on conviction on indictment, to a fine or to imprisonment for a term not exceeding five years or to both; or
(b) on summary conviction, to a fine not exceeding the statutory maximum [...][1] or to imprisonment for a term not exceeding six months, or to both.

Saving for necessary surgical operations

2.—(1) Subsection (1)(a) of section 1 shall not render unlawful the performance of a surgical operation if that operation— **41-002**
(a) is necessary for the physical or mental health of the person on whom it is performed and is performed by a registered medical practitioner; or
(b) is performed on a person who is in any stage of labour or has just given birth and is so performed for purposes connected with that labour or birth by—
(i) a registered medical practitioner or a registered midwife; or
(ii) a person undergoing a course of training with a view to becoming a registered medical practitioner or a registered midwife.

(2) In determining for the purposes of this section whether an operation is necessary for the mental health of a person, no account shall be taken of the effect on that person of any belief on the part of that or any other person that the operation is required as a matter of custom or ritual.

Sexual Offences Act 1985

CHAPTER 44

Soliciting of women by men

Kerb-crawling

1.—(1) A man commits an offence if he solicits a woman (or different women) for the purpose of prostitution— **42-001**
(a) from a motor vehicle while it is in a street or public place; or
(b) in a street or public place while in the immediate vicinity of a motor vehicle that he has just got out of or off,

persistently or, [...][2]in such manner or in such circumstances as to be likely to cause annoyance to the woman (or any of the women) solicited, or nuisance to other persons in the neighbourhood.

(2) A person guilty of an offence under this section shall be liable on summary conviction to a fine not exceeding level 3 on the standard scale [...][3].

(3) In this section "motor vehicle" has the same meaning as in [the Road Traffic Act 1988][4].

[1] Words repealed by Statute Law (Repeals) Act 1993 c.50 Sch 1 (XIV) para 1
[2] Words repealed by Statute Law (Repeals) Act 1993 c.50 Sch 1 (I) para 1
[3] Words repealed by Statute Law (Repeals) Act 1993 c.50 Sch 1 (XIV) para 1
[4] Words substituted by Road Traffic (Consequential Provisions) Act 1988 c.54 s 4 Sch 4 para 29

Persistent soliciting of women for the purpose of prostitution

42-002 **2.**—(1) A man commits an offence if in a street or public place he persistently solicits a woman (or different women) for the purpose of prostitution.

(2) A person guilty of an offence under this section shall be liable on summary conviction to a fine not exceeding level 3 on the standard scale [...][1].

Supplementary

Interpretation

42-003 **4.**—(1) References in this Act to a man soliciting a woman for the purpose of prostitution are references to his soliciting her for the purpose of obtaining her services as a prostitute.

(2) The use in any provision of this Act of the word "man" without the addition of the word "boy" shall not prevent the provision applying to any person to whom it would have applied if both words had been used, and similarly with the words "woman" and "girl".

(3) Paragraphs (a) and (b) of section 6 of the Interpretation Act 1978 (words importing the masculine gender to include the feminine, and vice versa) do not apply to this Act.

(4) For the purposes of this Act "street" includes any bridge, road, lane, footway, subway, square, court, alley or passage, whether a thoroughfare or not, which is for the time being open to the public; and the doorways and entrances of premises abutting on a street (as hereinbefore defined), and any ground adjoining and open to a street, shall be treated as forming part of the street.

Public Order Act 1986

CHAPTER 64

PART I

NEW OFFENCES

Riot

43-001 **1.**—(1) Where 12 or more persons who are present together use or threaten unlawful violence for a common purpose and the conduct of them (taken together) is such as would cause a person of reasonable firmness present at the scene to fear for his personal safety, each of the persons using unlawful violence for the common purpose is guilty of riot.

(2) It is immaterial whether or not the 12 or more use or threaten unlawful violence simultaneously.

(3) The common purpose may be inferred from conduct.

(4) No person of reasonable firmness need actually be, or be likely to be, present at the scene.

(5) Riot may be committed in private as well as in public places.

[1] Words repealed by Statute Law (Repeals) Act 1993 c.50 Sch 1 (XIV) para 1

(6) A person guilty of riot is liable on conviction on indictment to imprisonment for a term not exceeding ten years or a fine or both.

Violent disorder

2.—(1) Where 3 or more persons who are present together use or threaten unlawful violence and the conduct of them (taken together) is such as would cause a person of reasonable firmness present at the scene to fear for his personal safety, each of the persons using or threatening unlawful violence is guilty of violent disorder. **43-002**

(2) It is immaterial whether or not the 3 or more use or threaten unlawful violence simultaneously.

(3) No person of reasonable firmness need actually be, or be likely to be, present at the scene.

(4) Violent disorder may be committed in private as well as in public places.

(5) A person guilty of violent disorder is liable on conviction on indictment to imprisonment for a term not exceeding 5 years or a fine or both, or on summary conviction to imprisonment for a term not exceeding 6 months or a fine not exceeding the statutory maximum or both.

Affray

3.—(1) A person is guilty of affray if he uses or threatens unlawful violence towards another and his conduct is such as would cause a person of reasonable firmness present at the scene to fear for his personal safety. **43-003**

(2) Where 2 or more persons use or threaten the unlawful violence, it is the conduct of them taken together that must be considered for the purposes of subsection (1).

(3) For the purposes of this section a threat cannot be made by the use of words alone.

(4) No person of reasonable firmness need actually be, or be likely to be, present at the scene.

(5) Affray may be committed in private as well as in public places.

(6) A constable may arrest without warrant anyone he reasonably suspects is committing affray.

(7) A person guilty of affray is liable on conviction on indictment to imprisonment for a term not exceeding 3 years or a fine or both, or on summary conviction to imprisonment for a term not exceeding 6 months or a fine not exceeding the statutory maximum or both.

Fear or provocation of violence

4.—(1) A person is guilty of an offence if he— **43-004**

(a) uses towards another person threatening, abusive or insulting words or behaviour, or

(b) distributes or displays to another person any writing, sign or other visible representation which is threatening, abusive or insulting,

with intent to cause that person to believe that immediate unlawful violence will be used against him or another by any person, or to provoke the immediate use of unlawful violence by that person or another, or whereby that person is likely to believe that such violence will be used or it is likely that such violence will be provoked.

(2) An offence under this section may be committed in a public or a private place, except that no offence is committed where the words or behaviour are used, or the writing, sign or other visible representation is distributed or displayed, by

a person inside a dwelling and the other person is also inside that or another dwelling.

(3) A constable may arrest without warrant anyone he reasonably suspects is committing an offence under this section.

(4) A person guilty of an offence under this section is liable on summary conviction to imprisonment for a term not exceeding 6 months or a fine not exceeding level 5 on the standard scale or both.

[Intentional harassment, alarm or distress

43-005 **4A.**—(1) A person is guilty of an offence if, with intent to cause a person harassment, alarm or distress, he—

(a) uses threatening, abusive or insulting words or behaviour, or disorderly behaviour, or

(b) displays any writing, sign or other visible representation which is threatening, abusive or insulting,

thereby causing that or another person harassment, alarm or distress.

(2) An offence under this section may be committed in a public or a private place, except that no offence is committed where the words or behaviour are used, or the writing, sign or other visible representation is displayed, by a person inside a dwelling and the person who is harassed, alarmed or distressed is also inside that or another dwelling.

(3) It is a defence for the accused to prove—

(a) that he was inside a dwelling and had no reason to believe that the words or behaviour used, or the writing, sign or other visible representation displayed, would be heard or seen by a person outside that or any other dwelling, or

(b) that his conduct was reasonable.

(4) A constable may arrest without warrant anyone he reasonably suspects is committing an offence under this section.

(5) A person guilty of an offence under this section is liable on summary conviction to imprisonment for a term not exceeding 6 months or a fine not exceeding level 5 on the standard scale or both.][1]

Harassment, alarm or distress

43-006 **5.**—(1) A person is guilty of an offence if he—

(a) uses threatening, abusive or insulting words or behaviour, or disorderly behaviour, or

(b) displays any writing, sign or other visible representation which is threatening, abusive or insulting,

within the hearing or sight of a person likely to be caused harassment, alarm or distress thereby.

(2) An offence under this section may be committed in a public or a private place, except that no offence is committed where the words or behaviour are used, or the writing, sign or other visible representation is displayed, by a person inside a dwelling and the other person is also inside that or another dwelling.

(3) It is a defence for the accused to prove—

(a) that he had no reason to believe that there was any person within hearing or sight who was likely to be caused harassment, alarm or distress, or

[1] Added by Criminal Justice and Public Order Act 1994 c.33 Pt XII s 154

(b) that he was inside a dwelling and had no reason to believe that the words or behaviour used, or the writing, sign or other visible representation displayed, would be heard or seen by a person outside that or any other dwelling, or

(c) that his conduct was reasonable.

(4) A constable may arrest a person without warrant if—

(a) he engages in offensive conduct which [a][1] constable warns him to stop, and

(b) he engages in further offensive conduct immediately or shortly after the warning.

(5) In subsection (4) "offensive conduct" means conduct the constable reasonably suspects to constitute an offence under this section, and the conduct mentioned in paragraph (a) and the further conduct need not be of the same nature.

(6) A person guilty of an offence under this section is liable on summary conviction to a fine not exceeding level 3 on the standard scale.

Mental element: miscellaneous

6.—(1) A person is guilty of riot only if he intends to use violence or is aware that his conduct may be violent. **43-007**

(2) A person is guilty of violent disorder or affray only if he intends to use or threaten violence or is aware that his conduct may be violent or threaten violence.

(3) A person is guilty of an offence under section 4 only if he intends his words or behaviour, or the writing, sign or other visible representation, to be threatening, abusive or insulting, or is aware that it may be threatening, abusive or insulting.

(4) A person is guilty of an offence under section 5 only if he intends his words or behaviour, or the writing, sign or other visible representation, to be threatening, abusive or insulting, or is aware that it may be threatening, abusive or insulting or (as the case may be) he intends his behaviour to be or is aware that it may be disorderly.

(5) For the purposes of this section a person whose awareness is impaired by intoxication shall be taken to be aware of that of which he would be aware if not intoxicated, unless he shows either that his intoxication was not self-induced or that it was caused solely by the taking or administration of a substance in the course of medical treatment.

(6) In subsection (5) "intoxication" means any intoxication, whether caused by drink, drugs or other means, or by a combination of means.

(7) Subsections (1) and (2) do not affect the determination for the purposes of riot or violent disorder of the number of persons who use or threaten violence.

Procedure: miscellaneous

7.—(1) No prosecution for an offence of riot or incitement to riot may be instituted except by or with the consent of the Director of Public Prosecutions. **43-008**

(2) For the purposes of the rules against charging more than one offence in the same count or information, each of sections 1 to 5 creates one offence.

(3) If on the trial on indictment of a person charged with violent disorder or affray the jury find him not guilty of the offence charged, they may (without

[1] Word substitued by Public Order (Amendment) Act 1996 c.59 s 1

prejudice to section 6(3) of the Criminal Law Act 1967) find him guilty of an offence under section 4.

(4) The Crown Court has the same powers and duties in relation to a person who is by virtue of subsection (3) convicted before it of an offence under section 4 as a magistrates' court would have on convicting him of the offence.

Interpretation

43-009 **8.** In this Part—

"dwelling" means any structure or part of a structure occupied as a person's home or as other living accommodation (whether the occupation is separate or shared with others) but does not include any part not so occupied, and for this purpose "structure" includes a tent, caravan, vehicle, vessel or other temporary or movable structure;

"violence" means any violent conduct, so that—

(a) except in the context of affray, it includes violent conduct towards property as well as violent conduct towards persons, and

(b) it is not restricted to conduct causing or intended to cause injury or damage but includes any other violent conduct (for example, throwing at or towards a person a missile of a kind capable of causing injury which does not hit or falls short).

PART III

RACIAL HATRED

Meaning of "racial hatred"

Meaning of "racial hatred"

43-010 **17.** In this Part "racial hatred" means hatred against a group of persons defined by reference to colour, race, nationality (including citizenship) or ethnic or national origins.

Acts intended or likely to stir up racial hatred

Use of words or behaviour or display of written material

43-011 **18.**—(1) A person who uses threatening, abusive or insulting words or behaviour, or displays any written material which is threatening, abusive or insulting, is guilty of an offence if—

(a) he intends thereby to stir up racial hatred, or

(b) having regard to all the circumstances racial hatred is likely to be stirred up thereby.

(2) An offence under this section may be committed in a public or a private place, except that no offence is committed where the words or behaviour are used, or the written material is displayed, by a person inside a dwelling and are not heard or seen except by other persons in that or another dwelling.

(3) A constable may arrest without warrant anyone he reasonably suspects is committing an offence under this section.

(4) In proceedings for an offence under this section it is a defence for the accused to prove that he was inside a dwelling and had no reason to believe that

the words or behaviour used, or the written material displayed, would be heard or seen by a person outside that or any other dwelling.

(5) A person who is not shown to have intended to stir up racial hatred is not guilty of an offence under this section if he did not intend his words or behaviour, or the written material, to be, and was not aware that it might be, threatening, abusive or insulting.

(6) This section does not apply to words or behaviour used, or written material displayed, solely for the purpose of being included in a programme included in a programme service.

Publishing or distributing written material

19.—(1) A person who publishes or distributes written material which is threatening, abusive or insulting is guilty of an offence if— **43-012**

(a) he intends thereby to stir up racial hatred, or

(b) having regard to all the circumstances racial hatred is likely to be stirred up thereby.

(2) In proceedings for an offence under this section it is a defence for an accused who is not shown to have intended to stir up racial hatred to prove that he was not aware of the content of the material and did not suspect, and had no reason to suspect, that it was threatening, abusive or insulting.

(3) References in this Part to the publication or distribution of written material are to its publication or distribution to the public or a section of the public.

PART V

MISCELLANEOUS AND GENERAL

Contamination of or interference with goods with intention of causing public alarm or anxiety, etc

38.—(1) It is an offence for a person, with the intention— **43-013**

(a) of causing public alarm or anxiety, or

(b) of causing injury to members of the public consuming or using the goods, or

(c) of causing economic loss to any person by reason of the goods being shunned by members of the public, or

(d) of causing economic loss to any person by reason of steps taken to avoid any such alarm or anxiety, injury or loss,

to contaminate or interfere with goods, or make it appear that goods have been contaminated or interfered with, or to place goods which have been contaminated or interfered with, or which appear to have been contaminated or interfered with, in a place where goods of that description are consumed, used, sold or otherwise supplied.

(2) It is also an offence for a person, with any such intention as is mentioned in paragraph (a), (c) or (d) of subsection (1), to threaten that he or another will do, or to claim that he or another has done, any of the acts mentioned in that subsection.

(3) It is an offence for a person to be in possession of any of the following articles with a view to the commission of an offence under subsection (1)—

(a) materials to be used for contaminating or interfering with goods or making it appear that goods have been contaminated or interfered with, or

(b) goods which have been contaminated or interfered with, or which appear to have been contaminated or interfered with.

(4) A person guilty of an offence under this section is liable—

(a) on conviction on indictment to imprisonment for a term not exceeding 10 years or a fine or both, or

(b) on summary conviction to imprisonment for a term not exceeding six months or a fine not exceeding the statutory maximum or both.

(5) In this section "goods" includes substances whether natural or manufactured and whether or not incorporated in or mixed with other goods.

(6) The reference in subsection (2) to a person claiming that certain acts have been committed does not include a person who in good faith reports or warns that such acts have been, or appear to have been, committed.

Criminal Justice Act 1987

CHAPTER 38

PART I

FRAUD

Conspiracy to defraud

Charges of and penalty for conspiracy to defraud

44-001 **12.**—(1) If—

(a) a person agrees with any other person or persons that a course of conduct shall be pursued; and

(b) that course of conduct will necessarily amount to or involve the commission of any offence or offences by one or more of the parties to the agreement if the agreement is carried out in accordance with their intentions,

the fact that it will do so shall not preclude a charge of conspiracy to defraud being brought against any of them in respect of the agreement.

(3) A person guilty of conspiracy to defraud is liable on conviction on indictment to imprisonment for a term not exceeding 10 years or a fine or both.

Malicious Communications Act 1988

CHAPTER 27

Offence of sending letters etc. with intent to cause distress or anxiety

45-001 **1.**—(1) Any person who sends to another person—

(a) a letter, electronic communication or article of any description which conveys—

(i) a message which is indecent or grossly offensive;
(ii) a threat; or
(iii) information which is false and known or believed to be false by the sender; or
(b) any article or electronic communication which is, in whole or part, of an indecent or grossly offensive nature,

is guilty of an offence if his purpose, or one of his purposes, in sending it is that it should, so far as falling within paragraph (a) or (b) above, cause distress or anxiety to the recipient or to any other person to whom he intends that it or its contents or nature should be communicated.

(2) A person is not guilty of an offence by virtue of subsection (1)(a)(ii) above if he shows—

(a) that the threat was used to reinforce a demand made by him on reasonable grounds; and
(b) that he believed , and had reasonable grounds for believing, that the use of the threat was a proper means of reinforcing the demand.

(2A) In this section "electronic communication" includes–

(a) any oral or other communication by means of a telecommunication system (within the meaning of the Telecommunications Act 1984 c.12)); and
(b) any communication (however sent) that is in electronic form.

(3) In this section references to sending include references to delivering or transmitting and to causing to be sent , delivered or transmitted and "sender" shall be construed accordingly.

(4) A person guilty of an offence under this section shall be liable on summary conviction to imprisonment for a term not exceeding six months or to a fine not exceeding level 5 on the standard scale, or to both.

Criminal Justice Act 1988

CHAPTER 33

Jurisidiction

Common assault and battery to be summary offences

39. Common assault and battery shall be summary offences and a person guilty of either of them shall be liable to a fine not exceeding level 5 no the standard scale, to imprisonment for a term not exceeding six months, or to both. **46-001**

PART XI

MISCELLANEOUS

Torture

Torture

46-002 **134.**—(1) A public official or person acting in an official capacity, whatever his nationality, commits the offence of torture if in the United Kingdom or elsewhere he intentionally inflicts severe pain or suffering on another in the performance or purported performance of his official duties.

(2) A person not falling within subsection (1) above commits the offence of torture, whatever his nationality, if—

(a) in the United Kingdom or elsewhere he intentionally inflicts severe pain or suffering on another at the instigation or with the consent or acquiescence—

(i) of a public official; or

(ii) of a person acting in an official capacity; and

(b) the official or other person is performing or purporting to perform his official duties when he instigates the commission of the offence or consents to or acquiesces in it.

(3) It is immaterial whether the pain or suffering is physical or mental and whether it is caused by an act or an omission.

(4) It shall be a defence for a person charged with an offence under this section in respect of any conduct of his to prove that he had lawful authority, justification or excuse for that conduct.

(5) For the purposes of this section "lawful authority, justification or excuse"-means—

(a) in relation to pain or suffering inflicted in the United Kingdom, lawful authority, justification or excuse under the law of the part of the United Kingdom where it was inflicted;

(b) in relation to pain or suffering inflicted outside the United Kingdom—

(i) if it was inflicted by a United Kingdom official acting under the law of the United Kingdom or by a person acting in an official capacity under that law, lawful authority, justification or excuse under that law;

(ii) if it was inflicted by a United Kingdom official acting under the law of any part of the United Kingdom or by a person acting in an official capacity under such law, lawful authority, justification or excuse under the law of the part of the United Kingdom under whose law he was acting; and

(iii) in any other case, lawful authority, justification or excuse under the law of the place where it was inflicted.

(6) A person who commits the offence of torture shall be liable on conviction on indictment to imprisonment for life.

Articles with blades or points and offensive weapons

Offence of having article with blade or point in public place

139.—(1) Subject to subsections (4) and (5) below, any person who has an article to which this section applies with him in a public place shall be guilty of an offence. **46-003**

(2) Subject to subsection (3) below, this section applies to any article which has a blade or is sharply pointed except a folding pocketknife.

(3) This section applies to a folding pocketknife if the cutting edge of its blade exceeds 3 inches.

(4) It shall be a defence for a person charged with an offence under this section to prove that he had good reason or lawful authority for having the article with him in a public place.

(5) Without prejudice to the generality of subsection (4) above, it shall be a defence for a person charged with an offence under this section to prove that he had the article with him—

(a) for use at work;

(b) for religious reasons; or

(c) as part of any national costume.

(6) A person guilty of an offence under subsection (1) above shall be liable[—][1]

[(a) on summary conviction, to imprisonment for a term not exceeding six months, or a fine not exceeding the statutory maximum, or both;

(b) on conviction on indictment, to imprisonment for a term not exceeding two years, or a fine, or both.][2]

(7) In this section "public place" includes any place to which at the material time the public have or are permitted access, whether on payment or otherwise.

(8) This section shall not have effect in relation to anything done before it comes into force.

Offence of having article with blade or point (or offensive weapon) on school premises

139A.—(1) Any person who has an article to which section 139 of this Act applies with him on school premises shall be guilty of an offence. **46-004**

(2) Any person who has an offensive weapon within the meaning of section 1 of the Prevention of Crime Act 1953 with him on school premises shall be guilty of an offence.

(3) It shall be a defence for a person charged with an offence under subsection (1) or (2) above to prove that he had good reason or lawful authority for having the article or weapon with him on the premises in question.

(4) Without prejudice to the generality of subsection (3) above, it shall be a defence for a person charged with an offence under subsection (1) or (2) above to prove that he had the article or weapon in question with him—

(a) for use at work,

(b) for educational purposes,

(c) for religious reasons, or

(d) as part of any national costume.

(5) A person guilty of an offence—

(a) under subsection (1) above shall be liable—

[1] Words substituted by Offensive Weapons Act 1996 c.26 s 3 (1)
[2] Words substituted by Offensive Weapons Act 1996 c.26 s 3 (1)

(i) on summary conviction to imprisonment for a term not exceeding six months, or a fine not exceeding the statutory maximum, or both;

(ii) on conviction on indictment, to imprisonment for a term not exceeding two years, or a fine, or both;

(b) under subsection (2) above shall be liable—

(i) on summary conviction, to imprisonment for a term not exceeding six months, or a fine not exceeding the statutory maximum, or both;

(ii) on conviction on indictment, to imprisonment for a term not exceeding four years, or a fine, or both.

(6) In this section and section 139B, "school premises" means land used for the purposes of a school excluding any land occupied solely as a dwelling by a person employed at the school; and "school"has the meaning given by [section 4 of the Education Act 1996][1].

Offensive weapons

46-005 **141.**—(1) Any person who manufactures, sells or hires or offers for sale or hire, exposes or has in his possession for the purpose of sale or hire, or lends or gives to any other person, a weapon to which this section applies shall be guilty of an offence and liable on summary conviction to imprisonment for a term not exceeding six months or to a fine not exceeding level 5 on the standard scale or both.

(2) The Secretary of State may by order made by statutory instrument direct that this section shall apply to any description of weapon specified in the order except—

(a) any weapon subject to the Firearms Act 1968; and

(b) crossbows.

(3) A statutory instrument containing an order under this section shall not be made unless a draft of the instrument has been laid before Parliament and has been approved by a resolution of each House of Parliament.

(4) The importation of a weapon to which this section applies is hereby prohibited.

(5) It shall be a defence for any person charged in respect of any conduct of his relating to a weapon to which this section applies—

(a) with an offence under subsection (1) above; or

(b) with an offence under section 50(2) or (3) of the Customs and Excise Management Act 1979 (improper importation),

to prove that his conduct was only for the purposes of functions carried out on behalf of the Crown or of a visiting force.

(8) It shall be a defence for any person charged in respect of any conduct of his relating to a weapon to which this section applies—

(a) with an offence under subsection (1) above; or

(b) with an offence under section 50(2) or (3) of the Customs and Excise Management Act 1979,

to prove that the conduct in question was only for the purposes of making the weapon available to a museum or gallery to which this subsection applies.

(9) If a person acting on behalf of a museum or gallery to which subsection (8) above applies is charged with hiring or lending a weapon to which this section applies, it shall be a defence for him to prove that he had reasonable grounds for

[1] Words substituted by Education Act 1996 c.56 Sch 37 (I) para 69

believing that the person to whom he lent or hired it would use it only for cultural, artistic or educational purposes.

(10) Subsection (8) above applies to a museum or gallery only if it does not distribute profits.

(11) In this section "museum or gallery" includes any institution which has as its purpose, or one of its purposes, the preservation, display and interpretation of material of historical, artistic or scientific interest and gives the public access to it.

Sale of knives and certain articles with blade or point to persons under sixteen

141A.—(1) Any person who sells to a person under the age of sixteen years an article to which this section applies shall be guilty of an offence and liable on summary conviction to imprisonment for a term not exceeding six months, or a fine not exceeding level 5 on the standard scale, or both. **46-006**

(2) Subject to subsection (3) below, this section applies to—

(a) any knife, knife blade or razor blade,

(b) any axe, and

(c) any other article which has a blade or which is sharply pointed and which is made or adapted for use for causing injury to the person.

(3) This section does not apply to any article described in—

(a) section 1 of the Restriction of Offensive Weapons Act 1959.

(b) an order made under section 141(2) of this Act, or

(c) an order made by the Secretary of State under this section.

(4) It shall be a defence for a person charged with an offence under subsection (1) above to prove that he took all reasonable precautions and exercised all due diligence to avoid the commission of the offence.

Road Traffic Act 1988

CHAPTER 52

PART I

PRINCIPAL ROAD SAFETY PROVISIONS

Driving offences

Causing death by dangerous driving

1. A person who causes the death of another person by driving a mechanically propelled vehicle dangerously on a road or other public place is guilty of an offence. **47-001**

Dangerous driving

2. A person who drives a mechanically propelled vehicle dangerously on a road or other public place is guilty of an offence. **47-002**

Meaning of dangerous driving

47-003 **2A.**—(1) For the purposes of sections 1 and 2 above a person is to be regarded as driving dangerously if (and, subject to subsection (2) below, only if)—

(a) the way he drives falls far below what would be expected of a competent and careful driver, and

(b) it would be obvious to a competent and careful driver that driving in that way would be dangerous.

(2) A person is also to be regarded as driving dangerously for the purposes of sections 1 and 2 above if it would be obvious to a competent and careful driver that driving the vehicle in its current state would be dangerous.

(3) In subsections (1) and (2) above "dangerous" refers to danger either of injury to any person or of serious damage to property; and in determining for the purposes of those subsections what would be expected of, or obvious to, a competent and careful driver in a particular case, regard shall be had not only to the circumstances of which he could be expected to be aware but also to any circumstances shown to have been within the knowledge of the accused.

(4) In determining for the purposes of subsection (2) above the state of a vehicle, regard may be had to anything attached to or carried on or in it and to the manner in which it is attached or carried.

Careless, and inconsiderate, driving

47-004 **3.** If a person drives a mechanically propelled vehicle on a road or other public place without due care and attention, or without reasonable consideration for other persons using the road or place, he is guilty of an offence.

Motor vehicles: drink and drugs

Causing death by careless driving when under influence of drink or drugs

47-005 **3A.**—(1) If a person causes the death of another person by driving a mechanically propelled vehicle on a road or other public place without due care and attention, or without reasonable consideration for other persons using the road or place, and—

(a) he is, at the time when he is driving, unfit to drive through drink or drugs, or

(b) he has consumed so much alcohol that the proportion of it in his breath, blood or urine at that time exceeds the prescribed limit, or

(c) he is, within 18 hours after that time, required to provide a specimen in pursuance of section 7 of this Act, but without reasonable excuse fails to provide it,

he is guilty of an offence.

(2) For the purposes of this section a person shall be taken to be unfit to drive at any time when his ability to drive properly is impaired.

(3) Subsection (1)(b) and (c) above shall not apply in relation to a person driving a mechanically propelled vehicle other than a motor vehicle.

Driving, or being in charge, when under influence of drink or drugs

47-006 **4.**—(1) A person who, when driving or attempting to drive a mechanically propelled vehicle on a road or other public place, is unfit to drive through drink or drugs is guilty of an offence.

(2) Without prejudice to subsection (1) above, a person who, when in charge of a mechanically propelled vehicle which is on a road or other public place, is unfit to drive through drink or drugs is guilty of an offence.

(3) For the purposes of subsection (2) above, a person shall be deemed not to have been in charge of a mechanically propelled vehicle if he proves that at the material time the circumstances were such that there was no likelihood of his driving it so long as he remained unfit to drive through drink or drugs.

(4) The court may, in determining whether there was such a likelihood as is mentioned in subsection (3) above, disregard any injury to him and any damage to the vehicle.

(5) For the purposes of this section, a person shall be taken to be unfit to drive if his ability to drive properly is for the time being impaired.

(6) A constable may arrest a person without warrant if he has reasonable cause to suspect that that person is or has been committing an offence under this section.

(7) For the purpose of arresting a person under the power conferred by subsection (6) above, a constable may enter (if need be by force) any place where that person is or where the constable, with reasonable cause, suspects him to be.

Driving or being in charge of a motor vehicle with alcohol concentration above prescribed limit

5.—(1) If a person— **47-007**

(a) drives or attempts to drive a motor vehicle on a road or other public place, or

(b) is in charge of a motor vehicle on a road or other public place,

after consuming so much alcohol that the proportion of it in his breath, blood or urine exceeds the prescribed limit he is guilty of an offence.

(2) It is a defence for a person charged with an offence under subsection (1)(b) above to prove that at the time he is alleged to have committed the offence the circumstances were such that there was no likelihood of his driving the vehicle whilst the proportion of alcohol in his breath, blood or urine remained likely to exceed the prescribed limit.

(3) The court may, in determining whether there was such a likelihood as is mentioned in subsection (2) above, disregard any injury to him and any damage to the vehicle.

Breath tests

6.—(1) Where a constable in uniform has reasonable cause to suspect— **47-008**

(a) that a person driving or attempting to drive or in charge of a motor vehicle on a road or other public place has alcohol in his body or has committed a traffic offence whilst the vehicle was in motion, or

(b) that a person has been driving or attempting to drive or been in charge of a motor vehicle on a road or other public place with alcohol in his body and that that person still has alcohol in his body, or

(c) that a person has been driving or attempting to drive or been in charge of a motor vehicle on a road or other public place and has committed a traffic offence whilst the vehicle was in motion,

he may, subject to section 9 of this Act, require him to provide a specimen of breath for a breath test.

(2) If an accident occurs owing to the presence of a motor vehicle on a road or other public place, a constable may, subject to section 9 of this Act, require any person who he has reasonable cause to believe was driving or attempting to

drive or in charge of the vehicle at the time of the accident to provide a specimen of breath for a breath test.

(3) A person may be required under subsection (1) or subsection (2) above to provide a specimen either at or near the place where the requirement is made or, if the requirement is made under subsection (2) above and the constable making the requirement thinks fit, at a police station specified by the constable.

(4) A person who, without reasonable excuse, fails to provide a specimen of breath when required to do so in pursuance of this section is guilty of an offence.

(5) A constable may arrest a person without warrant if—

(a) as a result of a breath test he has reasonable cause to suspect that the proportion of alcohol in that person's breath or blood exceeds the prescribed limit, or

(b) that person has failed to provide a specimen of breath for a breath test when required to do so in pursuance of this section and the constable has reasonable cause to suspect that he has alcohol in his body,

but a person shall not be arrested by virtue of this subsection when he is at a hospital as a patient.

(6) A constable may, for the purpose of requiring a person to provide a specimen of breath under subsection (2) above in a case where he has reasonable cause to suspect that the accident involved injury to another person or of arresting him in such a case under subsection (5) above, enter (if need be by force) any place where that person is or where the constable, with reasonable cause, suspects him to be.

(8) In this section "traffic offence" means an offence under—

(a) any provision of Part II of the Public Passenger Vehicles Act 1981,

(b) any provision of the Road Traffic Regulation Act 1984,

(c) any provision of the Road Traffic Offenders Act 1988 except Part III, or

(d) any provision of this Act except Part V.

Provision of specimens for analysis

47-009 7.—(1) In the course of an investigation into whether a person has committed an offence under section 3A, 4 or 5 of this Act a constable may, subject to the following provisions of this section and section 9 of this Act, require him—

(a) to provide two specimens of breath for analysis by means of a device of a type approved by the Secretary of State, or

(b) to provide a specimen of blood or urine for a laboratory test.

(2) A requirement under this section to provide specimens of breath can only be made at a police station.

(3) A requirement under this section to provide a specimen of blood or urine can only be made at a police station or at a hospital; and it cannot be made at a police station unless—

(a) the constable making the requirement has reasonable cause to believe that for medical reasons a specimen of breath cannot be provided or should not be required, or

(b) at the time the requirement is made a device or a reliable device of the type mentioned in subsection (1)(a) above is not available at the police station or it is then for any other reason not practicable to use such a device there, or (bb) a device of the type mentioned in subsection (1)(a) above has been used at the police station but the constable who required the specimens of breath has reasonable cause to believe that the device has not produced a reliable indication of the proportion of alcohol in the breath of the person concerned, or

(c) the suspected offence is one under section 3A or 4 of this Act and the constable making the requirement has been advised by a medical practitioner that the condition of the person required to provide the specimen might be due to some drug;

but may then be made notwithstanding that the person required to provide the specimen has already provided or been required to provide two specimens of breath.

(4) If the provision of a specimen other than a specimen of breath may be required in pursuance of this section the question whether it is to be a specimen of blood or a specimen of urine shall be decided by the constable making the requirement, but if a medical practitioner is of the opinion that for medical reasons a specimen of blood cannot or should not be taken the specimen shall be a specimen of urine.

(5) A specimen of urine shall be provided within one hour of the requirement for its provision being made and after the provision of a previous specimen of urine.

(6) A person who, without reasonable excuse, fails to provide a specimen when required to do so in pursuance of this section is guilty of an offence.

(7) A constable must, on requiring any person to provide a specimen in pursuance of this section, warn him that a failure to provide it may render him liable to prosecution.

[Specimens of blood taken from persons incapable of consenting

7A—(1) A constable may make a request to a medical practitioner for him to take a specimen of blood from a person ('the person concerned') irrespective of whether that person consents if— **47-010**

(a) that person is a person from whom the constable would (in the absence of any incapacity of that person and of any objection under section 9) be entitled under section 7 to require the provision of a specimen of blood for a laboratory test;

(b) it appears to that constable that that person has been involved in an accident that constitutes or is comprised in the matter that is under investigation or the circumstances of that matter;

(c) it appears to that constable that that person is or may be incapable (whether or not he has purported to do so) of giving a valid consent to the taking of a specimen of blood; and

(d) it appears to that constable that that person's incapacity is attributable to medical reasons.

(2) A request under this section—

(a) shall not be made to a medical practitioner who for the time being has any responsibility (apart from the request) for the clinical care of the person concerned; and

(b) shall not be made to a medical practitioner other than a police medical practitioner unless—

(i) it is not reasonably practicable for the request to made to a police medical practitioner; or

(ii) it is not reasonably practicable for such a medical practitioner (assuming him to be willing to do so) to take the specimen.

(3) It shall be lawful for a medical practitioner to whom a request is made under this section, if he thinks fit—

(a) to take a specimen of blood from the person concerned irrespective of whether that person consents; and

(b) to provide the sample to a constable.

(4) If a specimen is taken in pursuance of a request under this section, the specimen shall not be subjected to a laboratory test unless the person from whom it was taken—

(a) has been informed that it was taken; and

(b) has been required by a constable to give his permission for a laboratory test of the specimen; and

(c) has given his permission.

(5) A constable must, on requiring a person to give his permission for the purposes of this section for a laboratory test of a specimen, warn that person that a failure to give the permission may render him liable to prosecution.

(6) A person who, without reasonable excuse, fails to give his permission for a laboratory test of a specimen of blood taken from him under this section is guilty of an offence.

(7) In this section 'police medical practitioner' means a medical practitioner who is engaged under any agreement to provide medical services for purposes connected with the activities of a police force.][1]

Choice of specimens of breath

47-011 **8.**—(1) Subject to subsection (2) below, of any two specimens of breath provided by any person in pursuance of section 7 of this Act that with the lower proportion of alcohol in the breath shall be used and the other shall be disregarded.

(2) If the specimen with the lower proportion of alcohol contains no more than 50 microgrammes of alcohol in 100 millilitres of breath, the person who provided it may claim that it should be replaced by such specimen as may be required under section 7(4) of this Act and, if he then provides such a specimen, neither specimen of breath shall be used.

(3) The Secretary of State may by regulations substitute another proportion of alcohol in the breath for that specified in subsection (2) above.

Protection for hospital patients

47-012 **9.**—(1) While a person is at a hospital as a patient he shall not be required to provide a specimen of breath for a breath test or to provide a specimen for a laboratory test unless the medical practitioner in immediate charge of his case has been notified of the proposal to make the requirement; and—

(a) if the requirement is then made, it shall be for the provision of a specimen at the hospital, but

(b) if the medical practitioner objects on the ground specified in subsection (2) below, the requirement shall not be made.

[(1A) While a person is at a hospital as a patient, no specimen of blood shall be taken from him under section 7A of this Act and he shall not be required to give his permission for a laboratory test of a specimen taken under that section unless the medical practitioner in immediate charge of his case—

[1] Added by Police Reform Act 2002 c.30 Pt 4 c 2 s 56 (1)

(a) has been notified of the proposal to take the specimen or to make the requirement; and
(b) has not objected on the ground specified in subsection (2).

(2) The ground on which the medical practitioner may object is—
(a) in a case falling within subsection (1), that the requirement or the provision of the specimen or (if one is required) the warning required by section 7(7) of this Act would be prejudicial to the proper care and treatment of the patient; and
(b) in a case falling within subsection (1A), that the taking of the specimen, the requirement or the warning required by section 7A(5) of this Act would be so prejudicial.][1]

Detention of persons affected by alcohol or a drug

10.—(1) Subject to subsections (2) and (3) below, a person required to provide a specimen of breath, blood or urine may afterwards be detained at a police station until it appears to the constable that, were that person then driving or attempting to drive a [mechanically propelled vehicle][2] on a road, he would not be committing an offence under section 4 or 5 of this Act. **47-013**

(2) A person shall not be detained in pursuance of this section if it appears to a constable that there is no likelihood of his driving or attempting to drive a [mechanically propelled vehicle][3] whilst his ability to drive properly is impaired or whilst the proportion of alcohol in his breath, blood or urine exceeds the prescribed limit.

(3) A constable must consult a medical practitioner on any question arising under this section whether a person's ability to drive properly is or might be impaired through drugs and must act on the medical practitioner's advice.

Interpretation of sections 4 to 10

11.—(1) The following provisions apply for the interpretation of [sections 3A to 10][4] of this Act. **47-014**

(2) In those sections—

"breath test" means a preliminary test for the purpose of obtaining, by means of a device of a type approved by the Secretary of State, an indication whether the proportion of alcohol in a person's breath or blood is likely to exceed the prescribed limit,

"drug" includes any intoxicant other than alcohol,

"fail" includes refuse,

"hospital" means an institution which provides medical or surgical treatment for in-patients or out-patients,

"the prescribed limit" means , as the case may require—
(a) 35 microgrammes of alcohol in 100 millilitres of breath,
(b) 80 milligrammes of alcohol in 100 millilitres of blood, or
(c) 107 milligrammes of alcohol in 100 millilitres of urine,

or such other proportion as may be prescribed by regulations made by the Secretary of State.

["registered health care professional" means a person (other than a medical practitioner) who is—
(a) a registered nurse; or

[1] Substituted for s 9 (2) by Police Reform Act 2002 c.30 Pt 4 c 2 s 56 (2)
[2] Words substituted by Road Traffic Act 1991 c.40 Sch 4 para 43
[3] Words substituted by Road Traffic Act 1991 c.40 Sch 4 para 43
[4] Word substituted by Road Traffic Act 1991 c.40 Sch 4 para 44

(b) a registered member of a health care profession which is designated for the purposes of this paragraph by an order made by the Secretary of State.][1]

[(2A) A health care profession is any profession mentioned in section 60(2) of the Health Act 1999 c.8) other than the profession of practising medicine and the profession of nursing.

(2B) An order under subsection (2) shall be made by statutory instrument; and any such statutory instrument shall be subject to annulment in pursuance of a resolution of either House of Parliament.][2]

(3) A person does not provide a specimen of breath for a breath test or for analysis unless the specimen—

(a) is sufficient to enable the test or the analysis to be carried out, and

(b) is provided in such a way as to enable the objective of the test or analysis to be satisfactorily achieved.

(4) A person provides a specimen of blood if and only if he consents to its being taken by a medical practitioner and it is so taken.

Official Secrets Act 1989

CHAPTER 6

Security and intelligence

48-001 **1.**—(1) A person who is or has been—

(a) a member of the security and intelligence services; or

(b) a person notified that he is subject to the provisions of this subsection,

is guilty of an offence if without lawful authority he discloses any information, document or other article relating to security or intelligence which is or has been in his possession by virtue of his position as a member of any of those services or in the course of his work while the notification is or was in force.

(2) The reference in subsection (1) above to disclosing information relating to security or intelligence includes a reference to making any statement which purports to be a disclosure of such information or is intended to be taken by those to whom it is addressed as being such a disclosure.

(3) A person who is or has been a Crown servant or government contractor is guilty of an offence if without lawful authority he makes a damaging disclosure of any information, document or other article relating to security or intelligence which is or has been in his possession by virtue of his position as such but otherwise than as mentioned in subsection (1) above.

(4) For the purposes of subsection (3) above a disclosure is damaging if—

(a) it causes damage to the work of, or of any part of, the security and intelligence services; or

(b) it is of information or a document or other article which is such that its unauthorised disclosure would be likely to cause such damage or which falls within a class or description of information, documents or articles the unauthorised disclosure of which would be likely to have that effect.

[1] Definition inserted by Police Reform Act 2002 c.30 Pt 4 c 2 s 55 (3)

[2] Added by Police Reform Act 2002 c.30 Pt 4 c 2 s 55 (4)

(5) It is a defence for a person charged with an offence under this section to prove that at the time of the alleged offence he did not know, and had no reasonable cause to believe, that the information, document or article in question related to security or intelligence or, in the case of an offence under subsection (3), that the disclosure would be damaging within the meaning of that subsection.

(6) Notification that a person is subject to subsection (1) above shall be effected by a notice in writing served on him by a Minister of the Crown; and such a notice may be served if, in the Minister's opinion, the work undertaken by the person in question is or includes work connected with the security and intelligence services and its nature is such that the interests of national security require that he should be subject to the provisions of that subsection.

(7) Subject to subsection (8) below, a notification for the purposes of subsection (1) above shall be in force for the period of five years beginning with the day on which it is served but may be renewed by further notices under subsection (6) above for periods of five years at a time.

(8) A notification for the purposes of subsection (1) above may at any time be revoked by a further notice in writing served by the Minister on the person concerned; and the Minister shall serve such a further notice as soon as, in his opinion, the work undertaken by that person ceases to be such as is mentioned in subsection (6) above.

(9) In this section "security or intelligence" means the work of, or in support of, the security and intelligence services or any part of them, and references to information relating to security or intelligence include references to information held or transmitted by those services or by persons in support of, or of any part of, them.

Defence

2.—(1) A person who is or has been a Crown servant or government contractor is guilty of an offence if without lawful authority he makes a damaging disclosure of any information, document or other article relating to defence which is or has been in his possession by virtue of his position as such. **48-002**

(2) For the purposes of subsection (1) above a disclosure is damaging if—

(a) it damages the capability of, or of any part of, the armed forces of the Crown to carry out their tasks or leads to loss of life or injury to members of those forces or serious damage to the equipment or installations of those forces; or

(b) otherwise than as mentioned in paragraph (a) above, it endangers the interests of the United Kingdom abroad, seriously obstructs the promotion or protection by the United Kingdom of those interests or endangers the safety of British citizens abroad; or

(c) it is of information or of a document or article which is such that its unauthorised disclosure would be likely to have any of those effects.

(3) It is a defence for a person charged with an offence under this section to prove that at the time of the alleged offence he did not know, and had no reasonable cause to believe, that the information, document or article in question related to defence or that its disclosure would be damaging within the meaning of subsection (1) above.

(4) In this section "defence" means—

(a) the size, shape, organisation, logistics, order of battle, deployment, operations, state of readiness and training of the armed forces of the Crown;

(b) the weapons, stores or other equipment of those forces and the invention, development, production and operation of such equipment and research relating to it;
(c) defence policy and strategy and military planning and intelligence;
(d) plans and measures for the maintenance of essential supplies and services that are or would be needed in time of war.

International relations

48-003 **3.**—(1) A person who is or has been a Crown servant or government contractor is guilty of an offence if without lawful authority he makes a damaging disclosure of—

(a) any information, document or other article relating to international relations; or
(b) any confidential information, document or other article which was obtained from a State other than the United Kingdom or an international organisation,

being information or a document or article which is or has been in his possession by virtue of his position as a Crown servant or government contractor.

(2) For the purposes of subsection (1) above a disclosure is damaging if—

(a) it endangers the interests of the United Kingdom abroad, seriously obstructs the promotion or protection by the United Kingdom of those interests or endangers the safety of British citizens abroad; or
(b) it is of information or of a document or article which is such that its unauthorised disclosure would be likely to have any of those effects.

(3) In the case of information or a document or article within subsection (1)(b) above—

(a) the fact that it is confidential, or
(b) its nature or contents,

may be sufficient to establish for the purposes of subsection (2)(b) above that the information, document or article is such that its unauthorised disclosure would be likely to have any of the effects there mentioned.

(4) It is a defence for a person charged with an offence under this section to prove that at the time of the alleged offence he did not know, and had no reasonable cause to believe, that the information, document or article in question was such as is mentioned in subsection (1) above or that its disclosure would be damaging within the meaning of that subsection.

(5) In this section "international relations" means the relations between States, between international organisations or between one or more States and one or more such organisations and includes any matter relating to a State other than the United Kingdom or to an international organisation which is capable of affecting the relations of the United Kingdom with another State or with an international organisation.

(6) For the purposes of this section any information, document or article obtained from a State or organisation is confidential at any time while the terms on which it was obtained require it to be held in confidence or while the circumstances in which it was obtained make it reasonable for the State or organisation to expect that it would be so held.

Crime and special investigation powers

48-004 **4.**—(1) A person who is or has been a Crown servant or government contractor is guilty of an offence if without lawful authority he discloses any information, document or other article to which this section applies and which is or has been in his possession by virtue of his position as such.

(2) This section applies to any information, document or other article—

(a) the disclosure of which—

(i) results in the commission of an offence; or

(ii) facilitates an escape from legal custody or the doing of any other act prejudicial to the safekeeping of persons in legal custody; or

(iii) impedes the prevention or detection of offences or the apprehension or prosecution of suspected offenders; or

(b) which is such that its unauthorised disclosure would be likely to have any of those effects.

(3) This section also applies to—

(a) any information obtained by reason of the interception of any communication in obedience to a warrant issued under section 2 of the Interception of Communications Act 1985 [or under the authority of an interception warrant under section 5 of the Regulation of Investigatory Powers Act 2000][1], any information relating to the obtaining of information by reason of any such interception and any document or other article which is or has been used or held for use in, or has been obtained by reason of, any such interception; and

(b) any information obtained by reason of action authorised by a warrant issued under section 3 of the Security Service Act 1989 [or under section 5 of the Intelligence Services Act 1994 or by an authorisation given under section 7 of that Act][2], any information relating to the obtaining of information by reason of any such action and any document or other article which is or has been used or held for use in, or has been obtained by reason of, any such action.

(4) It is a defence for a person charged with an offence under this section in respect of a disclosure falling within subsection (2)(a) above to prove that at the time of the alleged offence he did not know, and had no reasonable cause to believe, that the disclosure would have any of the effects there mentioned.

(5) It is a defence for a person charged with an offence under this section in respect of any other disclosure to prove that at the time of the alleged offence he did not know, and had no reasonable cause to believe, that the information, document or article in question was information or a document or article to which this section applies.

(6) In this section "legal custody" includes detention in pursuance of any enactment or any instrument made under an enactment.

Information resulting from unauthorised disclosures or entrusted in confidence

5.—(1) Subsection (2) below applies where— **48-005**

(a) any information, document or other article protected against disclosure by the foregoing provisions of this Act has come into a person's possession as a result of having been—

(i) disclosed (whether to him or another) by a Crown servant or government contractor without lawful authority; or

(ii) entrusted to him by a Crown servant or government contractor on terms requiring it to be held in confidence or in circumstances in

[1] Words added by Regulation of Investigatory Powers Act 2000 c.23 Sch 4 para 5

[2] Words added by Intelligence Services Act 1994 c.13 Sch 4 para 4

which the Crown servant or government contractor could reasonably expect that it would be so held; or

(iii) disclosed (whether to him or another) without lawful authority by a person to whom it was entrusted as mentioned in sub-paragraph (ii) above; and

(b) the disclosure without lawful authority of the information, document or article by the person into whose possession it has come is not an offence under any of those provisions.

(2) Subject to subsections (3) and (4) below, the person into whose possession the information, document or article has come is guilty of an offence if he discloses it without lawful authority knowing, or having reasonable cause to believe, that it is protected against disclosure by the foregoing provisions of this Act and that it has come into his possession as mentioned in subsection (1) above.

(3) In the case of information or a document or article protected against disclosure by sections 1 to 3 above, a person does not commit an offence under subsection (2) above unless—

(a) the disclosure by him is damaging; and

(b) he makes it knowing, or having reasonable cause to believe, that it would be damaging;

and the question whether a disclosure is damaging shall be determined for the purposes of this subsection as it would be in relation to a disclosure of that information, document or article by a Crown servant in contravention of section 1(3), 2(1) or 3(1) above.

(4) A person does not commit an offence under subsection (2) above in respect of information or a document or other article which has come into his possession as a result of having been disclosed—

(a) as mentioned in subsection (1)(a)(i) above by a government contractor; or

(b) as mentioned in subsection (1)(a)(iii) above,

unless that disclosure was by a British citizen or took place in the United Kingdom, in any of the Channel Islands or in the Isle of Man or a colony.

(5) For the purposes of this section information or a document or article is protected against disclosure by the foregoing provisions of this Act if—

(a) it relates to security or intelligence, defence or international relations within the meaning of section 1, 2 or 3 above or is such as is mentioned in section 3(1)(b) above; or

(b) it is information or a document or article to which section 4 above applies;

and information or a document or article is protected against disclosure by sections 1 to 3 above if it falls within paragraph (a) above.

(6) A person is guilty of an offence if without lawful authority he discloses any information, document or other article which he knows, or has reasonable cause to believe, to have come into his possession as a result of a contravention of section 1 of the Official Secrets Act 1911.

Information entrusted in confidence to other States or international organisations

48-006 **6.**—(1) This section applies where—

(a) any information, document or other article which—

(i) relates to security or intelligence, defence or international relations; and

(ii) has been communicated in confidence by or on behalf of the United Kingdom to another State or to an international organisation,

has come into a person's possession as a result of having been disclosed (whether to him or another) without the authority of that State or organisation or, in the case of an organisation, of a member of it; and

(b) the disclosure without lawful authority of the information, document or article by the person into whose possession it has come is not an offence under any of the foregoing provisions of this Act.

(2) Subject to subsection (3) below, the person into whose possession the information, document or article has come is guilty of an offence if he makes a damaging disclosure of it knowing, or having reasonable cause to believe, that it is such as is mentioned in subsection (1) above, that it has come into his possession as there mentioned and that its disclosure would be damaging.

(3) A person does not commit an offence under subsection (2) above if the information, document or article is disclosed by him with lawful authority or has previously been made available to the public with the authority of the State or organisation concerned or, in the case of an organisation, of a member of it.

(4) For the purposes of this section "security or intelligence", "defence" and "international relations" have the same meaning as in section 1, 2 and 3 above and the question whether a disclosure is damaging shall be determined as it would be in relation to a disclosure of the information, document or article in question by a Crown servant in contravention of section 1(3), 2(1) and 3(1) above.

(5) For the purposes of this section information or a document or article is communicated in confidence if it is communicated on terms requiring it to be held in confidence or in circumstances in which the person communicating it could reasonably expect that it would be so held.

Authorised disclosures

7.—(1) For the purposes of this Act a disclosure by— **48-007**

(a) a Crown servant; or

(b) a person, not being a Crown servant or government contractor, in whose case a notification for the purposes of section 1(1) above is in force,

is made with lawful authority if, and only if, it is made in accordance with his official duty.

(2) For the purposes of this Act a disclosure by a government contractor is made with lawful authority if, and only if, it is made—

(a) in accordance with an official authorisation; or

(b) for the purposes of the functions by virtue of which he is a government contractor and without contravening an official restriction.

(3) For the purposes of this Act a disclosure made by any other person is made with lawful authority if, and only if, it is made—

(a) to a Crown servant for the purposes of his functions as such; or

(b) in accordance with an official authorisation.

(4) It is a defence for a person charged with an offence under any of the foregoing provisions of this Act to prove that at the time of the alleged offence he believed that he had lawful authority to make the disclosure in question and had no reasonable cause to believe otherwise.

(5) In this section "official authorisation" and "official restriction" mean , subject to subsection (6) below, an authorisation or restriction duly given or

imposed by a Crown servant or government contractor or by or on behalf of a prescribed body or a body of a prescribed class.

(6) In relation to section 6 above "official authorisation" includes an authorisation duly given by or on behalf of the State or organisation concerned or, in the case of an organisation, a member of it.

Safeguarding of information

48-008 **8.**—(1) Where a Crown servant or government contractor, by virtue of his position as such, has in his possession or under his control any document or other article which it would be an offence under any of the foregoing provisions of this Act for him to disclose without lawful authority he is guilty of an offence if—

(a) being a Crown servant, he retains the document or article contrary to his official duty; or

(b) being a government contractor, he fails to comply with an official direction for the return or disposal of the document or article,

or if he fails to take such care to prevent the unauthorised disclosure of the document or article as a person in his position may reasonably be expected to take.

(2) It is a defence for a Crown servant charged with an offence under subsection (1)(a) above to prove that at the time of the alleged offence he believed that he was acting in accordance with his official duty and had no reasonable cause to believe otherwise.

(3) In subsections (1) and (2) above references to a Crown servant include any person, not being a Crown servant or government contractor, in whose case a notification for the purposes of section 1(1) above is in force.

(4) Where a person has in his possession or under his control any document or other article which it would be an offence under section 5 above for him to disclose without lawful authority, he is guilty of an offence if—

(a) he fails to comply with an official direction for its return or disposal; or

(b) where he obtained it from a Crown servant or government contractor on terms requiring it to be held in confidence or in circumstances in which that servant or contractor could reasonably expect that it would be so held, he fails to take such care to prevent its unauthorised disclosure as a person in his position may reasonably be expected to take.

(5) Where a person has in his possession or under his control any document or other article which it would be an offence under section 6 above for him to disclose without lawful authority, he is guilty of an offence if he fails to comply with an official direction for its return or disposal.

(6) A person is guilty of an offence if he discloses any official information, document or other article which can be used for the purpose of obtaining access to any information, document or other article protected against disclosure by the foregoing provisions of this Act and the circumstances in which it is disclosed are such that it would be reasonable to expect that it might be used for that purposes without authority.

(7) For the purposes of subsection (6) above a person discloses information or a document or article which is official if—

(a) he has or has had it in his possession by virtue of his position as a Crown servant or government contractor; or

(b) he knows or has reasonable cause to believe that a Crown servant or government contractor has or has had it in his possession by virtue of his position as such.

(8) Subsection (5) of section 5 above applies for the purposes of subsection (6) above as it applies for the purposes of that section.

(9) In this section "official direction" means a direction duly given by a Crown servant or government contractor or by or on behalf of a prescribed body or a body of a prescribed class.

Prosecutions

9.—(1) Subject to subsection (2) below, no prosecution for an offence under this Act shall be instituted in England and Wales or in Northern Ireland except by or with the consent of the Attorney General or, as the case may be, the Attorney General for Northern Ireland. **48-009**

(2) Subsection (1) above does not apply to an offence in respect of any such information, document or article as is mentioned in section 4(2) above but no prosecution for such an offence shall be instituted in England and Wales or in Northern Ireland except by or with the consent of the Director of Public Prosecutions or, as the case may be, the Director of Public Prosecutions for Northern Ireland.

Penalties

10.—(1) A person guilty of an offence under any provision of this Act other than section 8(1), (4) or (5) shall be liable— **48-010**

(a) on conviction on indictment, to imprisonment for a term not exceeding two years or a fine or both;

(b) on summary conviction, to imprisonment for a term not exceeding six months or a fine not exceeding the statutory maximum or both.

(2) A person guilty of an offence under section 8(1), (4) or (5) above shall be liable on summary conviction to imprisonment for a term not exceeding three months or a fine not exceeding level 5 on the standard scale or both.

"Crown servant" and "government contractor"

12.—(1) In this Act "Crown servant" means— **48-011**

(a) a Minister of the Crown;

[(aa) a member of the Scottish Executive or a junior Scottish Minister;][1]

(b) [...][2]

(c) any person employed in the civil service of the Crown, including Her Majesty's Diplomatic Service, Her Majesty's Overseas Civil Service, the civil service of Northern Ireland and the Northern Ireland Court Service;

(d) any member of the naval, military or air forces of the Crown, including any person employed by an association established for the purposes of [Part XI of the Reserve Forces Act 1996][3];

(e) any constable and any other person employed or appointed in or for the purposes of any police force (including a police force within the meaning of the [Police (Northern Ireland) Act 1998][4]) or of the National Criminal Intelligence Service or the National Crime Squad;

1 Added by Scotland Act 1998 c.46 Sch 8 para 26 (2)
2 Repealed by Northern Ireland Act 1998 c.47 Sch 15 para 1
3 Words substituted by Reserve Forces Act 1996 c.14 Sch 10 para 22
4 Words substituted by Police (Northern Ireland) Act 1998 c.32 Sch 4 para 17

(f) any person who is a member or employee of a prescribed body or a body of a prescribed class and either is prescribed for the purposes of this paragraph or belongs to a prescribed class of members or employees of any such body;

(g) any person who is the holder of a prescribed office or who is an employee of such a holder and either is prescribed for the purposes of this paragraph or belongs to a prescribed class of such employees.

(2) In this Act "government contractor" means, subject to subsection (3) below, any person who is not a Crown servant but who provides, or is employed in the provision of, goods or services—

(a) for the purposes of any Minister or person mentioned in paragraph (a) or (b) of subsection (1) above, of any office-holder in the Scottish Administration, of any of the services, forces or bodies mentioned in that subsection or of the holder of any office prescribed under that subsection; or

(aa) for the purposes of the National Assembly for Wales;

(b) under an agreement or arrangement certified by the Secretary of State as being one to which the government of a State other than the United Kingdom or an international organisation is a party or which is subordinate to, or made for the purposes of implementing, any such agreement or arrangement.

(3) Where an employee or class of employees of any body, or of any holder of an office, is prescribed by an order made for the purposes of subsection (1) above—

(a) any employee of that body, or of the holder of that office, who is not prescribed or is not within the prescribed class; and

(b) any person who does not provide, or is not employed in the provision of, goods or services for the purposes of the performance of those functions of the body or the holder of the office in connection with which the employee or prescribed class of employees is engaged,

shall not be a government contractor for the purposes of this Act.

(4) In this section "office-holder in the Scottish Administration" has the same meaning as in section 126(7)(a) of the Scotland Act 1998.

(5) This Act shall apply to the following as it applies to persons falling within the definition of Crown servant—

(a) the First Minister and deputy First Minister in Northern Ireland; and

(b) Northern Ireland Ministers and junior Ministers.

Other interpretation provisions

48-012 **13.**—(1) In this Act—

"disclose" and "disclosure", in relation to a document or other article, include parting with possession of it;

"international organisation" means , subject to subsections (2) and (3) below, an organisation of which only States are members and includes a reference to any organ of such an organisation;

"prescribed" means prescribed by an order made by the Secretary of State;

"State" includes the government of a State and any organ of its government and references to a State other than the United Kingdom include references to any territory outside the United Kingdom.

(2) In section 12(2)(b) above the reference to an international organisation includes a reference to any such organisation whether or not one of which only States are members and includes a commercial organisation.

(3) In determining for the purposes of subsection (1) above whether only States are members of an organisation, any member which is itself an organisation of which only States are members, or which is an organ of such an organisation, shall be treated as a State.

Computer Misuse Act 1990

CHAPTER 18

Computer misuse offences

Unauthorised access to computer material

1.—(1) A person is guilty of an offence if— **49-001**
(a) he causes a computer to perform any function with intent to secure access to any program or data held in any computer;
(b) the access he intends to secure is unauthorised; and
(c) he knows at the time when he causes the computer to perform the function that that is the case.

(2) The intent a person has to have to commit an offence under this section need not be directed at—
(a) any particular program or data;
(b) a program or data of any particular kind; or
(c) a program or data held in any particular computer.

(3) A person guilty of an offence under this section shall be liable on summary conviction to imprisonment for a term not exceeding six months or to a fine not exceeding level 5 on the standard scale or to both.

Unauthorised access with intent to commit or facilitate commission of further offences

2.—(1) A person is guilty of an offence under this section if he commits an offence under section 1 above ("the unauthorised access offence") with intent— **49-002**
(a) to commit an offence to which this section applies; or
(b) to facilitate the commission of such an offence (whether by himself or by any other person);

and the offence he intends to commit or facilitate is referred to below in this section as the further offence.

(2) This section applies to offences—
(a) for which the sentence is fixed by law; or
(b) for which a person who has attained the age of twenty-one years (eighteen in relation to England and Wales) and has no previous convictions may be sentenced to imprisonment for a term of five years (or, in England and Wales, might be so sentenced but for the restrictions imposed by section 33 of the Magistrates' Courts Act 1980).

(3) It is immaterial for the purposes of this section whether the further offence is to be committed on the same occasion as the unauthorised access offence or on any future occasion.

(4) A person may be guilty of an offence under this section even though the facts are such that the commission of the further offence is impossible.

(5) A person guilty of an offence under this section shall be liable—

(a) on summary conviction, to imprisonment for a term not exceeding six months or to a fine not exceeding the statutory maximum or to both; and

(b) on conviction on indictment, to imprisonment for a term not exceeding five years or to a fine or to both.

Unauthorised modification of computer material

49-003 **3.**—(1) A person is guilty of an offence if—

(a) he does any act which causes an unauthorised modification of the contents of any computer; and

(b) at the time when he does the act he has the requisite intent and the requisite knowledge.

(2) For the purposes of subsection (1)(b) above the requisite intent is an intent to cause a modification of the contents of any computer and by so doing—

(a) to impair the operation of any computer;

(b) to prevent or hinder access to any program or data held in any computer; or

(c) to impair the operation of any such program or the reliability of any such data.

(3) The intent need not be directed at—

(a) any particular computer;

(b) any particular program or data or a program or data of any particular kind; or

(c) any particular modification or a modification of any particular kind.

(4) For the purposes of subsection (1)(b) above the requisite knowledge is knowledge that any modification he intends to cause is unauthorised.

(5) It is immaterial for the purposes of this section whether an unauthorised modification or any intended effect of it of a kind mentioned in subsection (2) above is, or is intended to be, permanent or merely temporary.

(6) For the purposes of the Criminal Damage Act 1971 a modification of the contents of a computer shall not be regarded as damaging any computer or computer storage medium unless its effect on that computer or computer storage medium impairs its physical condition.

(7) A person guilty of an offence under this section shall be liable—

(a) on summary conviction, to imprisonment for a term not exceeding six months or to a fine not exceeding the statutory maximum or to both; and

(b) on conviction on indictment, to imprisonment for a term not exceeding five years or to a fine or to both.

Jurisdiction

Territorial scope of offences under this Act

49-004 **4.**—(1) Except as provided below in this section, it is immaterial for the purposes of any offence under section 1 or 3 above—

(a) whether any act or other event proof of which is required for conviction of the offence occurred in the home country concerned; or

(b) whether the accused was in the home country concerned at the time of any such act or event.

(2) Subject to subsection (3) below, in the case of such an offence at least one significant link with domestic jurisdiction must exist in the circumstances of the case for the offence to be committed.

(3) There is no need for any such link to exist for the commission of an offence under section 1 above to be established in proof of an allegation to that effect in proceedings for an offence under section 2 above.

(4) Subject to section 8 below, where—

(a) any such link does in fact exist in the case of an offence under section 1 above; and

(b) commission of that offence is alleged in proceedings for an offence under section 2 above;

section 2 above shall apply as if anything the accused intended to do or facilitate in any place outside the home country concerned which would be an offence to which section 2 applies if it took place in the home country concerned were the offence in question.

(6) References in this Act to the home country concerned are references—

(a) in the application of this Act to England and Wales, to England and Wales;

(b) in the application of this Act to Scotland, to Scotland; and

(c) in the application of this Act to Northern Ireland, to Northern Ireland.

Significant links with domestic jurisdiction

5.—(1) The following provisions of this section apply for the interpretation of section 4 above. **49-005**

(2) In relation to an offence under section 1, either of the following is a significant link with domestic jurisdiction—

(a) that the accused was in the home country concerned at the time when he did the act which caused the computer to perform the function; or

(b) that any computer containing any program or data to which the accused secured or intended to secure unauthorised access by doing that act was in the home country concerned at that time.

(3) In relation to an offence under section 3, either of the following is a significant link with domestic jurisdiction—

(a) that the accused was in the home country concerned at the time when he did the act which caused the unauthorised modification; or

(b) that the unauthorised modification took place in the home country concerned.

Territorial scope of inchoate offences related to offences under this Act

6.—(1) On a charge of conspiracy to commit an offence under this Act the following questions are immaterial to the accused's guilt— **49-006**

(a) the question where any person became a party to the conspiracy; and

(b) the question whether any act, omission or other event occurred in the home country concerned.

(2) On a charge of attempting to commit an offence under section 3 above the following questions are immaterial to the accused's guilt—

(a) the question where the attempt was made; and

(b) the question whether it had an effect in the home country concerned.

(3) On a charge of incitement to commit an offence under this Act the question where the incitement took place is immaterial to the accused's guilt.

(4) This section does not extend to Scotland.

Territorial scope of inchoate offences related to offences under external law corresponding to offences under this Act

49-007 **7.**—(4) Subject to section 8 below, if any act done by a person in England and Wales would amount to the offence of incitement to commit an offence under this Act but for the fact that what he had in view would not be an offence triable in England and Wales—

(a) what he had in view shall be treated as an offence under this Act for the purposes of any charge of incitement brought in respect of that act; and

(b) any such charge shall accordingly be triable in England and Wales.

Relevance of external law

49-008 **8.**—(1) A person is guilty of an offence triable by virtue of section 4(4) above only if what he intended to do or facilitate would involve the commission of an offence under the law in force where the whole or any part of it was intended to take place.

(3) A person is guilty of an offence triable by virtue of section 1(1A) of the Criminal Attempts Act 1981 or by virtue of section 7(4) above only if what he had in view would involve the commission of an offence under the law in force where the whole or any part of it was intended to take place.

(4) Conduct punishable under the law in force in any place is an offence under that law for the purposes of this section, however it is described in that law.

(5) Subject to subsection (7) below, a condition specified in subsection (1) or (3) above shall be taken to be satisfied unless not later than rules of court may provide the defence serve on the prosecution a notice—

(a) stating that, on the facts as alleged with respect to the relevant conduct, the condition is not in their opinion satisfied;

(b) showing their grounds for that opinion; and

(c) requiring the prosecution to show that it is satisfied.

(6) In subsection (5) above "the relevant conduct" means—

(a) where the condition in subsection (1) above is in question, what the accused intended to do or facilitate;

(c) where the condition in subsection (3) above is in question, what the accused had in view.

(7) The court, if it thinks fit, may permit the defence to require the prosecution to show that the condition is satisfied without the prior service of a notice under subsection (5) above.

(9) In the Crown Court the question whether the condition is satisfied shall be decided by the judge alone.

British citizenship immaterial

49-009 **9.**—(1) In any proceedings brought in England and Wales in respect of any offence to which this section applies it is immaterial to guilt whether or not the accused was a British citizen at the time of any act, omission or other event proof of which is required for conviction of the offence.

(2) This section applies to the following offences—

(a) any offence under this Act;

(c) any attempt to commit an offence under section 3 above; and

(d) incitement to commit an offence under this Act.

Miscellaneous and general

Conviction of an offence under section 1 in proceedings for an offence under section 2 or 3

12.—(1) If on the trial on indictment of a person charged with— **49-010**

(a) an offence under section 2 above; or

(b) an offence under section 3 above or any attempt to commit such an offence;

the jury find him not guilty of the offence charged, they may find him guilty of an offence under section 1 above if on the facts shown he could have been found guilty of that offence in proceedings for that offence brought before the expiry of any time limit under section 11 above applicable to such proceedings.

(2) The Crown Court shall have the same powers and duties in relation to a person who is by virtue of this section convicted before it of an offence under section 1 above as a magistrates' court would have on convicting him of the offence.

(3) This section is without prejudice to section 6(3) of the Criminal Law Act 1967 (conviction of alternative indictable offence on trial on indictment).

(4) This section does not extend to Scotland.

Interpretation

17.—(1) The following provisions of this section apply for the interpretation of this Act. **49-011**

(2) A person secures access to any program or data held in a computer if by causing a computer to perform any function he—

(a) alters or erases the program or data;

(b) copies or moves it to any storage medium other than that in which it is held or to a different location in the storage medium in which it is held;

(c) uses it; or

(d) has it output from the computer in which it is held (whether by having it displayed or in any other manner);

and references to access to a program or data (and to an intent to secure such access) shall be read accordingly.

(3) For the purposes of subsection (2)(c) above a person uses a program if the function the causes the computer to perform—

(a) causes the program to be executed; or

(b) is itself a function of the program.

(4) For the purposes of subsection (2)(d) above—

(a) a program is output if the instructions of which it consists are output; and

(b) the form in which any such instructions or any other data is output (and in particular whether or not it represents a form in which, in the case of instructions, they are capable of being executed or, in the case of data, it is capable of being processed by a computer) is immaterial.

(5) Access of any kind by any person to any program or data held in a computer is unauthorised if—

(a) he is not himself entitled to control access of the kind in question to the program or data; and

(b) he does not have consent to access by him of the kind in question to the program or data from any person who is so entitled.

but this subsection is subject to section 10.

(6) References to any program or data held in a computer include references to any program or data held in any removable storage medium which is for the time being in the computer; and a computer is to be regarded as containing any program or data held in any such medium.

(7) A modification of the contents of any computer takes place if, by the operation of any function of the computer concerned or any other computer—

(a) any program or data held in the computer concerned is altered or erased; or

(b) any program or data is added to its contents;

and any act which contributes towards causing such a modification shall be regarded as causing it.

(8) Such a modification is unauthorised if—

(a) the person whose act causes it is not himself entitled to determine whether the modification should be made; and

(b) he does not have consent to the modification from any person who is so entitled.

(9) References to the home country concerned shall be read in accordance with section 4(6) above.

(10) References to a program include references to part of a program.

Football (Offences) Act 1991

CHAPTER 19

Designated football matches

50-001 **1.**—(1) In this Act a "designated football match" means an association football match designated, or of a description designated, for the purposes of this Act by order of the Secretary of State.

Any such order shall be made by statutory instrument which shall be subject to annulment in pursuance of a resolution of either House of Parliament.

(2) References in this Act to things done at a designated football match include anything done at the ground—

(a) within the period beginning two hours before the start of the match or (if earlier) two hours before the time at which it is advertised to start and ending one hour after the end of the match; or

(b) where the match is advertised to start at a particular time on a particular day but does not take place on that day, within the period beginning two hours before and ending one hour after the advertised starting time.

Throwing of missiles

50-002 **2.** It is an offence for a person at a designated football match to throw anything at or towards—

(a) the playing area, or any area adjacent to the playing area to which spectators are not generally admitted, or

(b) any area in which spectators or other persons are or may be present,

without lawful authority or lawful excuse (which shall be for him to prove).

Indecent or racialist chanting

3.—(1) It is an offence to engage or take part in chanting of an indecent or racialist nature at a designated football match. **50-003**

(2) For this purpose—

(a) "chanting" means the repeated uttering of any words or sounds (whether alone or in concert with one or more others); and

(b) "of a racialist nature" means consisting of or including matter which is threatening, abusive or insulting to a person by reason of his colour, race, nationality (including citizenship) or ethnic or national origins.

Going onto the playing area

4. It is an offence for a person at a designated football match to go onto the playing area, or any area adjacent to the playing area to which spectators are not generally admitted, without lawful authority or lawful excuse (which shall be for him to prove). **50-004**

Supplementary provisions

5.—(2) A person guilty of an offence under this Act is liable on summary conviction to a fine not exceeding level 3 on the standard scale. **50-005**

Water Resources Act 1991

CHAPTER 57

PART III

CONTROL OF POLLUTION OF WATER RESOURCES

CHAPTER II

POLLUTION OFFENCES

Principal offences

Offences of polluting controlled waters

85.—(1) A person contravenes this section if he causes or knowingly permits any poisonous, noxious or polluting matter or any solid waste matter to enter any controlled waters. **51-001**

(2) A person contravenes this section if he causes or knowingly permits any matter, other than trade effluent or sewage effluent, to enter controlled waters by being discharged from a drain or sewer in contravention of a prohibition imposed under section 86 below.

(3) A person contravenes this section if he causes or knowingly permits any trade effluent or sewage effluent to be discharged—

(a) into any controlled waters; or

(b) from land in England and Wales, through a pipe, into the sea outside the seaward limits of controlled waters.

(4) A person contravenes this section if he causes or knowingly permits any trade effluent or sewage effluent to be discharged, in contravention of any prohibition imposed under section 86 below, from a building or from any fixed plant—

(a) on to or into any land; or

(b) into any waters of a lake or pond which are not inland freshwaters.

(5) A person contravenes this section if he causes or knowingly permits any matter whatever to enter any inland freshwaters so as to tend (either directly or in combination with other matter which he or another person causes or permits to enter those waters) to impeded the proper flow of the waters in a manner leading, or likely to lead, to a substantial aggravation of—

(a) pollution due to other causes; or

(b) the consequences of such pollution.

(6) Subject to the following provisions of this Chapter, a person who contravenes this section or the conditions of any consent given under this Chapter for the purposes of this section shall be guilty of an offence and liable—

(a) on summary conviction, to imprisonment for a term not exceeding three months or to a fine not exceeding £20,000 or to both;

(b) on conviction on indictment, to imprisonment for a term not exceeding two years or to a fine or to both.

Prohibition of certain discharges by notice or regulations

51-002 **86.**—(1) For the purposes of section 85 above a discharge of any effluent or other matter is, in relation to any person, in contravention of a prohibition imposed under this section if, subject to the following provisions of this section—

(a) the [Agency][1] has given that person notice prohibiting him from making or, as the case may be, continuing the discharge; or

(b) the [Agency][2] has given that person notice prohibiting him from making or, as the case may be, continuing the discharge unless specified conditions are observed, and those conditions are not observed.

(2) For the purposes of section 85 above a discharged of any effluent or other matter is also in contravention of a prohibition imposed under this section if the effluent or matter discharged—

(a) contains a prescribed substance or a prescribed concentration of such a substance; or

(b) derives from a prescribed process or from a process involving the use of prescribed substances or the use of such substances in quantities which exceed the prescribed amounts.

(3) Nothing in subsection (1) above shall authorise the giving of a notice for the purposes of that subsection in respect of discharges from a vessel; and nothing in any regulations made by virtue of subsection (2) above shall required any discharge from a vessel to be treated as a discharged in contravention of a prohibition imposed under this section.

(4) A notice given for the purposes of subsection (1) above shall expire at such time as may be specified in the notice.

(5) The time specified for the purposes of subsection (4) above shall not be before the end of the period of three months beginning with the day on which the notice is given, except in a case where the [Agency][3] is satisfied that there is an

[1] Words substituted by Environment Act 1995 c.25 Sch 22 para 128
[2] Words substituted by Environment Act 1995 c.25 Sch 22 para 128
[3] Words substituted by Environment Act 1995 c.25 Sch 22 para 128

emergency which requires the prohibition in question to come into force at such time before the end of that period as may be so specified.

(6) Where, in the case of such a notice for the purposes of subsection (1) above as (but for this subsection) would expire at a time at or after the end of the said period of three months, an application is made before that time for a consent under this Chapter in respect of the discharge to which the notice relates, that notice shall be deemed not to expire until the result of the application becomes final—

(a) on the grant or withdrawal of the application;

(b) on the expiration, without the bringing of an appeal with respect to the decision on the application, of any period prescribed as the period within which any such appeal must be brought; or

(c) on the withdrawal or determination of any such appeal.

Discharges into and from public sewers etc

87.—(1) This Section applies for the purposes of determining liability where sewage effluent is discharged as mentioned in subsection (3) or (4) of section 85 above from any sewer or works (ıthe discharging sewerı) vested in a sewerage undertaker (ıthe discharging undertakerı). **51-003**

(1A) If the discharging undertaker did not cause, or knowingly permit, the discharge it shall nevertheless be deemed to have caused the discharge if -

(a) matter included in the discharge was received by it into the discharging sewer or any other sewer of works vested in it;

(b) it was bound (either unconditionally or subject to conditions which were observed) to receive that matter into that sewer or works; and

(c) subsection (1B) below does not apply.

(1B) This subsection applies where the sewage effluent was, before being discharged from the discharging sewer, discharge through a main connection into that sewer or into any other sewer or works vested in the discharging undertaker by another sewerage undertaker (ıthe sending undertakerı) under an agreement having effect between the discharging undertaker and the sending undertaker under section 110A of the Water Industry Act 1991.

(1C) Where subsection (1B) above applies, the sending undertaker shall be deemed to have caused the discharge if, although it did not cause, or knowingly permit, the sewage effluent to be discharged into the discharging sewer, or into any other sewer or works of the discharging undertaker -

(a) matter included in the discharge was received by in into a sewer or works vested in it; and

(b) it was bound (either unconditionally or subject to conditions which were observed) to receive that matter into that sewer or works.

(2) A sewerage undertaker shall not be guilty of an offence under section 85 above by reason only of the fact that a discharge from a sewer or works vested in the undertaker contravenes conditions of a consent relating to the discharge if -

(a) the contravention is attributable to a discharge which another person caused or permitted to be made into the sewer or works;

(b) the undertaker either was not bound to receive the discharge into the sewer or works or was bound to receive it there subject to conditions which were not observed; and

(c) the undertaker could not reasonably have been expected to prevent the discharge into the sewer or works.

(3) A person shall not be guilty of an offence under section 85 above in respect of a discharge which he caused or permitted to be made into a sewer or

works vested in a sewerage undertaker if the undertaker was bound to receive the discharge there either unconditionally or subject to conditions which were observed.

(4) In this section ımain connectionı has the same meaning as in section 110A of the Water Industry Act 1991.

Defence to principal offences in respect of authorised discharges

51-004 **88.**—(1) Subject to the following provisions of this section, a person shall not be guilty of an offence under section 85 above in respect of the entry of any matter into any waters or any discharge if the entry occurs or the discharge is made under and in accordance with, or as a result of any act or omission under and in accordance with—

(a) a consent given under this Chapter or under Part II of the Control of Pollution Act 1974 (which makes corresponding provision for Scotland);

(aa) a permit granted, under regulations under section 2 of the Pollution Prevention and Control Act 1999, by an authority exercising functions under the regulations that are exercisable for the purpose of preventing or reducing emissions in to the air, water and land;

(b) an authorisation for a prescribed process designated for central control granted under Part I of the Environmental Protection Act 1990;

(c) a waste management or disposal licence;

(d) a licence granted under Part II of the Food and Environment Protection Act 1985;

(e) section 163 below or section 165 of the Water Industry Act 1991 (discharges for works purposes);

(f) any local statutory provision or statutory order which expressly confers power to discharge effluent into water; or

(g) any prescribed enactment.

(2) Schedule 10 to this Act shall have effect, subject to section 91 below, with respect to the making of applications for consents under this Chapter for the purposes of subsection (1)(a) above and with respect to the giving, revocation and modification of such consents.

(3) Nothing in any disposal licence shall be treated for the purposes of subsection (1) above as authorising—

(a) any such entry or discharge as is mentioned in subsections (2) to (4) of section 85 above; or

(b) any act or omission so far as it results in any such entry or discharge.

(4) In this section—

"disposal licence" means a licence issued in pursuance of section 5 of the Control of Pollution Act 1974;

"statutory order" means—

(a) any order under section 168 below or section 167 of the Water Industry Act 1991 (compulsory works orders); or

(b) any order, byelaw, scheme or award made under any other enactment, including an order or scheme confirmed by Parliament or brought into operation in accordance with special parliamentary procedure; and

"waste management licence" means such a licence granted under Part II of the Environmental Protection Act 1990.

Other defences to principal offences

89.—(1) A person shall not be guilty of an offences under section 85 above in respect of the entry of any matter into any waters or any discharge if— **51-005**

(a) the entry is caused or permitted, or the discharges is made, in an emergency in order to avoid danger to life or health;

(b) that person takes all such steps as are reasonably practicable in the circumstances for minimising the extent of the entry or discharge and of its polluting effects; and

(c) particulars of the entry of discharge are furnished to the Agency as soon as reasonably practicable after the entry occurs.

(2) A person shall not be guilty of an offence under section 85 above by reason of this causing or permitting any discharge of trade or sewage effluent from a vessel.

(3) A person shall not be guilty of an offence under section 85 above by reason only of his permitting water from an abandoned mine or an abandoned part of a mine to enter controlled waters.

(3A) Subsection (3) above shall not apply to the owner or former operator of any mine or part of a mine if the mine or part in question became abandoned after 31st December 1999.

(3B) In determining for the purposes of subsection (3A) above whether a mine or part of a mine became abandoned before, on or after 31st December 1999 in a case where the mine or part has become abandoned on two or more occasions, of which—

(a) at least one falls on or before that date, and

(b) at least one falls after that date,

the mine or part shall be regarded as becoming abandoned after that date (but without prejudice to the operation of subsection (3) above in relation to that mine or part at, or in relation to, any time before the first of those occasions which falls after that date).

(3C) Where, immediately before a part of a mine becomes abandoned, that part is the only part of the mine not falling to be regarded as abandoned for the time being, the abandonment of that part shall not be regarded for the purposes of subsection (3A) or (3B) above as constituting the abandonment of the mine, but only of that part of it.

(4) A person shall not, otherwise than in respect of the entry of any poisonous, noxious or polluting matter into any controlled waters, be guilty of an offence under section 85 above by reason of his depositing the solid refuse of a mine or quarry on any land so that it falls or is carried into inland freshwater if—

(a) he deposits the refuse on the land with the consent of the Agency;

(b) no other site for the deposit is reasonably practicable; and

(c) he takes all reasonably practicable steps to prevent the refuse from entering those inland freshwater.

(5) A highway authority or other person entitled to keep open a drain by virtue of section 100 of the Highways Act 1980 shall not be guilty of an offence under section 85 above by reason of his causing or permitting any discharge to be made from a drain kept open by virtue of that section unless the discharge is made in contravention of a prohibition imposed under section 86 above.

(6) In this section "mine" and "quarry" have the same meanings as in the Mines and Quarries Act 1954.

Prison Security Act 1992

CHAPTER 25

Offence of prison mutiny

52-001 **1.**—(1) Any prisoner who takes part in a prison mutiny shall be guilty of an offence and liable, on conviction on indictment, to imprisonment for a term not exceeding ten years or to a fine or to both.

(2) For the purposes of this section there is a prison mutiny where two or more prisoners, while on the premises of any prison, engage in conduct which is intended to further a common purpose of overthrowing lawful authority in that prison.

(3) For the purposes of this section the intentions and common purpose of prisoners may be inferred from the form and circumstances of their conduct and it shall be immaterial that conduct falling within subsection (2) above takes a different form in the case of different prisoners.

(4) Where there is a prison mutiny, a prisoner who has or is given a reasonable opportunity of submitting to lawful authority and fails, without reasonable excuse, to do so shall be regarded for the purposes of this section as taking part in the mutiny.

(5) Proceedings for an offence under this section shall not be brought except by or with the consent of the Director of Public Prosecutions.

(6) In this section—

"conduct" includes acts and omissions;

"prison" means any prison, young offender institution or remand centre which is under the general superintendence of, or is provided by, the Secretary of State under the Prison Act 1952, including a contracted out prison within the meaning of Part IV of the Criminal Justice Act 1991;

"prisoner" means any person for the time being in a prison as a result of any requirement imposed by a court or otherwise that he be detained in legal custody.

Sexual Offences (Amendment) Act 1992

CHAPTER 34

Anonymity of victims of certain offences

53-001 **1.**—(1) Where an allegation has been made that an offence to which this Act applies has been committed against a person, neither the name nor address, and no still or moving picture, of that person shall during that person's lifetime—

(a) be published in England and Wales or Northern Ireland in a written publication available to the public; or

(b) be included in a relevant programme for reception in England and Wales or Northern Ireland,

if it is likely to lead members of the public to identify that person as the person against whom the offence is alleged to have been committed.

(2) Where a person is accused of an offence to which this Act applies, no matter likely to lead members of the public to identify a person as the person against whom the offence is alleged to have been committed ("the complainant") shall during the complainant's lifetime—

(a) be published in England and Wales or Northern Ireland in a written publication available to the public; or

(b) be included in a relevant programme for reception in England and Wales or Northern Ireland.

(3) Subsections (1) and (2) are subject to any direction given under section 3.

(3A) The matter relating to a person in relation to which the restrictions imposed by subsection (1) or (2) apply (if their inclusion in any publication is likely to have the result mentioned in that subsection) include in particular -

(a) the person's name,

(b) the person's address,

(c) the identity of any school or other educational establishment attended by the person,

(d) the identity of any place of work, and

(e) any still or moving picture of the person.

(4) Nothing in this section prohibits the publication or inclusion in a relevant programme of matter consisting only of a report of criminal proceedings other than proceedings at, or intended to lead to, or on an appeal arising out of, a trial at which the accused is charged with the offence.

Offences to which this Act applies

2.—(1) This Act applies to the following offences— **53-002**

(a) any offence under any of the provisions of the Sexual Offences Act 1956 mentioned in subsection (2);

(aa) rape;

(ab) burglary with intent to commit rape;

(b) any offence under section 128 of the Mental Health Act 1959 (intercourse with mentally handicapped person by hospital staff etc.);

(c) any offence under section 1 of the Indecency with Children Act 1960 (indecent conduct towards young child);

(d) any offence under section 54 of the Criminal Law Act 1977 (incitement by man of his grand-daughter, daughter or sister under the age of 16 to commit incest with him);

(e) any attempt to commit any of the offences mentioned in paragraphs (a) to (d)[;][1]

(f) any conspiracy to commit any of those offences;

(g) any incitement of another to commit any of those offences.

(h) aiding, abetting, counselling or procuring the commission of any of the offences mentioned in paragraphs (aa) to (e) and (g).

(2) The provisions of the Act of 1956 are—

(a) section 2 (procurement of a woman by threats);

(b) section 3 (procurement of a woman by false pretences);

---

[1] Added by Criminal Justice and Public Order Act 1994 c.33 Sch 9 para 52 (2)

(c) section 4 (administering drugs to obtain intercourse with a woman);
(d) section 5 (intercourse with a girl under the age of 13);
(e) section 6 (intercourse with a girl between the ages of 13 and 16);
(f) section 7 (intercourse with a mentally handicapped person);
(g) section 9 (procurement of a mentally handicapped person);
(h) section 10 (incest by a man);
(i) section 11 (incest by a woman);
(j) section 12 (buggery);
(k) section 14 (indecent assault on a woman);
(l) section 15 (indecent assault on a man);
(m) section 16 (assault with intent to commit buggery).

Power to displace section 1

53-003 **3.**—(1) If, before the commencement of a trial at which a person is charged with an offence to which this Act applies, he or another person against whom the complainant may be expected to give evidence at the trial, applies to the judge for a direction under this subsection and satisfies the judge—

(a) that the direction is required for the purpose of inducing persons who are likely to be needed as witnesses at the trial to come forward; and
(b) that the conduct of the applicant's defence at the trial is likely to be substantially prejudiced if the direction is not given,

the judge shall direct that section 1 shall not, by virtue of the accusation alleging the offence in question, apply in relation to the complainant.

(2) If at a trial the judge is satisfied—

(a) that the effect of section 1 is to impose a substantial and unreasonable restriction upon the reporting of proceedings at the trial, and
(b) that it is in the public interest to remove or relax the restriction,

he shall direct that that section shall not apply to such matter as is specified in the direction.

(3) A direction shall not be given under subsection (2) by reason only of the outcome of the trial.

(4) If a person who has been convicted of an offence and has given notice of appeal against the conviction, or notice of an application for leave so to appeal, applies to the appellate court for a direction under this subsection and satisfies the court—

(a) that the direction is required for the purpose of obtaining evidence in support of the appeal; and
(b) that the applicant is likely to suffer substantial injustice if the direction is not given,

the court shall direct that section 1 shall not, by virtue of an accusation which alleges an offence to which this Act applies and is specified in the direction, apply in relation to a complainant so specified.

(5) A direction given under any provision of this section does not affect the operation of section 1 at any time before the direction is given.

(6) In subsections (1) and (2), "judge" means —

(a) in the case of an offence which is to be tried summarily or for which the mode of trial has not been determined, any justice of the peace acting for the petty sessions area concerned; and
(b) in any other case, any judge of the Crown Court in England and Wales.

(7) If, after the commencement of a trial at which a person is charged with an offence to which this Act applies, a new trial of the person for that offence is

ordered, the commencement of any previous trial shall be disregarded for the purposes of subsection (1).

Special rules for cases of incest or buggery

4.—(1) In this section— **53-004**

"section 10 offence" means an offence under section 10 of the Sexual Offences Act 1956 (incest by a man) or an attempt to commit that offence;

"section 11 offence" means an offence under section 11 of that Act (incest by a woman) or an attempt to commit that offence;

"section 12 offence" means an offence under section 12 of that Act (buggery) or an attempt to commit that offence.

(2) Section 1 does not apply to a woman against whom a section 10 offence is alleged to have been committed if she is accused of having committed a section 11 offence against the man who is alleged to have committed the section 10 offence against her.

(3) Section 1 does not apply to a man against whom a section 11 offence is alleged to have been committed if he is accused of having committed a section 10 offence against the woman who is alleged to have committed the section 11 offence against him.

(4) Section 1 does not apply to a person against whom a section 12 offence is alleged to have been committed if that person is accused of having committed a section 12 offence against the person who is alleged to have committed the section 12 offence against him.

(5) Subsection (2) does not affect the operation of this Act in relation to anything done at any time before the woman is accused.

(6) Subsection (3) does not affect the operation of this Act in relation to anything done at any time before the man is accused.

(7) Subsection (4) does not affect the operation of this Act in relation to anything done at any time before the person mentioned first in that subsection is accused.

Offences

5.—(1) If any matter is included in a publication in contravention of section 1, the following persons shall be guilty of an offence and liable on summary conviction to a fine not exceeding level 5 on the standard scale— **53-005**

(a) where the publication is a newspaper or periodical, any proprietor, any editor and any publisher of the newspaper or periodical;

(b) where the publication is a relevant programme—

(i) any body corporate or Scottish partnership engaged in providing the programme service in which the programme is included; and

(ii) any person having functions in relation to the programme corresponding to those of an editor of a newspaper;

(c) in the case of any other publication, any person publishing it.

(2) Where a person is charged with an offence under this section in respect of the publication of any matter or the inclusion of any matter in a relevant programme, it shall be a defence, subject to subsection (3), to prove that the publication or programme in which the matter appeared was one in respect of which the person against whom the offence mentioned in section 1 is alleged to have been committed had given written consent to the appearance of matter of that description.

(3) Written consent is not a defence if it is proved that any person interfered unreasonably with the peace or comfort of the person giving the consent, with intent to obtain it or that person was under the age of 16 at the time when it was given.

(5) Where a person is charged with an offence under this section it shall be a defence to prove that at the time of the alleged offence he was not aware, and neither suspected nor had reason to suspect, that the publication or programme in question included, the matter in question.

(5A) Where -

(a) a person is charged with an offence under this section, and

(b) the offence relates to the inclusion of any matter in a publication in contravention of section 1(1).

it shall be a defence to prove that at the time of the alleged offence he was not aware, and neither suspected nor had any reason to suspect, that the allegation in question had been made.

(6) Where an offence under this section committed by a body corporate is proved to have been committed with the consent or connivance of, or to be attributable to any neglect on the part of—

(a) a director, manager, secretary or other similar officer of the body corporate, or

(b) a person purporting to act in any such capacity,

he as well as the body corporate shall be guilty of the offence and liable to be proceeded against and punished accordingly.

(7) In relation to a body corporate whose affairs are managed by its members "director", in subsection (6), means a member of the body corporate.

Interpretation etc

53-006 6.—(1) In this Act—

"complainant" has the meaning given in section 1(2);

"picture" includes a likeness however produced;

"publication" means includes any speech, writing, relevant programme or other communication in whatever form, which is addressed to the public at large or any section of the public (and for this purpose every relevant programme shall be taken to be so addressed), but does not include an indictment or other document prepared for use in particular legal proceedings;

"relevant programme" means a programme included in a programme service, within the meaning of the Broadcasting Act 1990;

(2) For the purposes of this Act—

(a) where it is alleged that an offence to which this Act applies has been committed, the fact that any person has consented to an act which, on any prosecution for that offence, would fall to be proved by the prosecution, does not prevent that person from being regarded as a person against whom the alleged offence was committed; and

(b) where a person is accused of an offence of incest or buggery, the other party to the act in question shall be taken to be a person against whom the offence was committed even though he consented to that act.

(2A) For the purposes of this Act, where it is alleged or there is an accusation -

(a) that an offence of conspiracy or incitement of another to commit an offence mentioned in section 2(1)(aa) to (dd) or (3)(a) to (h) has been committed, or

(b) that an offence of aiding, abetting, counselling or procuring the commission of an offence of incitement of another to commit an offence mentioned in section 2(1)(aa) or (d) or (3)(a) to (h) has been committed,

the person against whom the substantive offence is alleged to have been intended to be committed shall be regarded as the person against whom the conspiracy or incitement is alleged to have been committed. In this subsection, "the substantive offence" means the offence to which the alleged conspiracy or incitement related.

(3) For the purposes of this Act, a person is accused of an offence, other than a service offence, if—

(a) an information is laid alleging that he has committed the offence,
(b) he appears before a court charged with the offence,
(c) a court before which he is appearing commits him for trial on a new charge alleging the offence, or
(d) a bill of indictment charging him with the offence is preferred before a court in which he may lawfully be indicted for the offence,

and references in subsection (2A) and in section 3 to an accusation alleging an offence shall be construed accordingly.

(4) Nothing in this Act affects any prohibition or restriction imposed by virtue of any other enactment upon a publication or upon matter included in a relevant programme.

Sexual Offences Act 1993

CHAPTER 30

Abolition of presumption of sexual incapacity

1. The presumption of criminal law that a boy under the age of fourteen is incapable of sexual intercourse (whether natural or unnatural) is hereby abolished. **54-001**

Criminal Justice Act 1993

CHAPTER 36

PART I

JURISDICTION

Offences to which this Part applies

1.—(1) This Part applies to two groups of offences— **55-001**

(a) any offence mentioned in subsection (2) (a "Group A offence"); and
(b) any offence mentioned in subsection (3) (a "Group B offence").

(2) The Group A offences are—

(a) an offence under any of the following provisions of the Theft Act 1968—

section 1 (theft);
section 15 (obtaining property by deception);
[section 15A (obtaining a money transfer by deception);][1]
section 16 (obtaining pecuniary advantage by deception);
section 17 (false accounting);
section 19 (false statements by company directors, etc.);
section 20(2) (procuring execution of valuable security by deception);
section 21 (blackmail);
section 22 (handling stolen goods);
[section 24A (retaining credits from dishonest sources, etc.);][2]

(b) an offence under either of the following provisions of the Theft Act 1978—

section 1 (obtaining services by deception);
section 2 (avoiding liability by deception);

(c) an offence under any of the following provisions of the Forgery and Counterfeiting Act 1981—

section 1 (forgery);
section 2 (copying a false instrument);
section 3 (using a false instrument);
section 4 (using a copy of a false instrument);
section 5 (offences which relate to money orders, share certificates, passports, etc.);
[section 14 (offences of counterfeiting notes and coins);
section 15 (offences of passing etc counterfeit notes and coins);
section 16 (offences involving the custody or control of counterfeit notes and coins);
section 17 (offences involving the making or custody or control of counterfeiting materials and implements);
section 20 (prohibition of importation of counterfeit notes and coins);
section 21 (prohibition of exportation of counterfeit notes and coins);][3]

(d) the common law offence of cheating in relation to the public revenue.

(3) The Group B offences are—

(a) conspiracy to commit a Group A offence;
(b) conspiracy to defraud;
(c) attempting to commit a Group A offence;
(d) incitement to commit a Group A offence.

(4) The Secretary of State may by order amend subsection (2) or (3) by adding or removing any offence.

(5) The power to make such an order shall be exercisable by statutory instrument.

(6) No order shall be made under subsection (4) unless a draft of it has been laid before and approved by a resolution of each House of Parliament.

[1] Words inserted by Theft (Amendment) Act 1996 c.62 s 3 (2)
[2] Words inserted by Theft (Amendment) Act 1996 c.62 s 3 (3)
[3] Words inserted by SI 2000/1878 art 2

Jurisdiction in respect of Group A offences

2.—(1) For the purposes of this Part, "relevant event", in relation to any Group A offence, means any act or omission or other event (including any result of one or more acts or omissions) proof of which is required for conviction of the offence. **55-002**

(2) For the purpose of determining whether or not a particular event is a relevant event in relation to a Group A offence, any question as to where it occurred is to be disregarded.

(3) A person may be guilty of a Group A offence if any of the events which are relevant events in relation to the offence occurred in England and Wales.

Questions immaterial to jurisdiction in the case of certain offences

3.—(1) A person may be guilty of a Group A or Group B offence whether or not— **55-003**

(a) he was a British citizen at any material time;

(b) he was in England and Wales at any such time.

(2) On a charge of conspiracy to commit a Group A offence, or on a charge of conspiracy to defraud in England and Wales, the defendant may be guilty of the offence whether or not—

(a) he became a party to the conspiracy in England and Wales;

(b) any act or omission or other event in relation to the conspiracy occurred in England and Wales.

(3) On a charge of attempting to commit a Group A offence, the defendant may be guilty of the offence whether or not—

(a) the attempt was made in England and Wales;

(b) it had an effect in England and Wales.

(4) Subsection (1)(a) does not apply where jurisdiction is given to try the offence in question by an enactment which makes provision by reference to the nationality of the person charged.

(5) Subsection (2) does not apply in relation to any charge under the Criminal Law Act 1977 brought by virtue of section 1A of that Act.

(6) Subsection (3) does not apply in relation to any charge under the Criminal Attempts Act 1981 brought by virtue of section 1A of that Act.

Rules for determining certain jurisdictional questions relating to the location of events

4. In relation to a Group A or Group B offence— **55-004**

(a) there is an obtaining of property in England and Wales if the property is either despatched from or received at a place in England and Wales; and

(b) there is a communication in England and Wales of any information, instruction, request, demand or other matter if it is sent by any means—

(i) from a place in England and Wales to a place elsewhere; or

(ii) from a place elsewhere to a place in England and Wales.

Conspiracy, attempt and incitement

5.—(3) A person may be guilty of conspiracy to defraud if— **55-005**

(a) a party to the agreement constituting the conspiracy, or a party's agent, did anything in England and Wales in relation to the agreement before its formation, or

(b) a party to it became a party in England and Wales (by joining it either in person or through an agent), or

(c) a party to it, or a party's agent, did or omitted anything in England and Wales in pursuance of it,

and the conspiracy would be triable in England and Wales but for the fraud which the parties to it had in view not being intended to take place in England and Wales.

(4) A person may be guilty of incitement to commit a Group A offence if the incitement—

(a) takes place in England and Wales; and

(b) would be triable in England and Wales but for what the person charged had in view not being an offence triable in England and Wales.

(5) Subsections (3) and (4) are subject to section 6.

Relevance of external law

55-006 **6.**—(1) A person is guilty of an offence triable by virtue of section 5(3), only if the pursuit of the agreed course of conduct would at some stage involve—

(a) an act or omission by one or more of the parties, or

(b) the happening of some other event,

constituting an offence under the law in force where the act, omission or other event was intended to take place.

(2) A person is guilty of an offence triable by virtue of section 1A of the Criminal Attempts Act 1981, or by virtue of section 5(4), only if what he had in view would involve the commission of an offence under the law in force where the whole or any part of it was intended to take place.

(3) Conduct punishable under the law in force in any place is an offence under that law for the purposes of this section, however it is described in that law.

(4) Subject to subsection (6), a condition specified in subsection (1) or (2) shall be taken to be satisfied unless, not later than rules of court may provide, the defence serve on the prosecution a notice—

(a) stating that, on the facts as alleged with respect to the relevant conduct, the condition is not in their opinion satisfied;

(b) showing their grounds for that opinion; and

(c) requiring the prosecution to show that it is satisfied.

(5) In subsection (4) "the relevant conduct" means—

(a) where the condition in subsection (1) is in question, the agreed course of conduct; and

(b) where the condition in subsection (2) is in question, what the defendant had in view.

(6) The court, if it thinks fit, may permit the defence to require the prosecution to show that the condition is satisfied without the prior service of a notice under subsection (4).

(7) In the Crown Court, the question whether the condition is satisfied shall be decided by the judge alone.

PART V

INSIDER DEALING

The offence of insider dealing

The offence

52.—(1) An individual who has information as an insider is guilty of insider dealing if, in the circumstances mentioned in subsection (3), he deals in securities that are price-affected securities in relation to the information. **55-007**

(2) An individual who has information as an insider is also guilty of insider dealing if—

(a) he encourages another person to deal in securities that are (whether or not that other knows it) price-affected securities in relation to the information, knowing or having reasonable cause to believe that the dealing would take place in the circumstances mentioned in subsection (3); or

(b) he discloses the information, otherwise than in the proper performance of the functions of his employment, office or profession, to another person.

(3) The circumstances referred to above are that the acquisition or disposal in question occurs on a regulated market, or that the person dealing relies on a professional intermediary or is himself acting as a professional intermediary.

(4) This section has effect subject to section 53.

Defences

53.—(1) An individual is not guilty of insider dealing by virtue of dealing in securities if he shows— **55-008**

(a) that he did not at the time expect the dealing to result in a profit attributable to the fact that the information in question was price-sensitive information in relation to the securities, or

(b) that at the time he believed on reasonable grounds that the information had been disclosed widely enough to ensure that none of those taking part in the dealing would be prejudiced by not having the information, or

(c) that he would have done what he did even if he had not had the information.

(2) An individual is not guilty of insider dealing by virtue of encouraging another person to deal in securities if he shows—

(a) that he did not at the time expect the dealing to result in a profit attributable to the fact that the information in question was price-sensitive information in relation to the securities, or

(b) that at the time he believed on reasonable grounds that the information had been or would be disclosed widely enough to ensure that none of those taking part in the dealing would be prejudiced by not having the information, or

(c) that he would have done what he did even if he had not had the information.

(3) An individual is not guilty of insider dealing by virtue of a disclosure of information if he shows—

(a) that he did not at the time expect any person, because of the disclosure, to deal in securities in the circumstances mentioned in subsection (3) of section 52; or

(b) that, although he had such an expectation at the time, he did not expect the dealing to result in a profit attributable to the fact that the information was price-sensitive information in relation to the securities.

(4) Schedule 1 (special defences) shall have effect.

(5) The Treasury may by order amend Schedule 1.

(6) In this section references to a profit include references to the avoidance of a loss.

Interpretation

Securities to which Part V applies

55-009 **54.**—(1) This Part applies to any security which—

(a) falls within any paragraph of Schedule 2; and

(b) satisfies any conditions applying to it under an order made by the Treasury for the purposes of this subsection;

and in the provisions of this Part (other than that Schedule) any reference to a security is a reference to a security to which this Part applies.

(2) The Treasury may by order amend Schedule 2.

"Dealing" in securities

55-010 **55.**—(1) For the purposes of this Part, a person deals in securities if—

(a) he acquires or disposes of the securities (whether as principal or agent); or

(b) he procures, directly or indirectly, an acquisition or disposal of the securities by any other person.

(2) For the purposes of this Part, "acquire", in relation to a security, includes—

(a) agreeing to acquire the security; and

(b) entering into a contract which creates the security

(3) For the purposes of this Part, "dispose", in relation to a security, includes—

(a) agreeing to dispose of the security; and

(b) bringing to an end a contract which created the security.

(4) For the purposes of subsection (1), a person procures an acquisition or disposal of a security if the security is acquired or disposed of by a person who is—

(a) his agent,

(b) his nominee, or

(c) a person who is acting at his direction,

in relation to the acquisition or disposal.

(5) Subsection (4) is not exhaustive as to the circumstances in which one person may be regarded as procuring an acquisition or disposal of securities by another.

"Inside information", etc

55-011 **56.**—(1) For the purposes of this section and section 57, "inside information" means information which—

(a) relates to particular securities or to a particular issuer of securities or to particular issuers of securities and not to securities generally or to issuers of securities generally;
(b) is specific or precise;
(c) has not been made public; and
(d) if it were made public would be likely to have a significant effect on the price of any securities.

(2) For the purposes of this Part, securities are "price-affected securities" in relation to inside information, and inside information is "price-sensitive information" in relation to securities, if and only if the information would, if made public, be likely to have a significant effect on the price of the securities.

(3) For the purposes of this section "price" includes value.

"Insiders"

57.—(1) For the purposes of this Part, a person has information as an insider if and only if— **55-012**

(a) it is, and he knows that it is, inside information, and
(b) he has it, and knows that he has it, from an inside source.

(2) For the purposes of subsection (1), a person has information from an inside source if and only if—

(a) he has it through—
 (i) being a director, employee or shareholder of an issuer of securities; or
 (ii) having access to the information by virtue of his employment, office or profession; or
(b) the direct or indirect source of his information is a person within paragraph (a).

Information "made public"

58.—(1) For the purposes of section 56, "made public", in relation to information, shall be construed in accordance with the following provisions of this section; but those provisions are not exhaustive as to the meaning of that expression. **55-013**

(2) Information is made public if—

(a) it is published in accordance with the rules of a regulated market for the purpose of informing investors and their professional advisers;
(b) it is contained in records which by virtue of any enactment are open to inspection by the public;
(c) it can be readily acquired by those likely to deal in any securities—
 (i) to which the information relates, or
 (ii) of an issuer to which the information relates; or
(d) it is derived from information which has been made public.

(3) Information may be treated as made public even though—

(a) it can be acquired only by persons exercising diligence or expertise;
(b) it is communicated to a section of the public and not to the public at large;
(c) it can be acquired only by observation;
(d) it is communicated only on payment of a fee; or
(e) it is published only outside the United Kingdom.

"Professional intermediary"

55-014 **59.**—(1) For the purposes of this Part, a "professional intermediary" is a person—

(a) who carries on a business consisting of an activity mentioned in subsection (2) and who holds himself out to the public or any section of the public (including a section of the public constituted by persons such as himself) as willing to engage in any such business; or

(b) who is employed by a person falling within paragraph (a) to carry out any such activity.

(2) The activities referred to in subsection (1) are—

(a) acquiring or disposing of securities (whether as principal or agent); or

(b) acting as an intermediary between persons taking part in any dealing in securities.

(3) A person is not to be treated as carrying on a business consisting of an activity mentioned in subsection (2)—

(a) if the activity in question is merely incidental to some other activity not falling within subsection (2); or

(b) merely because he occasionally conducts one of those activities.

(4) For the purposes of section 52, a person dealing in securities relies on a professional intermediary if and only if a person who is acting as a professional intermediary carries out an activity mentioned in subsection (2) in relation to that dealing.

Other interpretation provisions

55-015 **60.**—(1) For the purposes of this Part, "regulated market" means any market, however operated, which, by an order made by the Treasury, is identified (whether by name or by reference to criteria prescribed by the order) as a regulated market for the purposes of this Part.

(2) For the purposes of this Part an "issuer", in relation to any securities, means any company, public sector body or individual by which or by whom the securities have been or are to be issued.

(3) For the purposes of this Part—

(a) "company" means any body (whether or not incorporated and wherever incorporated or constituted) which is not a public sector body; and

(b) "public sector body" means —

(i) the government of the United Kingdom, of Northern Ireland or of any country or territory outside the United Kingdom;

(ii) a local authority in the United Kingdom or elsewhere;

(iii) any international organisation the members of which include the United Kingdom or another member state;

(iv) the Bank of England; or

(v) the central bank of any sovereign State.

(4) For the purposes of this Part, information shall be treated as relating to an issuer of securities which is a company not only where it is about the company but also where it may affect the company's business prospects.

Miscellaneous

Penalties and prosecution

55-016 **61.**—(1) An individual guilty of insider dealing shall be liable—

(a) on summary conviction, to a fine not exceeding the statutory maximum or imprisonment for a term not exceeding six months or to both; or

(b) on conviction on indictment, to a fine or imprisonment for a term not exceeding seven years or to both.

(2) Proceedings for offences under this Part shall not be instituted in England and Wales except by or with the consent of—

(a) the Secretary of State; or

(b) the Director of Public Prosecutions.

(3) In relation to proceedings in Northern Ireland for offences under this Part, subsection (2) shall have effect as if the reference to the Director of Public Prosecutions were a reference to the Director of Public Prosecutions for Northern Ireland.

Territorial scope of offence of insider dealing

62.—(1) An individual is not guilty of an offence falling within subsection (1) of section 52 unless— **55-017**

(a) he was within the United Kingdom at the time when he is alleged to have done any act constituting or forming part of the alleged dealing;

(b) the regulated market on which the dealing is alleged to have occurred is one which, by an order made by the Treasury, is identified (whether by name or by reference to criteria prescribed by the order) as being, for the purposes of this Part, regulated in the United Kingdom; or

(c) the professional intermediary was within the United Kingdom at the time when he is alleged to have done anything by means of which the offence is alleged to have been committed.

(2) An individual is not guilty of an offence falling within subsection (2) of section 52 unless—

(a) he was within the United Kingdom at the time when he is alleged to have disclosed the information or encouraged the dealing; or

(b) the alleged recipient of the information or encouragement was within the United Kingdom at the time when he is alleged to have received the information or encouragement.

Limits on section 52

63.—(1) Section 52 does not apply to anything done by an individual acting on behalf of a public sector body in pursuit of monetary policies or policies with respect to exchange rates or the management of public debt or foreign exchange reserves. **55-018**

(2) No contract shall be void or unenforceable by reason only of section 52.

SCHEDULES

Section 53(4)

Schedule 1

SPECIAL DEFENCES

Market makers

1.—(1) An individual is not guilty of insider dealing by virtue of dealing in securities or encouraging another person to deal if he shows that he acted in good faith in the course of— **55-019**

(a) his business as a market maker, or

(b) his employment in the business of a market maker.

(2) A market maker is a person who—

(a) holds himself out at all normal times in compliance with the rules of a regulated market or an approved organisation as willing to acquire or dispose of securities; and

(b) is recognised as doing so under those rules.

(3) In this paragraph "approved organisation" means an international securities self-regulating organisation approved [by the Treasury under any relevant order under section 22 of the Financial Services and Markets Act 2000][1].

Market information

55-020 **2.**— (1) An individual is not guilty of insider dealing by virtue of dealing in securities or encouraging another person to deal if he shows that—

(a) the information which he had as an insider was market information; and

(b) it was reasonable for an individual in his position to have acted as he did despite having that information as an insider at the time.

(2) In determining whether it is reasonable for an individual to do any act despite having market information at the time, there shall, in particular, be taken into account—

(a) the content of the information;

(b) the circumstances in which he first had the information and in what capacity; and

(c) the capacity in which he now acts.

55-021 **3.** An individual is not guilty of insider dealing by virtue of dealing in securities or encouraging another person to deal if he shows—

(a) that he acted—

(i) in connection with an acquisition or disposal which was under consideration or the subject of negotiation, or in the course of a series of such acquisitions or disposals; and

(ii) with a view to facilitating the accomplishment of the acquisition or disposal or the series of acquisitions or disposals; and

(b) that the information which he had as an insider was market information arising directly out of his involvement in the acquisition or disposal or series of acquisitions or disposals.

55-022 **4.** For the purposes of paragraphs 2 and 3 market information is information consisting of one or more of the following facts—

(a) that securities of a particular kind have been or are to be acquired or disposed of, or that their acquisition or disposal is under consideration or the subject of negotiation;

(b) that securities of a particular kind have not been or are not to be acquired or disposed of;

(c) the number of securities acquired or disposed of or to be acquired or disposed of or whose acquisition or disposal is under consideration or the subject of negotiation;

(d) the price (or range of prices) at which securities have been or are to be acquired or disposed of or the price (or range of prices) at which securities whose acquisition or disposal is under consideration or the subject of negotiation may be acquired or disposed of;

(e) the identity of the persons involved or likely to be involved in any capacity in an acquisition or disposal.

Price stabilisation

55-023 **5.**— (1) An individual is not guilty of insider dealing by virtue of dealing in securities or encouraging another person to deal if he shows that he acted in conformity with the price stabilisation rules.

[(2) "Price stabilisation rules" means rules made under section 144(1) of the Financial Services and Markets Act 2000.][2]

Section 54 Schedule 2

SECURITIES

Shares

55-024 **1.** Shares and stock in the share capital of a company ("shares").

[1] Words substituted by SI 2001/3649 Pt 8 art 341 (2)

[2] Substituted by SI 2001/3649 Pt 8 art 341 (3)

Debt securities

2. Any instrument creating or acknowledging indebtedness which is issued by a company or public sector body, including, in particular, debentures, debenture stock, loan stock, bonds and certificates of deposit ("debt securities"). **55-025**

Warrants

3. Any right (whether conferred by warrant or otherwise) to subscribe for shares or debt securities ("warrants"). **55-026**

Depositary receipts

4.—(1) The rights under any depositary receipt. **55-027**

(2) For the purposes of sub-paragraph (1) a "depositary receipt" means a certificate or other record (whether or not in the form of a document)—

(a) which is issued by or on behalf of a person who holds any relevant securities of a particular issuer; and

(b) which acknowledges that another person is entitled to rights in relation to the relevant securities or relevant securities of the same kind.

(3) In sub-paragraph (2) "relevant securities" means shares, debt securities and warrants.

Options

5. Any option to acquire or dispose of any security falling within any other paragraph of this Schedule. **55-028**

Futures

6.—(1) Rights under a contract for the acquisition or disposal of relevant securities under which delivery is to be made at a future date and at a price agreed when the contract is made. **55-029**

(2) In sub-paragraph (1)—

(a) the references to a future date and to a price agreed when the contract is made include references to a date and a price determined in accordance with terms of the contract; and

(b) "relevant securities" means any security falling within any other paragraph of this Schedule.

Contracts for differences

7.—(1) Rights under a contract which does not provide for the delivery of securities but whose purpose or pretended purpose is to secure a profit or avoid a loss by reference to fluctuations in— **55-030**

(a) a share index or other similar factor connected with relevant securities;

(b) the price of particular relevant securities; or

(c) the interest rate offered on money placed on deposit.

(2) In sub-paragraph (1) "relevant securities" means any security falling within any other paragraph of this Schedule.

Criminal Justice and Public Order Act 1994

CHAPTER 33

PART V

PUBLIC ORDER: COLLECTIVE TRESPASS OR NUISANCE ON LAND

Powers to remove trespassers on land

Power to remove trespassers on land

56-001 **61.**—(1) If the senior police officer present at the scene reasonably believes that two or more persons are trespassing on land and are present there with the common purpose of residing there for any period, that reasonable steps have been taken by or on behalf of the occupier to ask them to leave and—

(a) that any of those persons has caused damage to the land or to property on the land or used threatening, abusive or insulting words or behaviour towards the occupier, a member of his family or an employee or agent of his, or

(b) that those persons have between them six or more vehicles on the land,

he may direct those persons, or any of them, to leave the land and to remove any vehicles or other property they have with them on the land.

(2) Where the persons in question are reasonably believed by the senior police officer to be persons who were not originally trespassers but have become trespassers on the land, the officer must reasonably believe that the other conditions specified in subsection (1) are satisfied after those persons became trespassers before he can exercise the power conferred by that subsection.

(3) A direction under subsection (1) above, if not communicated to the persons referred to in subsection (1) by the police officer giving the direction, may be communicated to them by any constable at the scene.

(4) If a person knowing that a direction under subsection (1) above has been given which applies to him—

(a) fails to leave the land as soon as reasonably practicable, or

(b) having left again enters the land as a trespasser within the period of three months beginning with the day on which the direction was given,

he commits an offence and is liable on summary conviction to imprisonment for a term not exceeding three months or a fine not exceeding level 4 on the standard scale, or both.

(5) A constable in uniform who reasonably suspects that a person is committing an offence under this section may arrest him without a warrant.

(6) In proceedings for an offence under this section it is a defence for the accused to show—

(a) that he was not trespassing on the land, or

(b) that he had a reasonable excuse for failing to leave the land as soon as reasonably practicable or, as the case may be, for again entering the land as a trespasser.

(7) In its application in England and Wales to common land this section has effect as if in the preceding subsections of it—

(a) references to trespassing or trespassers were references to acts and persons doing acts which constitute either a trespass as against the occupier or an infringement of the commoners' rights; and

(b) references to "the occupier" included the commoners or any of them or, in the case of common land to which the public has access, the local authority as well as any commoner.

(8) Subsection (7) above does not—

(a) require action by more than one occupier; or

(b) constitute persons trespassers as against any commoner or the local authority if they are permitted to be there by the other occupier.

(9) In this section—

"common land" means common land as defined in section 22 of the Commons Registration Act 1965;

"commoner" means a person with rights of common as defined in section 22 of the Commons Registration Act 1965;

"land" does not include—

(a) buildings other than—

(i) agricultural buildings within the meaning of, in England and Wales, paragraphs 3 to 8 of Schedule 5 to the Local Government Finance Act 1988 or, in Scotland, section 7(2) of the Valuation and Rating (Scotland) Act 1956, or

(ii) scheduled monuments within the meaning of the Ancient Monuments and Archaeological Areas Act 1979;

(b) land forming part of—

(i) a highway unless it falls within the classifications in section 54 of the Wildlife and Countryside Act 1981 (footpath, bridleway or byway open to all traffic or road used as a public path) or is a cycle track under the Highways Act 1980 or the Cycle Tracks Act 1984; or

(ii) a road within the meaning of the Roads (Scotland) Act 1984 unless it falls within the definitions in section 151(2)(a)(ii) or (b) (footpaths and cycle tracks) of that Act or is a bridleway within the meaning of section 47 of the Countryside (Scotland) Act 1967;

"the local authority", in relation to common land, means any local authority which has powers in relation to the land under section 9 of the Commons Registration Act 1965;

"occupier" (and in subsection (8) "the other occupier") means—

(a) in England and Wales, the person entitled to possession of the land by virtue of an estate or interest held by him; and

(b) in Scotland, the person lawfully entitled to natural possession of the land;

"property", in relation to damage to property on land, means—

(a) in England and Wales, property within the meaning of section 10(1) of the Criminal Damage Act 1971; and

(b) in Scotland, either—

(i) heritable property other than land; or

(ii) corporeal movable property,

and "damage" includes the deposit of any substance capable of polluting the land;

"trespass" means, in the application of this section—

(a) in England and Wales, subject to the extensions effected by subsection (7) above, trespass as against the occupier of the land;

(b) in Scotland, entering, or as the case may be remaining on, land without lawful authority and without the occupier's consent; and

"trespassing" and "trespasser" shall be construed accordingly;

"vehicle" includes—

(a) any vehicle, whether or not it is in a fit state for use on roads, and includes any chassis or body, with or without wheels, appearing to have formed part of such a vehicle, and any load carried by, and anything attached to, such a vehicle; and

(b) a caravan as defined in section 29(1) of the Caravan Sites and Control of Development Act 1960;

and a person may be regarded for the purposes of this section as having a purpose of residing in a place notwithstanding that he has a home elsewhere.

Supplementary powers of seizure

56-002 **62.**—(1) If a direction has been given under section 61 and a constable reasonably suspects that any person to whom the direction applies has, without reasonable excuse—

(a) failed to remove any vehicle on the land which appears to the constable to belong to him or to be in his possession or under his control; or

(b) entered the land as a trespasser with a vehicle within the period of three months beginning with the day on which the direction was given,

the constable may seize and remove that vehicle.

(2) In this section "trespasser" and "vehicle" have the same meaning as in section 61.

Powers in relation to raves

Powers to remove persons attending or preparing for a rave

56-003 **63.**—(1) This section applies to a gathering on land in the open air of 100 or more persons (whether or not trespassers) at which amplified music is played during the night (with or without intermissions) and is such as, by reason of its loudness and duration and the time at which it is played, is likely to cause serious distress to the inhabitants of the locality; and for this purpose—

(a) such a gathering continues during intermissions in the music and, where the gathering extends over several days, throughout the period during which amplified music is played at night (with or without intermissions); and

(b) "music" includes sounds wholly or predominantly characterised by the emission of a succession of repetitive beats.

(2) If, as respects any land in the open air, a police officer of at least the rank of superintendent reasonably believes that—

(a) two or more persons are making preparations for the holding there of a gathering to which this section applies,

(b) ten or more persons are waiting for such a gathering to begin there, or

(c) ten or more persons are attending such a gathering which is in progress,

he may give a direction that those persons and any other persons who come to prepare or wait for or to attend the gathering are to leave the land and remove any vehicles or other property which they have with them on the land.

(3) A direction under subsection (2) above, if not communicated to the persons referred to in subsection (2) by the police officer giving the direction, may be communicated to them by any constable at the scene.

(4) Persons shall be treated as having had a direction under subsection (2) above communicated to them if reasonable steps have been taken to bring it to their attention.

(5) A direction under subsection (2) above does not apply to an exempt person.

(6) If a person knowing that a direction has been given which applies to him—

(a) fails to leave the land as soon as reasonably practicable, or

(b) having left again enters the land within the period of 7 days beginning with the day on which the direction was given,

he commits an offence and is liable on summary conviction to imprisonment for a term not exceeding three months or a fine not exceeding level 4 on the standard scale, or both.

(7) In proceedings for an offence under this section it is a defence for the accused to show that he had a reasonable excuse for failing to leave the land as soon as reasonably practicable or, as the case may be, for again entering the land.

(8) A constable in uniform who reasonably suspects that a person is committing an offence under this section may arrest him without a warrant.

(9) This section does not apply—

(a) in England and Wales, to a gathering licensed by an entertainment licence; or

(b) in Scotland, to a gathering in premises which, by virtue of section 41 of the Civic Government (Scotland) Act 1982, are licensed to be used as a place of public entertainment.

(10) In this section—

"entertainment licence" means a licence granted by a local authority under—

(a) Schedule 12 to the London Government Act 1963;

(b) section 3 of the Private Places of Entertainment (Licensing) Act 1967; or

(c) Schedule 1 to the Local Government (Miscellaneous Provisions) Act 1982;

"exempt person", in relation to land (or any gathering on land), means the occupier, any member of his family and any employee or agent of his and any person whose home is situated on the land;

"land in the open air" includes a place partly open to the air;

"local authority" means—

(a) in Greater London, a London borough council or the Common Council of the City of London;

(b) in England outside Greater London, a district council or the council of the Isles of Scilly;

(c) in Wales, a county council or county borough council; and

"occupier", "trespasser" and "vehicle" have the same meaning as in section 61.

Supplementary powers of entry and seizure

56-004 **64.**—(1) If a police officer of at least the rank of superintendent reasonably believes that circumstances exist in relation to any land which would justify the giving of a direction under section 63 in relation to a gathering to which that section applies he may authorise any constable to enter the land for any of the purposes specified in subsection (2) below.

(2) Those purposes are—

(a) to ascertain whether such circumstances exist; and

(b) to exercise any power conferred on a constable by section 63 or subsection (4) below.

(3) A constable who is so authorised to enter land for any purpose may enter the land without a warrant.

(4) If a direction has been given under section 63 and a constable reasonably suspects that any person to whom the direction applies has, without reasonable excuse—

(a) failed to remove any vehicle or sound equipment on the land which appears to the constable to belong to him or to be in his possession or under his control; or

(b) entered the land as a trespasser with a vehicle or sound equipment within the period of 7 days beginning with the day on which the direction was given,

the constable may seize and remove that vehicle or sound equipment.

(5) Subsection (4) above does not authorise the seizure of any vehicle or sound equipment of an exempt person.

(6) In this section—

"exempt person" has the same meaning as in section 63;

"sound equipment" means equipment designed or adapted for amplifying music and any equipment suitable for use in connection with such equipment, and "music" has the same meaning as in section 63; and

"vehicle" has the same meaning as in section 61.

Raves: power to stop persons from proceeding

56-005 **65.**—(1) If a constable in uniform reasonably believes that a person is on his way to a gathering to which section 63 applies in relation to which a direction under section 63(2) is in force, he may, subject to subsections (2) and (3) below—

(a) stop that person, and

(b) direct him not to proceed in the direction of the gathering.

(2) The power conferred by subsection (1) above may only be exercised at a place within 5 miles of the boundary of the site of the gathering.

(3) No direction may be given under subsection (1) above to an exempt person.

(4) If a person knowing that a direction under subsection (1) above has been given to him fails to comply with that direction, he commits an offence and is liable on summary conviction to a fine not exceeding level 3 on the standard scale.

(5) A constable in uniform who reasonably suspects that a person is committing an offence under this section may arrest him without a warrant.

(6) In this section, "exempt person" has the same meaning as in section 63.

Disruptive trespassers

Offence of aggravated trespass

68.—(1) A person commits the offence of aggravated trespass if he trespasses on land in the open air and, in relation to any lawful activity which persons are engaging in or are about to engage in on that or adjoining land in the open air, does there anything which is intended by him to have the effect— **56-006**

(a) of intimidating those persons or any of them so as to deter them or any of them from engaging in that activity,

(b) of obstructing that activity, or

(c) of disrupting that activity.

(2) Activity on any occasion on the part of a person or persons on land is "lawful" for the purposes of this section if he or they may engage in the activity on the land on that occasion without committing an offence or trespassing on the land.

(3) A person guilty of an offence under this section is liable on summary conviction to imprisonment for a term not exceeding three months or a fine not exceeding level 4 on the standard scale, or both.

(4) A constable in uniform who reasonably suspects that a person is committing an offence under this section may arrest him without a warrant.

(5) In this section "land" does not include—

(a) the highways and roads excluded from the application of section 61 by paragraph (b) of the definition of land in subsection (9) of that section; or

(b) a road within the meaning of the Roads (Northern Ireland) Order 1993.

Powers to remove persons committing or participating in aggravated trespass

69.—(1) If the senior police officer present at the scene reasonably believes— **56-007**

(a) that a person is committing, has committed or intends to commit the offence of aggravated trespass on land in the open air; or

(b) that two or more persons are trespassing on land in the open air and are present there with the common purpose of intimidating persons so as to deter them from engaging in a lawful activity or of obstructing or disrupting a lawful activity,

he may direct that person or (as the case may be) those persons (or any of them) to leave the land.

(2) A direction under subsection (1) above, if not communicated to the persons referred to in subsection (1) by the police officer giving the direction, may be communicated to them by any constable at the scene.

(3) If a person knowing that a direction under subsection (1) above has been given which applies to him—

(a) fails to leave the land as soon as practicable, or

(b) having left again enters the land as a trespasser within the period of three months beginning with the day on which the direction was given,

he commits an offence and is liable on summary conviction to imprisonment for a term not exceeding three months or a fine not exceeding level 4 on the standard scale, or both.

(4) In proceedings for an offence under subsection (3) it is a defence for the accused to show—

(a) that he was not trespassing on the land, or

(b) that he had a reasonable excuse for failing to leave the land as soon as practicable or, as the case may be, for again entering the land as a trespasser.

(5) A constable in uniform who reasonably suspects that a person is committing an offence under this section may arrest him without a warrant.

(6) In this section "lawful activity" and "land" have the same meaning as in section 68.

Powers to remove unauthorised campers

Power of local authority to direct unauthorised campers to leave land

56-008 77.—(1) If it appears to a local authority that persons are for the time being residing in a vehicle or vehicles within that authority's area—

(a) on any land forming part of a highway;

(b) on any other unoccupied land; or

(c) on any occupied land without the consent of the occupier,

the authority may give a direction that those persons and any others with them are to leave the land and remove the vehicle or vehicles and any other property they have with them on the land.

(2) Notice of a direction under subsection (1) must be served on the persons to whom the direction applies, but it shall be sufficient for this purpose for the direction to specify the land and (except where the direction applies to only one person) to be addressed to all occupants of the vehicles on the land, without naming them.

(3) If a person knowing that a direction under subsection (1) above has been given which applies to him—

(a) fails, as soon as practicable, to leave the land or remove from the land any vehicle or other property which is the subject of the direction, or

(b) having removed any such vehicle or property again enters the land with a vehicle within the period of three months beginning with the day on which the direction was given,

he commits an offence and is liable on summary conviction to a fine not exceeding level 3 on the standard scale.

(4) A direction under subsection (1) operates to require persons who re-enter the land within the said period with vehicles or other property to leave and remove the vehicles or other property as it operates in relation to the persons and vehicles or other property on the land when the direction was given.

(5) In proceedings for an offence under this section it is a defence for the accused to show that his failure to leave or to remove the vehicle or other property as soon as practicable or his re-entry with a vehicle was due to illness, mechanical breakdown or other immediate emergency.

(6) In this section—

"land" means land in the open air;

"local authority" means—

(a) in Greater London, a London borough or the Common Council of the City of London;

(b) in England outside Greater London, a county council, a district council or the Council of the Isles of Scilly;

(c) in Wales, a county council or a county borough council;

"occupier" means the person entitled to possession of the land by virtue of an estate or interest held by him;

"vehicle" includes—

(a) any vehicle, whether or not it is in a fit state for use on roads, and includes any body, with or without wheels, appearing to have formed part of such a vehicle, and any load carried by, and anything attached to, such a vehicle; and

(b) a caravan as defined in section 29(1) of the Caravan Sites and Control of Development Act 1960;

and a person may be regarded for the purposes of this section as residing on any land notwithstanding that he has a home elsewhere.

Orders for removal of persons and their vehicles unlawfully on land

78.—(1) A magistrates' court may, on a complaint made by a local authority, **56-009**
if satisfied that persons and vehicles in which they are residing are present on land within that authority's area in contravention of a direction given under section 77, make an order requiring the removal of any vehicle or other property which is so present on the land and any person residing in it.

(2) An order under this section may authorise the local authority to take such steps as are reasonably necessary to ensure that the order is complied with and, in particular, may authorise the authority, by its officers and servants—

(a) to enter upon the land specified in the order; and

(b) to take, in relation to any vehicle or property to be removed in pursuance of the order, such steps for securing entry and rendering it suitable for removal as may be so specified.

(3) The local authority shall not enter upon any occupied land unless they have given to the owner and occupier at least 24 hours notice of their intention to do so, or unless after reasonable inquiries they are unable to ascertain their names and addresses.

(4) A person who wilfully obstructs any person in the exercise of any power conferred on him by an order under this section commits an offence and is liable on summary conviction to a fine not exceeding level 3 on the standard scale.

(5) Where a complaint is made under this section, a summons issued by the court requiring the person or persons to whom it is directed to appear before the court to answer to the complaint may be directed—

(a) to the occupant of a particular vehicle on the land in question; or

(b) to all occupants of vehicles on the land in question, without naming him or them.

(6) Section 55(2) of the Magistrates' Courts Act 1980 (warrant for arrest of defendant failing to appear) does not apply to proceedings on a complaint made under this section.

(7) Section 77(6) of this Act applies also for the interpretation of this section.

Criminal Appeal Act 1995

CHAPTER 35

PART II

THE CRIMINAL CASES REVIEW COMMISSION

The Commission

The Commission

57-001 **8.**—(1) There shall be a body corporate to be known as the Criminal Cases Review Commission.

(2) The Commission shall not be regarded as the servant or agent of the Crown or as enjoying any status, immunity or privilege of the Crown; and the Commission's property shall not be regarded as property of, or held on behalf of, the Crown.

(3) The Commission shall consist of not fewer than eleven members.

(4) The members of the Commission shall be appointed by Her Majesty on the recommendation of the Prime Minister.

(5) At least one third of the members of the Commission shall be persons who are legally qualified; and for this purpose a person is legally qualified if—

(a) he has a ten year general qualification, within the meaning of section 71 of the Courts and Legal Services Act 1990, or

(b) he is a member of the Bar of Northern Ireland, or solicitor of the Supreme Court of Northern Ireland, of at least ten years' standing.

(6) At least two thirds of the members of the Commission shall be persons who appear to the Prime Minister to have knowledge or experience of any aspect of the criminal justice system and of them at least one shall be a person who appears to him to have knowledge or experience of any aspect of the criminal justice system in Northern Ireland; and for the purposes of this subsection the criminal justice system includes, in particular, the investigation of offences and the treatment of offenders.

(7) Schedule 1 (further provisions with respect to the Commission) shall have effect.

References to court

Cases dealt with on indictment in England and Wales

57-002 **9.**—(1) Where a person has been convicted of an offence on indictment in England and Wales, the Commission—

(a) may at any time refer the conviction to the Court of Appeal, and

(b) (whether or not they refer the conviction) may at any time refer to the Court of Appeal any sentence (not being a sentence fixed by law) imposed on, or in subsequent proceedings relating to, the conviction.

(2) A reference under subsection (1) of a person's conviction shall be treated for all purposes as an appeal by the person under section 1 of the 1968 Act against the conviction.

(3) A reference under subsection (1) of a sentence imposed on, or in subsequent proceedings relating to, a person's conviction on an indictment shall be treated for all purposes as an appeal by the person under section 9 of the 1968 Act against—

(a) the sentence, and
(b) any other sentence (not being a sentence fixed by law) imposed on, or in subsequent proceedings relating to, the conviction or any other conviction on the indictment.

(4) On a reference under subsection (1) of a person's conviction on an indictment the Commission may give notice to the Court of Appeal that any other conviction on the indictment which is specified in the notice is to be treated as referred to the Court of Appeal under subsection (1).

(5) Where a verdict of not guilty by reason of insanity has been returned in England and Wales in the case of a person, the Commission may at any time refer the verdict to the Court of Appeal; and a reference under this subsection shall be treated for all purposes as an appeal by the person under section 12 of the 1968 Act against the verdict.

(6) Where a jury in England and Wales has returned findings that a person is under a disability and that he did the act or made the omission charged against him, the Commission may at any time refer either or both of those findings to the Court of Appeal; and a reference under this subsection shall be treated for all purposes as an appeal by the person under section 15 of the 1968 Act against the finding or findings referred.

Cases dealt with summarily in England and Wales

11.—(1) Where a person has been convicted of an offence by a magistrates' court in England and Wales, the Commission— **57-003**

(a) may at any time refer the conviction to the Crown Court, and
(b) (Whether or not they refer the conviction) may at any time refer to the Crown Court any sentence imposed on, or in subsequent proceedings relating to, the conviction.

(2) A reference under subsection (1) of a person's conviction shall be treated for all purposes as an appeal by the person under section 108(1) of the Magistrates' Courts Act 1980 against the conviction (whether or not he pleaded guilty).

(3) A reference under subsection (1) of a sentence imposed on, or in subsequent proceedings relating to, a person's conviction shall be treated for all purposes as an appeal by the person under section 108(1) of the Magistrates' Courts Act 1980 against—

(a) the sentence, and
(b) any other sentence imposed on, or in subsequent proceedings relating to, the conviction or any related conviction.

(4) On a reference under subsection (1) of a person's conviction the Commission may give notice to the Crown Court that any related conviction which is specified in the notice is to be treated as referred to the Crown Court under subsection (1).

(5) For the purposes of this section convictions are related if they are convictions of the same person by the same court on the same day.

(6) On a reference under this section the Crown Court may not award any punishment more severe than that awarded by the court whose decision is referred.

(7) The Crown Court may grant bail to a person whose conviction or sentence has been referred under this section; and any time during which he is released on bail shall not count as part of any term of imprisonment or detention under his sentence.

Conditions for making of references

57-004 **13.**—(1) A reference of a conviction, verdict, finding or sentence shall not be made under any of section 9 to 12 unless—

(a) the Commission consider that there is a real possibility that the conviction, verdict, finding or sentence would not be upheld were the reference to be made,

(b) the Commission so consider—

(i) in the case of a conviction, verdict or finding, because of an argument, or evidence, not raised in the proceedings which led to it or on any appeal or application for leave to appeal against it, or

(ii) in the case of a sentence, because of an argument on a point of law, or information, not so raised, and

(c) an appeal against the conviction, verdict, finding or sentence has been determined or leave to appeal against it has been refused.

(2) Nothing in subsection (1)(b)(i) or (c) shall prevent the making of a reference if it appears to the Commission that there are exceptional circumstances which justify making it.

Further provisions about references

57-005 **14.**—(1) A reference of a conviction, verdict, finding or sentence may be made under any of sections 9 to 12 either after an application has been made by or on behalf of the person to whom it relates or without an application having been so made.

(2) In considering whether to make a reference of a conviction, verdict, finding or sentence under any of sections 9 to 12 the Commission shall have regard to—

(a) any application or representations made to the Commission by or on behalf of the person to whom it relates,

(b) any other representations made to the Commission in relation to it, and

(c) any other matters which appear to the Commission to be relevant.

(3) In considering whether to make a reference under section 9 or 10 the Commission may at any time refer any point on which they desire the assistance of the Court of Appeal to that Court for the Court's opinion on it; and on a reference under this subsection the Court of Appeal shall consider the point referred and furnish the Commission with the Court's opinion on the point.

(4) Where the Commission make a reference under any of sections 9 to 12 the Commission shall—

(a) give to the court to which the reference is made a statement of the Commission's reasons for making the reference, and

(b) send a copy of the statement to every person who appears to the Commission to be likely to be a party to any proceedings on the appeal arising from the reference.

(5) Where a reference under any of sections 9 to 12 is treated as an appeal against any conviction, verdict, finding or sentence, the appeal may be on any ground relating to the conviction, verdict, finding or sentence (whether or not the

ground is related to any reason given by the Commission for making the reference).

(6) In every case in which—

(a) an application has been made to the Commission by or on behalf of any person for the reference under any of sections 9 to 12 of any conviction, verdict, finding or sentence, but

(b) the Commission decide not to make a reference of the conviction, verdict, finding or sentence,

the Commission shall give a statement of the reasons for their decision to the person who made the application.

Investigations and assistance

Investigations for Court of Appeal

15.—(1) Where a direction is given by the Court of Appeal under section 23A(1) of the 1968 Act or section 25A(1) of the 1980 Act the Commission shall investigate the matter specified in the direction in such manner as the Commission think fit. **57-006**

(2) Where, in investigating a matter specified in such a direction, it appears to the Commission that—

(a) another matter (a "related matter") which is relevant to the determination of the case by the Court of Appeal ought, if possible, to be resolved before the case is determined by that Court, and

(b) an investigation of the related matter is likely to result in the Court's being able to resolve it,

the Commission may also investigate the related matter.

(3) The Commission shall—

(a) keep the Court of Appeal informed as to the progress of the investigation of any matter specified in a direction under section 23A(1) of the 1968 Act or section 25A(1) of the 1980 Act, and

(b) if they decide to investigate any related matter, notify the Court of Appeal of their decision and keep the Court informed as to the progress of the investigation.

(4) The Commission shall report to the Court of Appeal on the investigation of any matter specified in a direction under section 23A(1) of the 1968 Act or section 25A(1) of the 1980 Act when—

(a) they complete the investigation of that matter and of any related matter investigated by them, or

(b) they are directed to do so by the Court of Appeal,

whichever happens first.

(5) A report under subsection (4) shall include details of any inquiries made by or for the Commission in the investigation of the matter specified in the direction or any related matter investigated by them.

(6) Such a report shall be accompanied—

(a) by any statements and opinions received by the Commission in the investigation of the matter specified in the direction or any related matter investigated by them, and

(b) subject to subsection (7), by any reports so received.

(7) Such a report need not be accompanied by any reports submitted to the Commission under section 20(6) by an investigating officer.

Assistance in connection with prerogative of mercy

57-007 **16.**—(1) Where the Secretary of State refers to the Commission any matter which arises in the consideration of whether to recommend the exercise of Her Majesty's prerogative of mercy in relation to a conviction and on which he desires their assistance, the Commission shall—

(a) consider the matter referred, and

(b) give to the Secretary of State a statement of their conclusions on it;

and the Secretary of State shall, in considering whether so to recommend, treat the Commission's statement as conclusive of the matter referred.

(2) Where in any case the Commission are of the opinion that the Secretary of State should consider whether to recommend the exercise of Her Majesty's prerogative of mercy in relation to the case they shall give him the reasons for their opinion.

Supplementary powers

Power to obtain documents etc

57-008 **17.**—(1) This section applies where the Commission believe that a person serving in a public body has possession or control of a document or other material which may assist the Commission in the exercise of any of their functions.

(2) Where it is reasonable to do so, the Commission may require the person who is the appropriate person in relation to the public body—

(a) to produce the document or other material to the Commission or to give the Commission access to it, and

(b) to allow the Commission to take away the document or other material or to make and take away a copy of it in such form as they think appropriate,

and may direct that person that the document or other material must not be destroyed, damaged or altered before the direction is withdrawn by the Commission.

(3) The documents and other material covered by this section include, in particular, any document or other material obtained or created during any investigation or proceedings relating to—

(a) the case in relation to which the Commission's function is being or may be exercised, or

(b) any other case which may be in any way connected with that case (whether or not any function of the Commission could be exercised in relation to that other case).

(4) The duty to comply with a requirement under this section is not affected by any obligation of secrecy or other limitation on disclosure (including any such obligation or limitation imposed by or by virtue of an enactment) which would otherwise prevent the production of the document or other material to the Commission or the giving of access to it to the Commission.

Government documents etc. relating to current or old cases

57-009 **18.**—(1) Section 17 does not apply to any document or other material in the possession or control of a person serving in a government department if the document or other material—

(a) is relevant to a case to which this subsection applies, and

(b) is in the possession or control of the person in consequence of the Secretary of State's consideration of the case.

(2) Subsection (1) applies to a case if the Secretary of State—

(a) is, immediately before the day on which the repeal by this Act of section 17 of the 1968 Act or of section 14 of the 1980 Act comes into force, considering the case with a view to deciding whether to make a reference under that section or whether to recommend the exercise of Her Majesty's prerogative of mercy in relation to a conviction by a magistrates' court, or

(b) has at any earlier time considered the case with a view to deciding whether to make such a reference or whether so to recommend.

(3) The Secretary of State shall give to the Commission any document or other material which—

(a) contains representations made to him in relation to any case to which this subsection applies, or

(b) was received by him in connection with any such case otherwise than from a person serving in a government department,

and may give to the Commission any document or other material which is relevant to any such case but does not fall within paragraph (a) or (b).

(4) Subsection (3) applies to a case if—

(a) the Secretary of State is, immediately before the day on which the repeal by this Act of section 17 of the 1968 Act or of section 14 of the 1980 Act comes into force, considering the case with a view to deciding whether to make a reference under that section or whether to recommend the exercise of Her Majesty's prerogative of mercy in relation to a conviction by a magistrates' court, or

(b) the Secretary of State has at any earlier time considered the case with a view to deciding whether to make such a reference, or whether so to recommend, and the Commission at any time notify him that they wish subsection (3) to apply to the case.

Power to require appointment of investigating officers

19.—(1) Where the Commission believe that inquiries should be made for assisting them in the exercise of any of their functions in relation to any case they may require the appointment of an investigating officer to carry out the inquiries. **57-010**

(2) Where any offence to which the case relates was investigated by persons serving in a public body, a requirement under this section may be imposed—

(a) on the person who is the appropriate person in relation to the public body, or

(b) where the public body has ceased to exist, on any chief officer of police or on the person who is the appropriate person in relation to any public body which appears to the Commission to have functions which consist of or include functions similar to any of those of the public body which has ceased to exist.

(3) Where no offence to which the case relates was investigated by persons serving in a public body, a requirement under this section may be imposed on any chief officer of police.

(4) A requirement under this section imposed on a chief officer of police may be—

(a) a requirement to appoint a person serving in the police force in relation to which he is the chief officer of police, or

(b) a requirement to appoint a person serving in another police force selected by the chief officer.

(5) A requirement under this section imposed on a person who is the appropriate person in relation to a public body other than a police force may be—

(a) a requirement to appoint a person serving in the public body, or

(b) a requirement to appoint a person serving in a police force, or in a public body (other than a police force) having functions which consist of or include the investigation of offences, selected by the appropriate person.

(6) The Commission may direct—

(a) that a person shall not be appointed, or

(b) that a police force or other public body shall not be selected,

under subsection (4) or (5) without the approval of the Commission.

(7) Where an appointment is made under this section by the person who is the appropriate person in relation to any public body, that person shall inform the Commission of the appointment; and if the Commission are not satisfied with the person appointed they may direct that—

(a) the person who is the appropriate person in relation to the public body shall, as soon as is reasonably practicable, select another person in his place and notify the Commission of the proposal to appoint the other person, and

(b) the other person shall not be appointed without the approval of the Commission.

Inquiries by investigating officers

57-011 **20.**—(1) A person appointed as the investigating officer in relation to a case shall undertake such inquiries as the Commission may from time to time reasonably direct him to undertake in relation to the case.

(2) A person appointed as an investigating officer shall be permitted to act as such by the person who is the appropriate person in relation to the public body in which he is serving.

(3) Where the chief officer of an England and Wales police force appoints a member of the Royal Ulster Constabulary as an investigating officer, the member appointed shall have in England and Wales the same powers and privileges as a member of the police force has there as a constable; and where the Chief Constable of the Royal Ulster Constabulary appoints a member of an England and Wales police force as an investigating officer, the member appointed shall have in Northern Ireland the same powers and privileges as a member of the Royal Ulster Constabulary has there as a constable.

(4) The Commission may take any steps which they consider appropriate for supervising the undertaking of inquiries by an investigating officer.

(5) The Commission may at any time direct that a person appointed as the investigating officer in relation to a case shall cease to act as such; but the making of such a direction shall not prevent the Commission from imposing a requirement under section 19 to appoint another investigating officer in relation to the case.

(6) When a person appointed as the investigating officer in relation to a case has completed the inquiries which he has been directed by the Commission to undertake in relation to the case, he shall—

(a) prepare a report of his findings,

(b) submit it to the Commission, and

(c) send a copy of it to the person by whom he was appointed.

(7) When a person appointed as the investigating officer in relation to a case submits to the Commission a report of his findings he shall also submit to them any statements, opinions and reports received by him in connection with the inquiries which he was directed to undertake in relation to the case.

Other powers

21. Sections 17 to 20 are without prejudice to the taking by the Commission of any steps which they consider appropriate for assisting them in the exercise of any of their functions including, in particular— **57-012**

(a) undertaking, or arranging for others to undertake, inquiries, and
(b) obtaining, or arranging for others to obtain, statements, opinions and reports.

Meaning of "public body" etc

22.—(1) In sections 17, 19 and 20 and this section "public body" means— **57-013**

(a) any police force,
(b) any government department, local authority or other body constituted for purposes of the public service, local government or the administration of justice, or
(c) any other body whose members are appointed by Her Majesty, any Minister or any government department or whose revenues consist wholly or mainly of money provided by Parliament or appropriated by Measure of the Northern Ireland Assembly.

Police Act 1996

CHAPTER 16

PART V

MISCELLANEOUS AND GENERAL

Offences

Assaults on constables

89.—(1) Any person who assaults a constable in the execution of his duty, or a person assisting a constable in the execution of his duty, shall be guilty of an offence and liable on summary conviction to imprisonment for a term not exceeding six months or to a fine not exceeding level 5 on the standard scale, or to both. **58-001**

(2) Any person who resists or wilfully obstructs a constable in the execution of his duty, or a person assisting a constable in the execution of his duty, shall be guilty of an offence and liable on summary conviction to imprisonment for a term not exceeding one month or to a fine not exceeding level 3 on the standard scale, or to both.

(3) This section also applies to a constable who is a member of a police force maintained in Scotland or Northern Ireland when he is executing a warrant, or

otherwise acting in England or Wales, by virtue of any enactment conferring powers on him in England and Wales.

(4) In this section references to a person assisting a constable in the execution of his duty include references to any person who is neither a constable nor in the company of a constable but who—

(a) is a member of an international joint investigation team that is led by a member of a police force or by a member of the National Criminal Intelligence Service or of the National Crime Squad; and
(b) is carrying out his functions as a member of that team.

(5) In this section 'international joint investigation team' means any investigation team formed in accordance with—

(a) any framework decision on joint investigation teams adopted under Article 34 of the Treaty on European Union;
(b) the Convention on Mutual Assistance in Criminal Matters between the Member States of the European Union, and the Protocol to that Convention, established in accordance with that Article of that Treaty; or
(c) any international agreement to which the United Kingdom is a party and which is specified for the purposes of this section in an order made by the Secretary of State.

(6) A statutory instrument containing an order under subsection (5) shall be subject to annulment in pursuance of a resolution of either House of Parliament.

Law Reform (Year and a Day Rule) Act 1996

CHAPTER 19

Abolition of "year and a day rule"

59-001 **1.** The rule known as the "year and a day rule" (that is, the rule that, for the purposes of offences involving death and of suicide, an act or omission is conclusively presumed not to have caused a person's death if more than a year and a day elapsed before he died) is abolished for all purposes.

Restriction on institution of proceedings for a fatal offence

59-002 **2.**—(1) Proceedings to which this section applies may only be instituted by or with the consent of the Attorney General.

(2) This section applies to proceedings against a person for a fatal offence if—

(a) the injury alleged to have caused the death was sustained more than three years before the death occurred, or
(b) the person has previously been convicted of an offence committed in circumstances alleged to be connected with the death.

(3) In subsection (2)"fatal offence" means —

(a) murder, manslaughter, infanticide or any other offence of which one of the elements is causing a person's death, or
(b) the offence of aiding, abetting, counselling or procuring a person's suicide.

(4) No provision that proceedings may be instituted only by or with the consent of the Director of Public Prosecutions shall apply to proceedings to which this section applies.

(5) In the application of this section to Northern Ireland—

(a) the reference in subsection (1) to the Attorney General is to the Attorney General for Northern Ireland, and

(b) the reference in subsection (4) to the Director of Public Prosecutions is to the Director of Public Prosecutions for Northern Ireland.

Short title, commencement and extent

3.—(1) This Act may be cited as the Law Reform (Year and a Day Rule) Act 1996. **59-003**

(2) Section 1 does not affect the continued application of the rule referred to in that section to a case where the act or omission (or the last of the acts or omissions) which caused the death occurred before the day on which this Act is passed.

Criminal Procedure and Investigations Act 1996

CHAPTER 25

PART VII

MISCELLANEOUS AND GENERAL

Tainted acquittals

Acquittals tainted by intimidation etc

54.—(1) This section applies where— **60-001**

(a) a person has been acquitted of an offence, and

(b) a person has been convicted of an administration of justice offence involving interference with or intimidation of a juror or a witness (or potential witness) in any proceedings which led to the acquittal.

(2) Where it appears to the court before which the person was convicted that—

(a) there is a real possibility that, but for the interference or intimidation, the acquitted person would not have been acquitted, and

(b) subsection (5) does not apply,

the court shall certify that it so appears.

(3) Where a court certifies under subsection (2) an application may be made to the High Court for an order quashing the acquittal, and the Court shall make the order if (but shall not do so unless) the four conditions in section 55 are satisfied.

(4) Where an order is made under subsection (3) proceedings may be taken against the acquitted person for the offence of which he was acquitted.

(5) This subsection applies if, because of lapse of time or for any other reason, it would be contrary to the interests of justice to take proceedings against the acquitted person for the offence of which he was acquitted.

(6) For the purposes of this section the following offences are administration of justice offences—

(a) the offence of perverting the course of justice;

(b) the offence under section 51(1) of the Criminal Justice and Public Order Act 1994 (intimidation etc. of witnesses, jurors and others);

(c) an offence of aiding, abetting, counselling, procuring, suborning or inciting another person to commit an offence under section 1 of the Perjury Act 1911.

(7) This section applies in relation to acquittals in respect of offences alleged to be committed on or after the appointed day.

(8) The reference in subsection (7) to the appointed day is to such day as is appointed for the purposes of this section by the Secretary of State by order.

Conditions for making order

60-002 **55.**—(1) The first condition is that it appears to the High Court likely that, but for the interference or intimidation, the acquitted person would not have been acquitted.

(2) The second condition is that it does not appear to the Court that, because of lapse of time or for any other reason, it would be contrary to the interests of justice to take proceedings against the acquitted person for the offence of which he was acquitted.

(3) The third condition is that it appears to the Court that the acquitted person has been given a reasonable opportunity to make written representations to the Court.

(4) The fourth condition is that it appears to the Court that the conviction for the administration of justice offence will stand.

(5) In applying subsection (4) the Court shall—

(a) take into account all the information before it, but

(b) ignore the possibility of new factors coming to light.

(6) Accordingly, the fourth condition has the effect that the Court shall not make an order under section 54(3) if (for instance) it appears to the Court that any time allowed for giving notice of appeal has not expired or that an appeal is pending.

Time limits for proceedings

60-003 **56.**—(1) Where—

(a) an order is made under section 54(3) quashing an acquittal.

(b) by virtue of section 54(4) it is proposed to take proceedings against the acquitted person for the offence of which he was acquitted, and

(c) apart from this subsection, the effect of an enactment would be that the proceedings must be commenced before a specified period calculated by reference to the commission of the offence,

in relation to the proceedings the enactment shall have effect as if the period were instead one calculated by reference to the time the order is made under section 54(3).

(2) Subsection (1)(c) applies however the enactment is expressed so that (for instance) it applies in the case of—

(a) paragraph 10 of Schedule 2 to the Sexual Offences Act 1956 (prosecution for certain offences may not be commenced more than 12 months after offence);

(b) section 127(1) of the Magistrates' Courts Act 1980 (magistrates' court not to try information unless it is laid within 6 months from time when offence committed);
(c) an enactment that imposes a time limit only in certain circumstances (as where proceedings are not instituted by or with the consent of the Director of Public Prosecutions).

Sexual Offences (Conspiracy and Incitement) Act 1996

CHAPTER 29

England and Wales and Northern Ireland

Incitement to commit certain sexual acts outside the United Kingdom

2.—(1) This section applies where— **61-001**
(a) any act done by a person in England and Wales would amount to the offence of incitement to commit a listed sexual offence but for the fact that what he had in view would not be an offence triable in England and Wales,
(b) the whole or part of what he had in view was intended to take place in a country or territory outside the United Kingdom, and
(c) what he had in view would involve the commission of an offence under the law in force in that country or territory.

(2) Where this section applies—
(a) what he had in view is to be treated as that listed sexual offence for the purposes of any charge of incitement brought in respect of that act, and
(b) any such charge is accordingly triable in England and Wales.

(3) Any act of incitement by means of a message (however communicated) is to be treated as done in England and Wales if the message is sent or received in England and Wales.

Sections 1 and 2: supplementary

3.—(1) Conduct punishable under the law in force in any country or **61-002**
territory is an offence under that law for the purposes of section 2 however it is described in that law.

(2) Subject to subsection (3), a condition in section 2(1)(c) is to be taken to be satisfied unless, not later than rules of court may provide, the defence serve on the prosecution a notice—
(a) stating that, on the facts as alleged with respect to what the accused had in view, the condition is not in their opinion satisfied,
(b) showing their grounds for that opinion, and
(c) requiring the prosecution to show that it is satisfied.

(4) The court, if it thinks fit, may permit the defence to require the prosecution to show that the condition is satisfied without the prior service of a notice under subsection (2).

(5) In the Crown Court the question whether the condition is satisfied is to be decided by the judge alone.

(6) In any proceedings in respect of any offence triable by virtue of section 2 it is immaterial to guilt whether or not the accused was a British citizen at the time of any act or other event proof of which is required for conviction of the offence.

(8) References to an offence of incitement to commit a listed sexual offence include an offence triable in England and Wales as such an incitement by virtue of section 2 (without prejudice to subsection (2) of that section).

(9) Subsection (8) applies to references in any enactment, instrument or document (except those in section 2 of this Act and in Part I of the Criminal Law Act 1977).

Interpretation

61-003 **5.** In this Act "listed sexual offence" has the meaning given by the Schedule.

Section 5.. Schedule

LISTED SEXUAL OFFENCES

England and Wales

61-004 1.—(1) In relation to England and Wales, the following are listed sexual offences:

(a) offences under the following provisions of the Sexual Offences Act 1956—
  (i) section 1 (rape),
  (ii) section 5 (intercourse with girl under the age of thirteen),
  (iii) section 6 (intercourse with girl under the age of sixteen),
  (iv) section 12 (buggery),
  (v) section 14 (indecent assault on a girl), and
  (vi) section 15 (indecent assault on a boy),

(b) an offence under section 1 of the Indecency with Children Act 1960 (indecent conduct towards young child).

(2) In sub-paragraph (1)(a), sub-paragraphs (i), (iv), (v) and (vi) do not apply where the victim of the offence has attained the age of sixteen years.

Knives Act 1997

CHAPTER 21

The offences

Unlawful marketing of knives

62-001 **1.**—(1) A person is guilty of an offence if he markets a knife in a way which—

(a) indicates, or suggests, that it is suitable for combat; or

(b) is otherwise likely to stimulate or encourage violent behaviour involving the use of the knife as a weapon.

(2) "Suitable for combat" and "violent behaviour" are defined in section 10.

(3) For the purposes of this Act, an indication or suggestion that a knife is suitable for combat may, in particular, be given or made by a name or description—

(a) applied to the knife;

(b) on the knife or on any packaging in which it is contained; or

(c) included in any advertisement which, expressly or by implication, relates to the knife.

(4) For the purposes of this Act, a person markets a knife if—

(a) he sells or hires it;

(b) he offers, or exposes, it for sale or hire; or

(c) he has it in his possession for the purpose of sale or hire.

(5) A person who is guilty of an offence under this section is liable—

(a) on summary conviction to imprisonment for a term not exceeding six months or to a fine not exceeding the statutory maximum, or to both;

(b) on conviction on indictment to imprisonment for a term not exceeding two years or to a fine, or to both.

Publications

2.—(1) A person is guilty of an offence if he publishes any written, pictorial or other material in connection with the marketing of any knife and that material— **62-002**

(a) indicates, or suggests, that the knife is suitable for combat; or

(b) is otherwise likely to stimulate or encourage violent behaviour involving the use of the knife as a weapon.

(2) A person who is guilty of an offence under this section is liable—

(a) on summary conviction to imprisonment for a term not exceeding six months or to a fine not exceeding the statutory maximum, or to both;

(b) on conviction on indictment to imprisonment for a term not exceeding two years or to a fine, or to both.

The defences

Exempt trades

3.—(1) It is a defence for a person charged with an offence under section 1 to prove that— **62-003**

(a) the knife was marketed—

(i) for use by the armed forces of any country;

(ii) as an antique or curio; or

(iii) as falling within such other category (if any) as may be prescribed;

(b) it was reasonable for the knife to be marketed in that way; and

(c) there were no reasonable grounds for suspecting that a person into whose possession the knife might come in consequence of the way in which it was marketed would use it for an unlawful purpose.

(2) It is a defence for a person charged with an offence under section 2 to prove that—

(a) the material was published in connection with marketing a knife—

(i) for use by the armed forces of any country;

(ii) as an antique or curio; or

(iii) as falling within such other category (if any) as may be prescribed;

(b) it was reasonable for the knife to be marketed in that way; and

(c) there were no reasonable grounds for suspecting that a person into whose possession the knife might come in consequence of the publishing of the material would use it for an unlawful purpose.

(3) In this section "prescribed" means prescribed by regulations made by the Secretary of State.

Other defences

62-004 **4.**—(1) It is a defence for a person charged with an offence under section 1 to prove that he did not know or suspect, and had no reasonable grounds for suspecting, that the way in which the knife was marketed—

(a) amounted to an indication or suggestion that the knife was suitable for combat; or

(b) was likely to stimulate or encourage violent behaviour involving the use of the knife as a weapon.

(2) It is a defence for a person charged with an offence under section 2 to prove that he did not know or suspect, and had no reasonable grounds for suspecting, that the material—

(a) amounted to an indication or suggestion that the knife was suitable for combat; or

(b) was likely to stimulate or encourage violent behaviour involving the use of the knife as a weapon.

(3) It is a defence for a person charged with an offence under section 1 or 2 to prove that he took all reasonable precautions and exercised all due diligence to avoid committing the offence.

Miscellaneous

Interpretation

62-005 **10.** In this Act—

"the court" means —

(a) in relation to England and Wales or Northern Ireland, the Crown Court or a magistrate's court;

(b) in relation to Scotland, the sheriff;

"knife" means an instrument which has a blade or is sharply pointed;

"marketing" and related expressions are to be read with section 1(4);

"publication" includes a publication in electronic form and, in the case of a publication which is, or may be, produced from electronic data, any medium on which the data are stored;

"suitable for combat" means suitable for use as a weapon for inflicting injury on a person or causing a person to fear injury;

"violent behaviour" means an unlawful act inflicting injury on a person or causing a person to fear injury.

Protection from Harassment Act 1997

CHAPTER 40

England and Wales

Prohibition of harassment

1.—(1) A person must not pursue a course of conduct— **63-001**

(a) which amounts to harassment of another, and

(b) which he knows or ought to know amounts to harassment of the other.

(2) For the purposes of this section, the person whose course of conduct is in question ought to know that it amounts to harassment of another if a reasonable person in possession of the same information would think the course of conduct amounted to harassment of the other.

(3) Subsection (1) does not apply to a course of conduct if the person who pursued it shows—

(a) that it was pursued for the purpose of preventing or detecting crime,

(b) that it was pursued under any enactment or rule of law or to comply with any condition or requirement imposed by any person under any enactment, or

(c) that in the particular circumstances the pursuit of the course of conduct was reasonable.

Offence of harassment

2.—(1) A person who pursues a course of conduct in breach of section 1 is guilty of an offence. **63-002**

(2) A person guilty of an offence under this section is liable on summary conviction to imprisonment for a term not exceeding six months, or a fine not exceeding level 5 on the standard scale, or both.

Civil remedy

3.—(1) An actual or apprehended breach of section 1 may be the subject of a claim in civil proceedings by the person who is or may be the victim of the course of conduct in question. **63-003**

(2) On such a claim, damages may be awarded for (among other things) any anxiety caused by the harassment and any financial loss resulting from the harassment.

(3) Where—

(a) in such proceedings the High Court or a county court grants an injunction for the purpose of restraining the defendant from pursuing any conduct which amounts to harassment, and

(b) the plaintiff considers that the defendant has done anything which he is prohibited from doing by the injunction,

the plaintiff may apply for the issue of a warrant for the arrest of the defendant.

(4) An application under subsection (3) may be made—

(a) where the injunction was granted by the High Court, to a judge of that court, and

(b) where the injunction was granted by a county court, to a judge or district judge of that or any other county court.

(5) The judge or district judge to whom an application under subsection (3) is made may only issue a warrant if—

(a) the application is substantiated on oath, and

(b) the judge or district judge has reasonable grounds for believing that the defendant has done anything which he is prohibited from doing by the injunction.

(6) Where—

(a) the High Court or a county court grants an injunction for the purpose mentioned in subsection (3)(a), and

(b) without reasonable excuse the defendant does anything which he is prohibited from doing by the injunction,

he is guilty of an offence.

(7) Where a person is convicted of an offence under subsection (6) in respect of any conduct, that conduct is not punishable as a contempt of court.

(8) A person cannot be convicted of an offence under subsection (6) in respect of any conduct which has been punished as a contempt of court.

(9) A person guilty of an offence under subsection (6) is liable—

(a) on conviction on indictment, to imprisonment for a term not exceeding five years, or a fine, or both, or

(b) on summary conviction, to imprisonment for a term not exceeding six months, or a fine not exceeding the statutory maximum, or both.

Putting people in fear of violence

63-004 **4.**—(1) A person whose course of conduct causes another to fear, on at least two occasions, that violence will be used against him is guilty of an offence if he knows or ought to know that his course of conduct will cause the other so to fear on each of those occasions.

(2) For the purposes of this section, the person whose course of conduct is in question ought to know that it will cause another to fear that violence will be used against him on any occasion if a reasonable person in possession of the same information would think the course of conduct would cause the other so to fear on that occasion.

(3) It is a defence for a person charged with an offence under this section to show that—

(a) his course of conduct was pursued for the purpose of preventing or detecting crime,

(b) his course of conduct was pursued under any enactment or rule of law or to comply with any condition or requirement imposed by any person under any enactment, or

(c) the pursuit of his course of conduct was reasonable for the protection of himself or another or for the protection of his or another's property.

(4) A person guilty of an offence under this section is liable—

(a) on conviction on indictment, to imprisonment for a term not exceeding five years, or a fine, or both, or

(b) on summary conviction, to imprisonment for a term not exceeding six months, or a fine not exceeding the statutory maximum, or both.

(5) If on the trial on indictment of a person charged with an offence under this section the jury find him not guilty of the offence charged, they may find him guilty of an offence under section 2.

(6) The Crown Court has the same powers and duties in relation to a person who is by virtue of subsection (5) convicted before it of an offence under section 2 as a magistrates' court would have on convicting him of the offence.

Restraining orders

5.—(1) A court sentencing or otherwise dealing with a person ("the defendant") convicted of an offence under section 2 or 4 may (as well as sentencing him or dealing with him in any other way) make an order under this section. **63-005**

(2) The order may, for the purpose of protecting the victim of the offence, or any other person mentioned in the order, from further conduct which—

(a) amounts to harassment, or

(b) will cause a fear of violence,

prohibit the defendant from doing anything described in the order.

(3) The order may have effect for a specified period or until further order.

(4) The prosecutor, the defendant or any other person mentioned in the order may apply to the court which made the order for it to be varied or discharged by a further order.

(5) If without reasonable excuse the defendant does anything which he is prohibited from doing by an order under this section, he is guilty of an offence.

(6) A person guilty of an offence under this section is liable—

(a) on conviction on indictment, to imprisonment for a term not exceeding five years, or a fine, or both, or

(b) on summary conviction, to imprisonment for a term not exceeding six months, or a fine not exceeding the statutory maximum, or both.

Interpretation of this group of sections

7.—(1) This section applies for the interpretation of sections 1 to 5. **63-006**

(2) References to harassing a person include alarming the person or causing the person distress.

(3) A "course of conduct" must involve conduct on at least two occasions.

(3A) A person's conduct on any occasion shall be taken, if aided, abetted, counselled or procured by another–

(a) to be conduct on that occasion of the other (as well as conduct of the person whose conduct it is); and

(b) to be conduct in relation to which the other's knowledge and purpose, and what he ought to have known, are the same as they were in relation to what was contemplated or reasonably foreseeable at the time of the aiding, abetting, counselling or procuring.

(4) "Conduct" includes speech.

General

National security, etc

12.—(1) If the Secretary of State certifies that in his opinion anything done by a specified person on a specified occasion related to— **63-007**

(a) national security,

(b) the economic well-being of the United Kingdom, or

(c) the prevention or detection of serious crime,

and was done on behalf of the Crown, the certificate is conclusive evidence that this Act does not apply to any conduct of that person on that occasion.

(2) In subsection (1), "specified" means specified in the certificate in question.

(3) A document purporting to be a certificate under subsection (1) is to be received in evidence and, unless the contrary is proved, be treated as being such a certificate.

Sex Offenders Act 1997

CHAPTER 51

PART II

SEXUAL OFFENCES COMMITTED OUTSIDE THE UNITED KINGDOM

Extension of jurisdiction: England and Wales and Northern Ireland

64-001 **7.**—(1) Subject to subsection (2) below, any act done by a person in a country or territory outside the United Kingdom which—

(a) constituted an offence under the law in force in that country or territory; and

(b) would constitute a sexual offence to which this section applies if it had been done in England and Wales, or in Northern Ireland,

shall constitute that sexual offence under the law of that part of the United Kingdom.

(2) No proceedings shall by virtue of this section be brought against any person unless he was at the commencement of this section, or has subsequently become, a British citizen or resident in the United Kingdom.

(3) An act punishable under the law in force in any country or territory constitutes an offence under that law for the purposes of this section, however it is described in that law.

(4) Subject to subsection (5) below, the condition in subsection (1)(a) above shall be taken to be satisfied unless, not later than rules of court may provide, the defence serve on the prosecution a notice—

(a) stating that, on the facts as alleged with respect to the act in question, the condition is not in their opinion satisfied;

(b) showing their grounds for that opinion; and

(c) requiring the prosecution to show that it is satisfied.

(5) The court, if it thinks fit, may permit the defence to require the prosecution to show that the condition is satisfied without the prior service of a notice under subsection (4) above.

(6) In the Crown Court the question whether the condition is satisfied is to be decided by the judge alone.

(7) Schedule 2 to this Act which lists the sexual offences to which this section applies) shall have effect.

SCHEDULES

Section 7(7). Schedule 2

SEXUAL OFFENCES TO WHICH SECTION 7 APPLIES

England and Wales

1.— (1) In relation to England and Wales, the following are sexual offences to which section 7 of this Act applies, namely— **64-002**

(a) offences under the following provisions of the Sexual Offences Act 1956—
   (i) section 1 (rape);
   (ii) section 5 (intercourse with girl under 13);
   (iii) section 6 (intercourse with girl between 13 and 16);
   (iv) section 12 (buggery);
   (v) section 14 (indecent assault on a girl);
   (vi) section 15 (indecent assault on a boy); and
   (vii) section 16 (assault with intent to commit buggery);
(b) an offence under section 1 of the Indecency with Children Act 1960 (indecent conduct towards young child); and
(c) an offence under section 1 of the Protection of Children Act 1978 (indecent photographs of children).

(2) In sub-paragraph (1)(a) above, sub-paragraphs (i) and (iv) to (vii) do not apply where the victim of the offence was 16 or over at the time of the offence.

Crime and Disorder Act 1998

CHAPTER 37

PART II

CRIMINAL LAW

Racially or religiously aggravated offences: England and Wales

Meaning of "racially or religiously aggravated"

28.—(1) An offence is racially or religiously aggravated for the purposes of sections 29 to 32 below if— **65-001**

(a) at the time of committing the offence, or immediately before or after doing so, the offender demonstrates towards the victim of the offence hostility based on the victim's membership (or presumed membership) of a racial or religious group; or
(b) the offence is motivated (wholly or partly) by hostility towards members of a racial or religious group based on their membership of that group.

(2) In subsection (1)(a) above—

"membership", in relation to a racial or religious group, includes association with members of that group;

"presumed" means presumed by the offender.

(3) It is immaterial for the purposes of paragraph (a) or (b) of subsection (1) above whether or not the offender's hostility is also based, to any extent, on any other factor not mentioned in that paragraph.

(4) In this section "racial group" means a group of persons defined by reference to race, colour, nationality (including citizenship) or ethnic or national origins.

(5) In this section "religious group" means a group of persons defined by reference to religious belief or lack of religious belief.

Racially or religiously aggravated assaults

65-002 **29.**—(1) A person is guilty of an offence under this section if he commits—

(a) an offence under section 20 of the Offences Against the Person Act 1861 (malicious wounding or grievous bodily harm);

(b) an offence under section 47 of that Act (actual bodily harm); or

(c) common assault,

which is racially or religiously aggravated for the purposes of this section.

(2) A person guilty of an offence falling within subsection (1)(a) or (b) above shall be liable—

(a) on summary conviction, to imprisonment for a term not exceeding six months or to a fine not exceeding the statutory maximum, or to both;

(b) on conviction on indictment, to imprisonment for a term not exceeding seven years or to a fine, or to both.

(3) A person guilty of an offence falling within subsection (1)(c) above shall be liable—

(a) on summary conviction, to imprisonment for a term not exceeding six months or to a fine not exceeding the statutory maximum, or to both;

(b) on conviction on indictment, to imprisonment for a term not exceeding two years or to a fine, or to both.

Racially or religiously aggravated criminal damage

65-003 **30.**—(1) A person is guilty of an offence under this section if he commits an offence under section 1(1) of the Criminal Damage Act 1971 (destroying or damaging property belonging to another) which is racially or religiously aggravated for the purposes of this section.

(2) A person guilty of an offence under this section shall be liable—

(a) on summary conviction, to imprisonment for a term not exceeding six months or to a fine not exceeding the statutory maximum, or to both;

(b) on conviction on indictment, to imprisonment for a term not exceeding fourteen years or to a fine, or to both.

(3) For the purposes of this section, section 28(1)(a) above shall have effect as if the person to whom the property belongs or is treated as belonging for the purposes of that Act were the victim of the offence.

Racially or religiously aggravated public order offences

65-004 **31.**—(1) A person is guilty of an offence under this section if he commits—

(a) an offence under section 4 of the Public Order Act 1986 (fear or provocation of violence);

(b) an offence under section 4A of that Act (intentional harassment, alarm or distress); or

(c) an offence under section 5 of that Act (harassment, alarm or distress),

which is racially or religiously aggravated for the purposes of this section.

(2) A constable may arrest without warrant anyone whom he reasonably suspects to be committing an offence falling within subsection (1)(a) or (b) above.

(3) A constable may arrest a person without warrant if—

(a) he engages in conduct which a constable reasonably suspects to constitute an offence falling within subsection (1)(c) above;

(b) he is warned by that constable to stop; and

(c) he engages in further such conduct immediately or shortly after the warning.

The conduct mentioned in paragraph (a) above and the further conduct need not be of the same nature.

(4) A person guilty of an offence falling within subsection (1)(a) or (b) above shall be liable—

(a) on summary conviction, to imprisonment for a term not exceeding six months or to a fine not exceeding the statutory maximum, or to both;

(b) on conviction on indictment, to imprisonment for a term not exceeding two years or to a fine, or to both.

(5) A person guilty of an offence falling within subsection (1)(c) above shall be liable on summary conviction to a fine not exceeding level 4 on the standard scale.

(6) If, on the trial on indictment of a person charged with an offence falling within subsection (1)(a) or (b) above, the jury find him not guilty of the offence charged, they may find him guilty of the basic offence mentioned in that provision.

(7) For the purposes of subsection (1)(c) above, section 28(1)(a) above shall have effect as if the person likely to be caused harassment, alarm or distress were the victim of the offence.

Racially or religiously aggravated harassment etc

32.—(1) A person is guilty of an offence under this section if he commits— **65-005**

(a) an offence under section 2 of the Protection from Harassment Act 1997 (offence of harassment); or

(b) an offence under section 4 of that Act (putting people in fear of violence),

which is racially or religiously aggravated for the purposes of this section.

(3) A person guilty of an offence falling within subsection (1)(a) above shall be liable—

(a) on summary conviction, to imprisonment for a term not exceeding six months or to a fine not exceeding the statutory maximum, or to both;

(b) on conviction on indictment, to imprisonment for a term not exceeding two years or to a fine, or to both.

(4) A person guilty of an offence falling within subsection (1)(b) above shall be liable—

(a) on summary conviction, to imprisonment for a term not exceeding six months or to a fine not exceeding the statutory maximum, or to both;

(b) on conviction on indictment, to imprisonment for a term not exceeding seven years or to a fine, or to both.

(5) If, on the trial on indictment of a person charged with an offence falling within subsection (1)(a) above, the jury find him not guilty of the offence charged, they may find him guilty of the basic offence mentioned in that provision.

(6) If, on the trial on indictment of a person charged with an offence falling within subsection (1)(b) above, the jury find him not guilty of the offence charged, they may find him guilty of an offence falling within subsection (1)(a) above.

(7) Section 5 of the Protection from Harassment Act 1997 (restraining orders) shall have effect in relation to a person convicted of an offence under this section as if the reference in subsection (1) of that section to an offence under section 2 or 4 included a reference to an offence under this section.

Miscellaneous

Abolition of rebuttable presumption that a child is doli incapax

65-006 **34.** The rebuttable presumption of criminal law that a child aged 10 or over is incapable of committing an offence is hereby abolished.

Human Rights Act 1998

CHAPTER 42

Introduction

The Convention Rights

66-001 **1.**—(1) In this Act "the Convention rights" means the rights and fundamental freedoms set out in—

(a) Articles 2 to 12 and 14 of the Convention,
(b) Articles 1 to 3 of the First Protocol, and
(c) Articles 1 and 2 of the Sixth Protocol,

as read with Articles 16 to 18 of the Convention.

(2) Those Articles are to have effect for the purposes of this Act subject to any designated derogation or reservation (as to which see sections 14 and 15).

(3) The Articles are set out in Schedule 1.

(4) The Lord Chancellor may by order make such amendments to this Act as he considers appropriate to reflect the effect, in relation to the United Kingdom, of a protocol.

(5) In subsection (4) "protocol" means a protocol to the Convention—

(a) which the United Kingdom has ratified; or
(b) which the United Kingdom has signed with a view to ratification.

(6) No amendment may be made by an order under subsection (4) so as to come into force before the protocol concerned is in force in relation to the United Kingdom.

Interpretation of Convention rights

66-002 **2.**—(1) A court or tribunal determining a question which has arisen in connection with a Convention right must take into account any—

(a) judgment, decision, declaration or advisory opinion of the European Court of Human Rights,
(b) opinion of the Commission given in a report adopted under Article 31 of the Convention,

(c) decision of the Commission in connection with Article 26 or 27(2) of the Convention, or
(d) decision of the Committee of Ministers taken under Article 46 of the Convention,

whenever made or given, so far as, in the opinion of the court or tribunal, it is relevant to the proceedings in which that question has arisen.

(2) Evidence of any judgment, decision, declaration or opinion of which account may have to be taken under this section is to be given in proceedings before any court or tribunal in such manner as may be provided by rules.

(3) In this section "rules" means rules of court or, in the case of proceedings before a tribunal, rules made for the purposes of this section—

(a) by the Lord Chancellor or the Secretary of State, in relation to any proceedings outside Scotland;
(b) by the Secretary of State, in relation to proceedings in Scotland; or
(c) by a Northern Ireland department, in relation to proceedings before a tribunal in Northern Ireland—
    (i) which deals with transferred matters; and
    (ii) for which no rules made under paragraph (a) are in force.

Legislation

Interpretation of legislation

3.—(1) So far as it is possible to do so, primary legislation and subordinate legislation must be read and given effect in a way which is compatible with the Convention rights. **66-003**

(2) This section—

(a) applies to primary legislation and subordinate legislation whenever enacted;
(b) does not affect the validity, continuing operation or enforcement of any incompatible primary legislation; and
(c) does not affect the validity, continuing operation or enforcement of any incompatible subordinate legislation if (disregarding any possibility of revocation) primary legislation prevents removal of the incompatibility.

Declaration of incompatibility

4.—(1) Subsection (2) applies in any proceedings in which a court determines whether a provision of primary legislation is compatible with a Convention right. **66-004**

(2) If the court is satisfied that the provision is incompatible with a Convention right, it may make a declaration of that incompatibility.

(3) Subsection (4) applies in any proceedings in which a court determines whether a provision of subordinate legislation, made in the exercise of a power conferred by primary legislation, is compatible with a Convention right.

(4) If the court is satisfied—

(a) that the provision is incompatible with a Convention right, and
(b) that (disregarding any possibility of revocation) the primary legislation concerned prevents removal of the incompatibility,

it may make a declaration of that incompatibility.

(5) In this section "court" means —

(a) the House of Lords;
(b) the Judicial Committee of the Privy Council;

(c) the Courts-Martial Appeal Court;

(d) in Scotland, the High Court of Justiciary sitting otherwise than as a trial court or the Court of Session;

(e) in England and Wales or Northern Ireland, the High Court or the Court of Appeal.

(6) A declaration under this section ("a declaration of incompatibility")—

(a) does not affect the validity, continuing operation or enforcement of the provision in respect of which it is given; and

(b) is not binding on the parties to the proceedings in which it is made.

Right of Crown to intervene

66-005 **5.**—(1) Where a court is considering whether to make a declaration of incompatibility, the Crown is entitled to notice in accordance with rules of court.

(2) In any case to which subsection (1) applies—

(a) a Minister of the Crown (or a person nominated by him),

(b) a member of the Scottish Executive,

(c) a Northern Ireland Minister,

(d) a Northern Ireland department,

is entitled, on giving notice in accordance with rules of court, to be joined as a party to the proceedings.

(3) Notice under subsection (2) may be given at any time during the proceedings.

(4) A person who has been made a party to criminal proceedings (other than in Scotland) as the result of a notice under subsection (2) may, with leave, appeal to the House of Lords against any declaration of incompatibility made in the proceedings.

(5) In subsection (4)—

"criminal proceedings" includes all proceedings before the Courts-Martial Appeal Court; and

"leave" means leave granted by the court making the declaration of incompatibility or by the House of Lords.

Public authorities

Acts of public authorities

66-006 **6.**—(1) It is unlawful for a public authority to act in a way which is incompatible with a Convention right.

(2) Subsection (1) does not apply to an act if—

(a) as the result of one or more provisions of primary legislation, the authority could not have acted differently; or

(b) in the case of one or more provisions of, or made under, primary legislation which cannot be read or given effect in a way which is compatible with the Convention rights, the authority was acting so as to give effect to or enforce those provisions.

(3) In this section "public authority" includes—

(a) a court or tribunal, and

(b) any person certain of whose functions are functions of a public nature,

but does not include either House of Parliament or a person exercising functions in connection with proceedings in Parliament.

(4) In subsection (3) "Parliament" does not include the House of Lords in its judicial capacity.

(5) In relation to a particular act, a person is not a public authority by virtue only of subsection (3)(b) if the nature of the act is private.

(6) "An act" includes a failure to act but does not include a failure to—

(a) introduce in, or lay before, Parliament a proposal for legislation; or

(b) make any primary legislation or remedial order.

Proceedings

7.—(1) A person who claims that a public authority has acted (or proposes to act) in a way which is made unlawful by section 6(1) may— **66-007**

(a) bring proceedings against the authority under this Act in the appropriate court or tribunal, or

(b) rely on the Convention right or rights concerned in any legal proceedings,

but only if he is (or would be) a victim of the unlawful act.

(2) In subsection (1)(a) "appropriate court or tribunal" means such court or tribunal as may be determined in accordance with rules; and proceedings against an authority include a counterclaim or similar proceedings.

(3) If the proceedings are brought on an application for judicial review, the applicant is to be taken to have a sufficient interest in relation to the unlawful act only if he is, or would be, a victim of that act.

(4) If the proceedings are made by way of a petition for judicial review in Scotland, the applicant shall be taken to have title and interest to sue in relation to the unlawful act only if he is, or would be, a victim of that act.

(5) Proceedings under subsection (1)(a) must be brought before the end of—

(a) the period of one year beginning with the date on which the act complained of took place; or

(b) such longer period as the court or tribunal considers equitable having regard to all the circumstances,

but that is subject to any rule imposing a stricter time limit in relation to the procedure in question.

(6) In subsection (1)(b) "legal proceedings" includes—

(a) proceedings brought by or at the instigation of a public authority; and

(b) an appeal against the decision of a court or tribunal.

(7) For the purposes of this section, a person is a victim of an unlawful act only if he would be a victim for the purposes of Article 34 of the Convention if proceedings were brought in the European Court of Human Rights in respect of that act.

(8) Nothing in this Act creates a criminal offence.

(9) In this section "rules" means —

(a) in relation to proceedings before a court or tribunal outside Scotland, rules made by the Lord Chancellor or the Secretary of State for the purposes of this section or rules of court,

(b) in relation to proceedings before a court or tribunal in Scotland, rules made by the Secretary of State for those purposes,

(c) in relation to proceedings before a tribunal in Northern Ireland—

(i) which deals with transferred matters; and

(ii) for which no rules made under paragraph (a) are in force,

rules made by a Northern Ireland department for those purposes,

and includes provision made by order under section 1 of the Courts and Legal Services Act 1990.

(10) In making rules, regard must be had to section 9.

(11) The Minister who has power to make rules in relation to a particular tribunal may, to the extent he considers it necessary to ensure that the tribunal can provide an appropriate remedy in relation to an act (or proposed act) of a public authority which is (or would be) unlawful as a result of section 6(1), by order add to—

(a) the relief or remedies which the tribunal may grant; or

(b) the grounds on which it may grant any of them.

(12) An order made under subsection (11) may contain such incidental, supplemental, consequential or transitional provision as the Minister making it considers appropriate.

(13) "The Minister" includes the Northern Ireland department concerned.

Judicial remedies

66-008 **8.**—(1) In relation to any act (or proposed act) of a public authority which the court finds is (or would be) unlawful, it may grant such relief or remedy, or make such order, within its powers as it considers just and appropriate.

(2) But damages may be awarded only by a court which has power to award damages, or to order the payment of compensation, in civil proceedings.

(3) No award of damages is to be made unless, taking account of all the circumstances of the case, including—

(a) any other relief or remedy granted, or order made, in relation to the act in question (by that or any other court), and

(b) the consequences of any decision (of that or any other court) in respect of that act,

the court is satisfied that the award is necessary to afford just satisfaction to the person in whose favour it is made.

(4) In determining—

(a) whether to award damages, or

(b) the amount of an award,

the court must take into account the principles applied by the European Court of Human Rights in relation to the award of compensation under Article 41 of the Convention.

(5) A public authority against which damages are awarded is to be treated—

(a) in Scotland, for the purposes of section 3 of the Law Reform (Miscellaneous Provisions) (Scotland) Act 1940 as if the award were made in an action of damages in which the authority has been found liable in respect of loss or damage to the person to whom the award is made;

(b) for the purposes of the Civil Liability (Contribution) Act 1978 as liable in respect of damage suffered by the person to whom the award is made.

(6) In this section—

"court" includes a tribunal;

"damages" means damages for an unlawful act of a public authority; and

"unlawful" means unlawful under section 6(1).

Judicial acts

66-009 **9.**—(1) Proceedings under section 7(1)(a) in respect of a judicial act may be brought only—

(a) by exercising a right of appeal;

(b) on an application (in Scotland a petition) for judicial review; or

(c) in such other forum as may be prescribed by rules.

(2) That does not affect any rule of law which prevents a court from being the subject of judicial review.

(3) In proceedings under this Act in respect of a judicial act done in good faith, damages may not be awarded otherwise than to compensate a person to the extent required by Article 5(5) of the Convention.

(4) An award of damages permitted by subsection (3) is to be made against the Crown; but no award may be made unless the appropriate person, if not a party to the proceedings, is joined.

(5) In this section—

"appropriate person" means the Minister responsible for the court concerned, or a person or government department nominated by him;

"court" includes a tribunal;

"judge" includes a member of a tribunal, a justice of the peace and a clerk or other officer entitled to exercise the jurisdiction of a court;

"judicial act" means a judicial act of a court and includes an act done on the instructions, or on behalf, of a judge; and

"rules" has the same meaning as in section 7(9).

Remedial action

Power to take remedial action

10.—(1) This section applies if— **66-010**

(a) a provision of legislation has been declared under section 4 to be incompatible with a Convention right and, if an appeal lies—

(i) all persons who may appeal have stated in writing that they do not intend to do so;

(ii) the time for bringing an appeal has expired and no appeal has been brought within that time; or

(iii) an appeal brought within that time has been determined or abandoned; or

(b) it appears to a Minister of the Crown or Her Majesty in Council that, having regard to a finding of the European Court of Human Rights made after the coming into force of this section in proceedings against the United Kingdom, a provision of legislation is incompatible with an obligation of the United Kingdom arising from the Convention.

(2) If a Minister of the Crown considers that there are compelling reasons for proceeding under this section, he may by order make such amendments to the legislation as he considers necessary to remove the incompatibility.

(3) If, in the case of subordinate legislation, a Minister of the Crown considers—

(a) that it is necessary to amend the primary legislation under which the subordinate legislation in question was made, in order to enable the incompatibility to be removed, and

(b) that there are compelling reasons for proceeding under this section,

he may by order make such amendments to the primary legislation as he considers necessary.

(4) This section also applies where the provision in question is in subordinate legislation and has been quashed, or declared invalid, by reason of incompatibility with a Convention right and the Minister proposes to proceed under paragraph 2(b) of Schedule 2.

(5) If the legislation is an Order in Council, the power conferred by subsection (2) or (3) is exercisable by Her Majesty in Council.

(6) In this section "legislation" does not include a Measure of the Church Assembly or of the General Synod of the Church of England.

(7) Schedule 2 makes further provision about remedial orders.

Other rights and proceedings

Safeguard for existing human rights

66-011 **11.** A person's reliance on a Convention right does not restrict—

(a) any other right or freedom conferred on him by or under any law having effect in any part of the United Kingdom; or

(b) his right to make any claim or bring any proceedings which he could make or bring apart from sections 7 to 9.

Freedom of expression

66-012 **12.**—(1) This section applies if a court is considering whether to grant any relief which, if granted, might affect the exercise of the Convention right to freedom of expression.

(2) If the person against whom the application for relief is made ("the respondent") is neither present nor represented, no such relief is to be granted unless the court is satisfied—

(a) that the applicant has taken all practicable steps to notify the respondent; or

(b) that there are compelling reasons why the respondent should not be notified.

(3) No such relief is to be granted so as to restrain publication before trial unless the court is satisfied that the applicant is likely to establish that publication should not be allowed.

(4) The court must have particular regard to the importance of the Convention right to freedom of expression and, where the proceedings relate to material which the respondent claims, or which appears to the court, to be journalistic, literary or artistic material (or to conduct connected with such material), to—

(a) the extent to which—

(i) the material has, or is about to, become available to the public; or

(ii) it is, or would be, in the public interest for the material to be published;

(b) any relevant privacy code.

(5) In this section—

"court" includes a tribunal; and

"relief" includes any remedy or order (other than in criminal proceedings).

Freedom of thought, conscience and religion

66-013 **13.**—(1) If a court's determination of any question arising under this Act might affect the exercise by a religious organisation (itself or its members collectively) of the Convention right to freedom of thought, conscience and religion, it must have particular regard to the importance of that right.

(2) In this section "court" includes a tribunal.

Derogations and reservations

Derogations

14.—[(1) In this Act "designated derogation" means any derogation by the United Kingdom from an Article of the Convention, or of any protocol to the Convention, which is designated for the purposes of this Act in an order made by the [Lord Chancellor][1].][2] **66-014**

(2) [...][3]

(3) If a designated derogation is amended or replaced it ceases to be a designated derogation.

(4) But subsection (3) does not prevent the [Lord Chancellor][4] from exercising his power under subsection (1) [...][5] to make a fresh designation order in respect of the Article concerned.

(5) The [Lord Chancellor][6] must by order make such amendments to Schedule 3 as he considers appropriate to reflect—

(a) any designation order; or
(b) the effect of subsection (3).

(6) A designation order may be made in anticipation of the making by the United Kingdom of a proposed derogation.

Reservations

15.—(1) In this Act "designated reservation" means— **66-015**

(a) the United Kingdom's reservation to Article 2 of the First Protocol to the Convention; and
(b) any other reservation by the United Kingdom to an Article of the Convention, or of any protocol to the Convention, which is designated for the purposes of this Act in an order made by the [Lord Chancellor][7].

(2) The text of the reservation referred to in subsection (1)(a) is set out in Part II of Schedule 3.

(3) If a designated reservation is withdrawn wholly or in part it ceases to be a designated reservation.

(4) But subsection (3) does not prevent the [Lord Chancellor][8] from exercising his power under subsection (1)(b) to make a fresh designation order in respect of the Article concerned.

(5) The [Lord Chancellor][9] must by order make such amendments to this Act as he considers appropriate to reflect—

(a) any designation order; or
(b) the effect of subsection (3).

Period for which designated derogations have effect

16.—[(1) If it has not already been withdrawn by the United Kingdom, a designated derogation ceases to have effect for the purposes of this Act, at the end **66-016**

[1] Words substituted by SI 2001/3500 Sch 2 (I) para 7 (b)
[2] Substituted by SI 2001/1216 art 2 (a)
[3] Repealed by SI 2001/1216 art 2 (b)
[4] Words substituted by SI 2001/3500 Sch 2 (I) para 7 (b)
[5] Word repealed by SI 2001/1216 art 2 (c)
[6] Words substituted by SI 2001/3500 Sch 2 (I) para 7 (b)
[7] Words substituted by SI 2001/3500 Sch 2 (I) para 7 (c)
[8] Words substituted by SI 2001/3500 Sch 2 (I) para 7 (c)
[9] Words substituted by SI 2001/3500 Sch 2 (I) para 7 (c)

of the period of five years beginning with the date on which the order designating it was made.][1]

(2) At any time before the period—

(a) fixed by subsection (1)[...][2], or

(b) extended by an order under this subsection,

comes to an end, the [Lord Chancellor][3] may by order extend it by a further period of five years.

(3) An order under [...][4][section 14(1)][5] ceases to have effect at the end of the period for consideration, unless a resolution has been passed by each House approving the order.

(4) Subsection (3) does not affect—

(a) anything done in reliance on the order; or

(b) the power to make a fresh order under section 14(1)[...][6].

(5) In subsection (3) "period for consideration" means the period of forty days beginning with the day on which the order was made.

(6) In calculating the period for consideration, no account is to be taken of any time during which—

(a) Parliament is dissolved or prorogued; or

(b) both Houses are adjourned for more than four days.

(7) If a designated derogation is withdrawn by the United Kingdom, the [Lord Chancellor][7] must by order make such amendments to this Act as he considers are required to reflect that withdrawal.

Periodic review of designated reservations

66-017 **17.**—(1) The appropriate Minister must review the designated reservation referred to in section 15(1)(a)—

(a) before the end of the period of five years beginning with the date on which section 1(2) came into force; and

(b) if that designation is still in force, before the end of the period of five years beginning with the date on which the last report relating to it was laid under subsection (3).

(2) The appropriate Minister must review each of the other designated reservations (if any)—

(a) before the end of the period of five years beginning with the date on which the order designating the reservation first came into force; and

(b) if the designation is still in force, before the end of the period of five years beginning with the date on which the last report relating to it was laid under subsection (3).

(3) The Minister conducting a review under this section must prepare a report on the result of the review and lay a copy of it before each House of Parliament.

1 Substituted by SI 2001/1216 art 3 (a)
2 Words repealed by SI 2001/1216 art 3 (b)
3 Words substituted by SI 2001/3500 Sch 2 (I) para 7 (d)
4 Word repealed by SI 2001/1216 art 3 (c)
5 Word repealed by SI 2001/1216 art 3 (c)
6 Word repealed by SI 2001/1216 art 3 (d)
7 Words substituted by SI 2001/3500 Sch 2 (I) para 7 (d)

SCHEDULES

Section 1(3) Schedule 1

THE ARTICLES

THE CONVENTION

RIGHTS AND FREEDOMS

Right to life

Article 2 **66-018**

1. Everyone's right to life shall be protected by law. No one shall be deprived of his life intentionally save in the execution of a sentence of a court following his conviction of a crime for which this penalty is provided by law.

2. Deprivation of life shall not be regarded as inflicted in contravention of this Article when it results from the use of force which is no more than absolutely necessary:
   (a) in defence of any person from unlawful violence;
   (b) in order to effect a lawful arrest or to prevent the escape of a person lawfully detained;
   (c) in action lawfully taken for the purpose of quelling a riot or insurrection.

Prohibition of torture

Article 3 **66-019**

No one shall be subjected to torture or to inhuman or degrading treatment or punishment.

Prohibition of slavery and forced labour

Article 4 **66-020**

1. No one shall be held in slavery or servitude.
2. No one shall be required to perform forced or compulsory labour.
3. For the purpose of this Article the term "forced or compulsory labour" shall not include:
   (a) any work required to be done in the ordinary course of detention imposed according to the provisions of Article 5 of this Convention or during conditional release from such detention;
   (b) any service of a military character or, in case of conscientious objectors in countries where they are recognised, service exacted instead of compulsory military service;
   (c) any service exacted in case of an emergency or calamity threatening the life or well-being of the community;
   (d) any work or service which forms part of normal civic obligations.

Right to liberty and security

Article 5 **66-021**

1. Everyone has the right to liberty and security of a person. No one shall be deprived of his liberty save in the following cases and in accordance with a procedure prescribed by law:
   (a) the lawful detention of a person after conviction by a competent court;
   (b) the lawful arrest or detention of a person for non-compliance with the lawful order of a court or in order to secure the fulfilment of any obligation prescribed by law;
   (c) the lawful arrest or detention of a person effected for the purpose of bringing him before the competent legal authority on reasonable suspicion of having committed an offence or when it is reasonably considered necessary to prevent his committing an offence or fleeing after having done so;
   (d) the detention of a minor by lawful order for the purpose of educational supervision or his lawful detention for the purpose of bringing him before the competent legal authority;

(e) the lawful detention of persons for the prevention of the spreading of infectious diseases, of persons of unsound mind, alcoholics or drug addicts or vagrants;
(f) the lawful arrest or detention of a person to prevent his effecting an unauthorised entry into the country or of a person against whom action is being taken with a view to deportation or extradition.

2. Everyone who is arrested shall be informed promptly, in a language which he understands, of the reasons for his arrest and of any charge against him.

3. Everyone arrested or detained in accordance with the provisions of paragraph 1(c) of this Article shall be brought promptly before a judge or other officer authorised by law to exercise judicial power and shall be entitled to trial within a reasonable time or to release pending trial. Release may be conditioned by guarantees to appear for trial.

4. Everyone who is deprived of his liberty by arrest or detention shall be entitled to take proceedings by which the lawfulness of his detention shall be decided speedily by a court and his release ordered if the detention is not lawful.

5. Everyone who has been the victim of arrest or detention in contravention of the provisions of this Article shall have an enforceable right to compensation.

Right to a fair trial

66-022 **Article 6**

1. In the determination of his civil rights and obligations or of any criminal charge against him, everyone is entitled to a fair and public hearing within a reasonable time by an independent and impartial tribunal established by law. Judgment shall be pronounced publicly but the press and public may be excluded from all or part of the trial in the interest of morals, public order or national security in a democratic society, where the interests of juveniles or the protection of the private life of the parties so require, or to the extent strictly necessary in the opinion of the court in special circumstances where publicity would prejudice the interests of justice.

2. Everyone charged with a criminal offence shall be presumed innocent until proved guilty according to law.

3. Everyone charged with a criminal offence has the following minimum rights:
(a) to be informed promptly, in a language which he understands and in detail, of the nature and cause of the accusation against him;
(b) to have adequate time and facilities for the preparation of his defence;
(c) to defend himself in person or through legal assistance of his own choosing or, if he has not sufficient means to pay for legal assistance, to be given it free when the interests of justice so require;
(d) to examine or have examined witnesses against him and to obtain the attendance and examination of witnesses on his behalf under the same conditions as witnesses against him;
(e) to have the free assistance of an interpreter if he cannot understand or speak the language used in court.

No punishment without law

66-023 **Article 7**

1. No one shall be held guilty of any criminal offence on account of any act or omission which did not constitute a criminal offence under national or international law at the time when it was committed. Nor shall a heavier penalty be imposed than the one that was applicable at the time the criminal offence was committed.

2. This Article shall not prejudice the trial and punishment of any person for any act or omission which, at the time when it was committed, was criminal according to the general principles of law recognised by civilised nations.

Right to respect for private and family life

66-024 **Article 8**

1. Everyone has the right to respect for his private and family life, his home and his correspondence.

2. There shall be no interference by a public authority with the exercise of this right except such as is in accordance with the law and is necessary in a democratic society in the interests of national security, public safety or the economic well-being of the country, for the prevention of disorder or

crime, for the protection of health or morals, or for the protection of the rights and freedoms of others.

Freedom of thought, conscience and religion

Article 9 **66-025**

1. Everyone has the right to freedom of thought, conscience and religion, this right includes freedom to change his religion or belief and freedom, either alone or in community with others and in public or private, to manifest his religion or belief, in worship, teaching, practice and observance.

2. Freedom to manifest one's religion or beliefs shall be subject only to such limitation as are prescribed by law and are necessary in a democratic society in the interests of public safety, for the protection of public order, health or morals, or for the protection of the rights and freedoms of others.

Freedom of expression

Article 10 **66-026**

1. Everyone has the right to freedom of expression. This right shall include freedom to hold opinions and to receive and impart information and ideas without interference by public authority and regardless of frontiers. This Article shall not prevent States from requiring the licensing of broadcasting, television or cinema enterprises.

2. The exercise of these freedoms, since it carries with it duties and responsibilities, may be subject to such formalities, conditions, restrictions or penalties as are prescribed by law and are necessary in a democratic society, in the interests of national security, territorial integrity or public safety, for the prevention of disorder or crime, for the protection of health or morals, for the protection of the reputation or rights of others, for preventing the disclosure of information received in confidence, or for maintaining the authority and impartiality of the judiciary.

Freedom of assembly and association

Article 11 **66-027**

1. Everyone has the right to freedom of peaceful assembly and to freedom of association with others, including the right to form and to join trade unions for the protection of his interests.

2. No restrictions shall be placed on the exercise of these rights other than such as are prescribed by law and are necessary in a democratic society in the interests of national security or public safety, for the prevention of disorder or crime, for the protection of health or morals or for the protection of the rights and freedoms of others. This Article shall not prevent the imposition of lawful restrictions on the exercise of these rights by members of the armed forces, of the police or of the administration of the State.

Right to marry

Article 12 **66-028**

Men and women of marriageable age have the right to marry and to found a family, according to the national laws governing the exercise of this right.

Prohibition of discrimination

Article 14 **66-029**

The enjoyment of the rights and freedoms set forth in this Convention shall be secured without discrimination on any ground such as sex, race, colour, language, religion, political or other opinion, national or social origin, association with a national minority, property, birth or other status.

Restrictions on political activity of aliens

Article 16 **66-030**

Nothing in Articles 10, 11 and 14 shall be regarded as preventing the High Contracting Parties from imposing restrictions on the political activity of aliens.

Prohibition of abuse of rights

66-031 Article 17

Nothing in this Convention may be interpreted as implying for any State, group or person any right to engage in any activity or perform any act aimed at the destruction of any of the rights and freedoms set forth herein or at their limitation to a greater extent than is provided for in the Convention.

Limitation on use of restrictions on rights

66-032 Article 18

The restrictions permitted under this Convention to the said rights and freedoms shall not be applied for any purpose other than those for which they have been prescribed.

THE FIRST PROTOCOL

Protection of property

66-033 Article 1

Every natural or legal person is entitled to the peaceful enjoyment of his possessions. No one shall be deprived of his possessions except in the public interest and subject to the conditions provided for by law and by the general principles of international law.

The preceding provisions shall not, however, in any way impair the right of a State to enforce such laws as it deems necessary to control the use of property in accordance with the general interest or to secure the payment of taxes or other contributions or penalties.

Right to education

66-034 Article 2

No person shall be denied the right to education. In the exercise of any functions which it assumes in relation to education and to teaching, the State shall respect the right of parents to ensure such education and teaching in conformity with their own religious and philosophical convictions.

Right to free elections

66-035 Article 3

The High Contracting Parties undertake to hold free elections at reasonable intervals by secret ballot, under conditions which will ensure the free expression of the opinion of the people in the choice of the legislature.

THE SIXTH PROTOCOL

Abolition of the death penalty

66-036 Article 1

The death penalty shall be abolished. No one shall be condemned to such penalty or executed.

Death penalty in time of war

66-037 Article 2

A State may make provision in its law for the death penalty in respect of acts committed in time of war or of imminent threat of war; such penalty shall be applied only in the instances laid down in the law and in accordance with its provisions. The State shall communicate to the Secretary General of the Council of Europe the relevant provisions of that law.

Criminal Cases Review (Insanity) Act 1999

CHAPTER 25

Reference of former verdict of guilty but insane

1.—(1) Where a verdict was returned in England and Wales or Northern Ireland to the effect that a person was guilty of the act or omission charged against him but was insane at the time, the Criminal Cases Review Commission may at any time refer the verdict to the Court of Appeal if subsection (2) below applies. **67-001**

(2) This subsection applies if the Commission consider that there is a real possibility that the verdict would not be upheld were the reference to be made and either—

(a) the Commission so consider because of an argument, or evidence, not raised in the proceedings which led to the verdict, or

(b) it appears to the Commission that there are exceptional circumstances which justify the making of the reference.

(3) Section 14 of the Criminal Appeal Act 1995 (supplementary provision about the reference of a verdict) shall apply in relation to a reference under subsection (1) above as it applies in relation to references under section 9 or 10 of that Act.

Reference treated as appeal: England and Wales

2.—(1) A reference under section 1(1)above of a verdict returned in England and Wales in the case of a person shall be treated for all purposes as an appeal by the person under section 12 of the Criminal Appeal Act 1968. **67-002**

(2) In their application to such a reference by virtue of subsection (1) above, sections 13 and 14 of that Act shall have effect—

(a) as if references to the verdict of not guilty by reason of insanity were to the verdict referred under section 1(1) above, and

(b) as if, in section 14(1)(b), for the words from the beginning to "that he" there were substituted "the accused was under a disability and"

Reference treated as appeal: Northern Ireland

3.—(1) A reference under section 1(1) above of a verdict returned in Northern Ireland in the case of a person shall be treated for all purposes as an appeal by the person under section 12 of the Criminal Appeal (Northern Ireland) Act 1980. **67-003**

(2) In their application to such a reference by virtue of subsection (1) above, sections 12 and 13 of that Act shall have effect—

(a) as if references to the finding of not guilty on the ground of insanity were to the verdict referred under section 1(1) above, and

(b) as if, in section 13(5A), for the words "there should have been findings that the accused was unfit to be tried and that he" there were substituted "the accused was unfit to be tried and".

Extent and short title

67-004 **4.**—(1) Section 1 above and this section extend to England and Wales and Northern Ireland.

(2) Section 2 above extends to England and Wales.

(3) Section 3 above extends to Northern Ireland.

(4) This Act may be cited as the Criminal Cases Review (Insanity) Act 1999.

Financial Services and Markets Act 2000

CHAPTER 8

PART XXVII

OFFENCES

Miscellaneous offences

Misleading statements and practices

68-001 **397.**—(1) This subsection applies to a person who–

(a) makes a statement, promise or forecast which he knows to be misleading, false or deceptive in a material particular;

(b) dishonestly conceals any materials facts whether in connection with a statement, promise or forecast made by him or otherwise; or

(c) recklessly makes (dishonestly or otherwise) a statement, promise or forecast which is misleading, false or deceptive in a material particular.

(2) A person to whom subsection (1) applies is guilty of an offence if he makes the statement, promise or forecast or conceals the facts for the purpose of inducing, or is reckless as to whether it may induce, another person (whether or not the person to whom the statement, promise or forecast is made)–

(a) to enter or offer to enter into, or to refrain from entering or offering to enter into, a relevant agreement; or

(b) to exercise, or refrain from exercising, any rights conferred by a relevant investment.

(3) Any person who does any act or engages in any course of conduct which creates a false or misleading impression as to the market in or the price or value of any relevant investments is guilty of an offence if he does so for the purpose of creating that impression and of thereby inducing another person to acquire, dispose of, subscribe for or underwrite those investments or to refrain from doing so or to exercise, or refrain from exercising, any rights conferred by those investments.

(4) In proceedings for an offence under subsection (2) brought against a person to whom subsection (1) applies as a result of paragraph (a) of that subsection, it is a defence for him to show that the statement, promise or forecast was made in conformity with price stabilising rules or control of information rules.

(5) In proceedings brought against any person for an offence under subsection (3) it is a defence for him to show–

(a) that he reasonably believed that his act or conduct would not create an impression that was false or misleading as to the matters mentioned in that subsection;

(b) that he acted or engaged in the conduct–

(i) for the purpose of stabilising the price of investments; and

(ii) in conformity with price stabilising rules; or

(c) that he acted or engaged in the conduct in conformity with control of information rules.

(6) Subsections (1) and (2) do not apply unless–

(a) the statement, promise or forecast is made in or from, or the facts are concealed in or from the United Kingdom or arrangements are made in or from the United Kingdom for the statement, promise or forecast to be made or the facts to be concealed;

(b) the person on whom the inducement is intended to or may have effect is in the United Kingdom; or

(c) the agreement is or would be entered into or the rights are or would be exercised in the United Kingdom.

(7) Subsection (3) does not apply unless–

(a) the act is done, or the course of conduct is engaged in, in the United Kingdom; or

(b) the false or misleading impression is created there.

(8) A person guilty of an offence under this section is liable–

(a) on summary conviction, to imprisonment for a term not exceeding six months or a fine not exceeding the statutory maximum, or both;

(b) on conviction on indictment, to imprisonment for a term not exceeding seven years or a fine, or both.

(9) "Relevant agreement" means an agreement–

(a) the entering into or performance of which by either party constitutes an activity of a specified kind or one which falls within a specified class of activity; and

(b) which relates to a relevant investment.

(10) "Relevant investment" means an investment of a specified kind or one which falls within a prescribed class of investment.

(11) Schedule 2 (except paragraphs 25 and 26) applies for the purposes of subsections (9) and (10) with references to section 22 being read as references to each of those subsections.

(12) Nothing in Schedule 2, as applied by subsection (11), limits the power conferred by subsection (9) or (10).

(13) "Investment" includes any asset, right or interest.

(14) "Specified" means specified in an order made by the Treasury.

Bodies corporate and partnerships

Offences by bodies corporate etc

400.—(1) If an offence under this Act committed by a body corporate is shown– **68-002**

(a) to have been committed with the consent or connivance of an officer, or

(b) to be attributable to any neglect on his part,

the officer as well as the body corporate is guilty of the offence and liable to be proceeded against and punished accordingly.

(2) If the affairs of a body corporate are managed by its members, subsection (1) applies in relation to the acts and defaults of a member in connection with his functions of management as if he were a director of the body.

(3) If an offence under this Act committed by a partnership is shown–

(a) to have been committed with the consent or connivance of a partner, or

(b) to be attributable to any neglect on his part,

the partner as well as the partnership is guilty of the offence and liable to be proceeded against and punished accordingly.

(4) In subsection (3) "partner" includes a person purporting to act as a partner.

(5) "Officer", in relation to a body corporate, means–

(a) a director, member of the committee of management, chief executive, manager, secretary or other similar officer of the body, or a person purporting to act in any such capacity; and

(b) an individual who is a controller of the body.

(6) If an offence under this Act committed by an unincorporated association (other than a partnership) is shown–

(a) to have been committed with the consent or connivance of an officer of the association or a member of its governing body, or

(b) to be attributable to any neglect on the part of such an officer or member,

that officer or member as well as the association is guilty of the offence and liable to be proceeded against and punished accordingly.

(7) Regulations may provide for the application of any provision of this section, with such modifications as the Treasury consider appropriate, to a body corporate or unincorporated association formed or recognised under the law of a territory outside the United Kingdom.

Terrorism Act 2000

CHAPTER 11

PART I

INTRODUCTORY

Terrorism: interpretation

69-001 **1.**—(1) In this Act "terrorism" means the use or threat of action where–

(a) the action falls within subsection (2),

(b) the use or threat is designed to influence the government or to intimidate the public or a section of the public, and

(c) the use or threat is made for the purpose of advancing a political, religious or ideological cause.

(2) Action falls within this subsection if it–

(a) involves serious violence against a person,

(b) involves serious damage to property,

(c) endangers a person's life, other than that of the person committing the action,

(d) creates a serious risk to the health or safety of the public or a section of the public, or

(e) is designed seriously to interfere with or seriously to disrupt an electronic system.

(3) The use or threat of action falling within subsection (2) which involves the use of firearms or explosives is terrorism whether or not subsection (1)(b) is satisfied.

(4) In this section–

(a) "action" includes action outside the United Kingdom,

(b) a reference to any person or to property is a reference to any person, or to property, wherever situated,

(c) a reference to the public includes a reference to the public of a country other than the United Kingdom, and

(d) "the government" means the government of the United Kingdom, of a Part of the United Kingdom or of a country other than the United Kingdom.

(5) In this Act a reference to action taken for the purposes of terrorism includes a reference to action taken for the benefit of a proscribed organisation.

PART III

TERRORIST PROPERTY

Interpretation

Terrorist property

14.—(1) In this Act "terrorist property" means– **69-002**

(a) money or other property which is likely to be used for the purposes of terrorism (including any resources of a proscribed organisation),

(b) proceeds of the commission of acts of terrorism, and

(c) proceeds of acts carried out for the purposes of terrorism.

(2) In subsection (1)–

(a) a reference to proceeds of an act includes a reference to any property which wholly or partly, and directly or indirectly, represents the proceeds of the act (including payments or other rewards in connection with its commission), and

(b) the reference to an organisation's resources includes a reference to any money or other property which is applied or made available, or is to be applied or made available, for use by the organisation.

Offences

Fund-raising

15.—(1) A person commits an offence if he– **69-003**

(a) invites another to provide money or other property, and

(b) intends that it should be used, or has reasonable cause to suspect that it may be used, for the purposes of terrorism.

(2) A person commits an offence if he–

(a) receives money or other property, and

(b) intends that it should be used, or has reasonable cause to suspect that it may be used, for the purposes of terrorism.

(3) A person commits an offence if he–

(a) provides money or other property, and

(b) knows or has reasonable cause to suspect that it will or may be used for the purposes of terrorism.

(4) In this section a reference to the provision of money or other property is a reference to its being given, lent or otherwise made available, whether or not for consideration.

Use and possession

69-004 **16.**—(1) A person commits an offence if he uses money or other property for the purposes of terrorism.

(2) A person commits an offence if he–

(a) possesses money or other property, and

(b) intends that it should be used, or has reasonable cause to suspect that it may be used, for the purposes of terrorism.

Funding arrangements

69-005 **17.** A person commits an offence if–

(a) he enters into or becomes concerned in an arrangement as a result of which money or other property is made available or is to be made available to another, and

(b) he knows or has reasonable cause to suspect that it will or may be used for the purposes of terrorism.

Money laundering

69-006 **18.**—(1) A person commits an offence if he enters into or becomes concerned in an arrangement which facilitates the retention or control by or on behalf of another person of terrorist property–

(a) by concealment,

(b) by removal from the jurisdiction,

(c) by transfer to nominees, or

(d) in any other way.

(2) It is a defence for a person charged with an offence under subsection (1) to prove that he did not know and had no reasonable cause to suspect that the arrangement related to terrorist property.

Disclosure of information: duty

69-007 **19.**—(1) This section applies where a person–

(a) believes or suspects that another person has committed an offence under any of sections 15 to 18, and

(b) bases his belief or suspicion on information which comes to his attention in the course of a trade, profession, business or employment.

[(1A) But this section does not apply if the information came to the person in the course of a business in the regulated sector.][1]

(2) The person commits an offence if he does not disclose to a constable as soon as is reasonably practicable–

(a) his belief or suspicion, and

(b) the information on which it is based.

[1] Added by Anti-terrorism, Crime and Security Act 2001 c.24 Sch 2 (3) para 5 (3)

(3) It is a defence for a person charged with an offence under subsection (2) to prove that he had a reasonable excuse for not making the disclosure.

(4) Where–

(a) a person is in employment,

(b) his employer has established a procedure for the making of disclosures of the matters specified in subsection (2), and

(c) he is charged with an offence under that subsection,

it is a defence for him to prove that he disclosed the matters specified in that subsection in accordance with the procedure.

(5) Subsection (2) does not require disclosure by a professional legal adviser of–

(a) information which he obtains in privileged circumstances, or

(b) a belief or suspicion based on information which he obtains in privileged circumstances.

(6) For the purpose of subsection (5) information is obtained by an adviser in privileged circumstances if it comes to him, otherwise than with a view to furthering a criminal purpose–

(a) from a client or a client's representative, in connection with the provision of legal advice by the adviser to the client,

(b) from a person seeking legal advice from the adviser, or from the person's representative, or

(c) from any person, for the purpose of actual or contemplated legal proceedings.

(7) For the purposes of subsection (1)(a) a person shall be treated as having committed an offence under one of sections 15 to 18 if–

(a) he has taken an action or been in possession of a thing, and

(b) he would have committed an offence under one of those sections if he had been in the United Kingdom at the time when he took the action or was in possession of the thing.

[(7A) The reference to a business in the regulated sector must be construed in accordance with Schedule 3A.

(7B) The reference to a constable includes a reference to a person authorised for the purposes of this section by the Director General of the National Criminal Intelligence Service.][1]

(8) A person guilty of an offence under this section shall be liable–

(a) on conviction on indictment, to imprisonment for a term not exceeding five years, to a fine or to both, or

(b) on summary conviction, to imprisonment for a term not exceeding six months, or to a fine not exceeding the statutory maximum or to both.

Disclosure of information: permission

20.—(1) A person may disclose to a constable– **69-008**

(a) a suspicion or belief that any money or other property is terrorist property or is derived from terrorist property;

(b) any matter on which the suspicion or belief is based.

(2) A person may make a disclosure to a constable in the circumstances mentioned in section 19(1) and (2).

(3) Subsections (1) and (2) shall have effect notwithstanding any restriction on the disclosure of information imposed by statute or otherwise.

(4) Where–

(a) a person is in employment, and

[1] Added by Anti-terrorism, Crime and Security Act 2001 c.24 Sch 2 (3) para 5 (4)

(b) his employer has established a procedure for the making of disclosures of the kinds mentioned in subsection (1) and section 19(2),

subsections (1) and (2) shall have effect in relation to that person as if any reference to disclosure to a constable included a reference to disclosure in accordance with the procedure.

[(5) References to a constable include references to a person authorised for the purposes of this section by the Director General of the National Criminal Intelligence Service.][1]

Cooperation with police

69-009 **21.**—(1) A person does not commit an offence under any of sections 15 to 18 if he is acting with the express consent of a constable.

(2) Subject to subsections (3) and (4), a person does not commit an offence under any of sections 15 to 18 by involvement in a transaction or arrangement relating to money or other property if he discloses to a constable–

(a) his suspicion or belief that the money or other property is terrorist property, and

(b) the information on which his suspicion or belief is based.

(3) Subsection (2) applies only where a person makes a disclosure–

(a) after he becomes concerned in the transaction concerned,

(b) on his own initiative, and

(c) as soon as is reasonably practicable.

(4) Subsection (2) does not apply to a person if–

(a) a constable forbids him to continue his involvement in the transaction or arrangement to which the disclosure relates, and

(b) he continues his involvement.

(5) It is a defence for a person charged with an offence under any of sections 15(2) and (3) and 16 to 18 to prove that–

(a) he intended to make a disclosure of the kind mentioned in subsections (2) and (3), and

(b) there is reasonable excuse for his failure to do so.

(6) Where–

(a) a person is in employment, and

(b) his employer has established a procedure for the making of disclosures of the same kind as may be made to a constable under subsection (2),

this section shall have effect in relation to that person as if any reference to disclosure to a constable included a reference to disclosure in accordance with the procedure.

(7) A reference in this section to a transaction or arrangement relating to money or other property includes a reference to use or possession.

[Failure to disclose: regulated sector

69-010 **21A**—(1) A person commits an offence if each of the following three conditions is satisfied.

(2) The first condition is that he—

(a) knows or suspects, or

(b) has reasonable grounds for knowing or suspecting,

that another person has committed an offence under any of sections 15 to 18.

(3) The second condition is that the information or other matter—

(a) on which his knowledge or suspicion is based, or

[1] Added by Anti-terrorism, Crime and Security Act 2001 c.24 Sch 2 (3) para 5 (5)

(b) which gives reasonable grounds for such knowledge or suspicion,
came to him in the course of a business in the regulated sector.

(4) The third condition is that he does not disclose the information or other matter to a constable or a nominated officer as soon as is practicable after it comes to him.

(5) But a person does not commit an offence under this section if—

(a) he has a reasonable excuse for not disclosing the information or other matter;
(b) he is a professional legal adviser and the information or other matter came to him in privileged circumstances.

(6) In deciding whether a person committed an offence under this section the court must consider whether he followed any relevant guidance which was at the time concerned—

(a) issued by a supervisory authority or any other appropriate body,
(b) approved by the Treasury, and
(c) published in a manner it approved as appropriate in its opinion to bring the guidance to the attention of persons likely to be affected by it.

(7) A disclosure to a nominated officer is a disclosure which—

(a) is made to a person nominated by the alleged offender's employer to receive disclosures under this section, and
(b) is made in the course of the alleged offender's employment and in accordance with the procedure established by the employer for the purpose.

(8) Information or other matter comes to a professional legal adviser in privileged circumstances if it is communicated or given to him—

(a) by (or by a representative of) a client of his in connection with the giving by the adviser of legal advice to the client,
(b) by (or by a representative of) a person seeking legal advice from the adviser, or
(c) by a person in connection with legal proceedings or contemplated legal proceedings.

(9) But subsection (8) does not apply to information or other matter which is communicated or given with a view to furthering a criminal purpose.

(10) Schedule 3A has effect for the purpose of determining what is—

(a) a business in the regulated sector;
(b) a supervisory authority.

(11) For the purposes of subsection (2) a person is to be taken to have committed an offence there mentioned if—

(a) he has taken an action or been in possession of a thing and
(b) he would have committed the offence if he had been in the United Kingdom at the time when he took the action or was in possession of the thing.

(12) A person guilty of an offence under this section is liable—

(a) on conviction on indictment, to imprisonment for a term not exceeding five years or to a fine or to both;
(b) on summary conviction, to imprisonment for a term not exceeding six months or to a fine not exceeding the statutory maximum or to both.

(13) An appropriate body is any body which regulates or is representative of any trade, profession, business or employment carried on by the alleged offender.

(14) The reference to a constable includes a reference to a person authorised for the purposes of this section by the Director General of the National Criminal Intelligence Service.][1]

[Protected disclosures

69-011 **21B**—(1) A disclosure which satisfies the following three conditions is not to be taken to breach any restriction on the disclosure of information (however imposed).

(2) The first condition is that the information or other matter disclosed came to the person making the disclosure (the discloser) in the course of a business in the regulated sector.

(3) The second condition is that the information or other matter—

(a) causes the discloser to know or suspect, or

(b) gives him reasonable grounds for knowing or suspecting,

that another person has committed an offence under any of sections 15 to 18.

(4) The third condition is that the disclosure is made to a constable or a nominated officer as soon as is practicable after the information or other matter comes to the discloser.

(5) A disclosure to a nominated officer is a disclosure which—

(a) is made to a person nominated by the discloser's employer to receive disclosures under this section, and

(b) is made in the course of the discloser's employment and in accordance with the procedure established by the employer for the purpose.

(6) The reference to a business in the regulated sector must be construed in accordance with Schedule 3A.

(7) The reference to a constable includes a reference to a person authorised for the purposes of this section by the Director General of the National Criminal Intelligence Service.][2]

Penalties

69-012 **22.** A person guilty of an offence under any of sections 15 to 18 shall be liable–

(a) on conviction on indictment, to imprisonment for a term not exceeding 14 years, to a fine or to both, or

(b) on summary conviction, to imprisonment for a term not exceeding six months, to a fine not exceeding the statutory maximum or to both.

PART IV

TERRORIST INVESTIGATIONS

Information and evidence

[Information about acts of terrorism

69-013 **38B**—(1) This section applies where a person has information which he knows or believes might be of material assistance—

(a) in preventing the commission by another person of an act of terrorism, or

[1] Added by Anti-terrorism, Crime and Security Act 2001 c.24 Sch 2 (3) para 5 (2)

[2] Added by Anti-terrorism, Crime and Security Act 2001 c.24 Sch 2 (3) para 5 (2)

(b) in securing the apprehension, prosecution or conviction of another person, in the United Kingdom, for an offence involving the commission, preparation or instigation of an act of terrorism.

(2) The person commits an offence if he does not disclose the information as soon as reasonably practicable in accordance with subsection (3).

(3) Disclosure is in accordance with this subsection if it is made—

(a) in England and Wales, to a constable,

(b) in Scotland, to a constable, or

(c) in Northern Ireland, to a constable or a member of Her Majesty's forces.

(4) It is a defence for a person charged with an offence under subsection (2) to prove that he had a reasonable excuse for not making the disclosure.

(5) A person guilty of an offence under this section shall be liable—

(a) on conviction on indictment, to imprisonment for a term not exceeding five years, or to a fine or to both, or

(b) on summary conviction, to imprisonment for a term not exceeding six months, or to a fine not exceeding the statutory maximum or to both.

(6) Proceedings for an offence under this section may be taken, and the offence may for the purposes of those proceedings be treated as having been committed, in any place where the person to be charged is or has at any time been since he first knew or believed that the information might be of material assistance as mentioned in subsection (1).][1]

PART VI

MISCELLANEOUS

Terrorist offences

Possession for terrorist purposes

57.—(1) A person commits an offence if he possesses an article in circumstances which give rise to a reasonable suspicion that his possession is for a purpose connected with the commission, preparation or instigation of an act of terrorism. **69-014**

(2) It is a defence for a person charged with an offence under this section to prove that his possession of the article was not for a purpose connected with the commission, preparation or instigation of an act of terrorism.

(3) In proceedings for an offence under this section, if it is proved that an article–

(a) was on any premises at the same time as the accused, or

(b) was on premises of which the accused was the occupier or which he habitually used otherwise than as a member of the public,

the court may assume that the accused possessed the article, unless he proves that he did not know of its presence on the premises or that he had no control over it.

(4) A person guilty of an offence under this section shall be liable–

(a) on conviction on indictment, to imprisonment for a term not exceeding 10 years, to a fine or to both, or

(b) on summary conviction, to imprisonment for a term not exceeding six months, to a fine not exceeding the statutory maximum or to both.

[1] Inserted by Anti-terrorism, Crime and Security Act 2001 c.24 Pt 13 s 117 (2)

Collection of information

69-015 **58.**—(1) A person commits an offence if–

(a) he collects or makes a record of information of a kind likely to be useful to a person committing or preparing an act of terrorism, or

(b) he possesses a document or record containing information of that kind.

(2) In this section "record" includes a photographic or electronic record.

(3) It is a defence for a person charged with an offence under this section to prove that he had a reasonable excuse for his action or possession.

(4) A person guilty of an offence under this section shall be liable–

(a) on conviction on indictment, to imprisonment for a term not exceeding 10 years, to a fine or to both, or

(b) on summary conviction, to imprisonment for a term not exceeding six months, to a fine not exceeding the statutory maximum or to both.

(5) A court by or before which a person is convicted of an offence under this section may order the forfeiture of any document or record containing information of the kind mentioned in subsection (1)(a).

(6) Before making an order under subsection (5) a court must give an opportunity to be heard to any person, other than the convicted person, who claims to be the owner of or otherwise interested in anything which can be forfeited under that subsection.

(7) An order under subsection (5) shall not come into force until there is no further possibility of it being varied, or set aside, on appeal (disregarding any power of a court to grant leave to appeal out of time).

PART VIII

GENERAL

Defences

69-016 **118.**—(1) Subsection (2) applies where in accordance with a provision mentioned in subsection (5) it is a defence for a person charged with an offence to prove a particular matter.

(2) If the person adduces evidence which is sufficient to raise an issue with respect to the matter the court or jury shall assume that the defence is satisfied unless the prosecution proves beyond reasonable doubt that it is not.

(3) Subsection (4) applies where in accordance with a provision mentioned in subsection (5) a court–

(a) may make an assumption in relation to a person charged with an offence unless a particular matter is proved, or

(b) may accept a fact as sufficient evidence unless a particular matter is proved.

(4) If evidence is adduced which is sufficient to raise an issue with respect to the matter mentioned in subsection (3)(a) or (b) the court shall treat it as proved unless the prosecution disproves it beyond reasonable doubt.

(5) The provisions in respect of which subsections (2) and (4) apply are–

(a) sections 12(4), 39(5)(a), 54, 57, 58, 77 and 103 of this Act, and

(b) sections 13, 32 and 33 of the Northern Ireland (Emergency Provisions) Act 1996 (possession and information offences) as they have effect by virtue of Schedule 1 to this Act.

Anti-terrorism, Crime and Security Act 2001

CHAPTER 24

PART 13

MISCELLANEOUS

Dangerous substances

Use of noxious substances or things to cause harm and intimidate

113.—(1) A person who takes any action which— **70-001**

(a) involves the use of a noxious substance or other noxious thing;

(b) has or is likely to have an effect falling within subsection (2); and

(c) is designed to influence the government or to intimidate the public or a section of the public,

is guilty of an offence.

(2) Action has an effect falling within this subsection if it—

(a) causes serious violence against a person anywhere in the world;

(b) causes serious damage to real or personal property anywhere in the world;

(c) endangers human life or creates a serious risk to the health or safety of the public or a section of the public; or

(d) induces in members of the public the fear that the action is likely to endanger their lives or create a serious risk to their health or safety;

but any effect on the person taking the action is to be disregarded.

(3) A person who—

(a) makes a threat that he or another will take any action which constitutes an offence under subsection (1); and

(b) intends thereby to induce in a person anywhere in the world the fear that the threat is likely to be carried out,

is guilty of an offence.

(4) A person guilty of an offence under this section is liable—

(a) on summary conviction, to imprisonment for a term not exceeding six months or a fine not exceeding the statutory maximum (or both); and

(b) on conviction on indictment, to imprisonment for a term not exceeding fourteen years or a fine (or both).

(5) In this section—

"the government" means the government of the United Kingdom, of a part of the United Kingdom or of a country other than the United Kingdom; and

"the public" includes the public of a country other than the United Kingdom.

Hoaxes involving noxious substances or things

70-002 **114.**—(1) A person is guilty of an offence if he—

(a) places any substance or other thing in any place; or

(b) sends any substance or other thing from one place to another (by post, rail or any other means whatever);

with the intention of inducing in a person anywhere in the world a belief that it is likely to be (or contain) a noxious substance or other noxious thing and thereby endanger human life or create a serious risk to human health.

(2) A person is guilty of an offence if he communicates any information which he knows or believes to be false with the intention of inducing in a person anywhere in the world a belief that a noxious substance or other noxious thing is likely to be present (whether at the time the information is communicated or later) in any place and thereby endanger human life or create a serious risk to human health.

(3) A person guilty of an offence under this section is liable—

(a) on summary conviction, to imprisonment for a term not exceeding six months or a fine not exceeding the statutory maximum (or both); and

(b) on conviction on indictment, to imprisonment for a term not exceeding seven years or a fine (or both).

Sections 113 and 114: supplementary

70-003 **115.**—(1) For the purposes of sections 113 and 114 "substance" includes any biological agent and any other natural or artificial substance (whatever its form, origin or method of production).

(2) For a person to be guilty of an offence under section 113(3) or 114 it is not necessary for him to have any particular person in mind as the person in whom he intends to induce the belief in question.

The Code for Crown Prosecutors

I. Code for Crown Prosecutors

The Crown Prosecution Service is a public service for England and Wales headed by the Director of Public Prosecutions. It is answerable to Parliament through the Attorney General. The Crown Prosecution Service is a national organisation consisting of 42 Areas. Each area is headed by a Chief Crown Prosecutor, and corresponds to a single police force area, with one for London. It was set up in 1986 to prosecute cases instituted by the police. The police are responsible for the investigation of crime. Although the Crown Prosecution Service works closely with the Police, it is independent of them. **A–001**

The Director of Public Prosecutions is responsible for issuing a code for Crown Prosecutions under section 10 of the *Prosecution of Offences Act 1985*, giving guidance on the general principles to be applied when making decisions about prosecutions. This is the fourth edition of the Code and replaces all earlier versions. For the purposes of this Code, "Crown Prosecutor" includes members of staff in the Crown Prosecution Service who are designated by the Director of Public Prosecutions under section 7A of the Act and are exercising powers under that section.

1. Introduction

1.1. The decision to prosecute an individual is a serious step. Fair and effective prosecution is essential to the maintenance of law and order. Even in a small case a prosecution has serious implications for all involved - victims, witnesses and defendants. The Crown Prosecution Service applies the Code for Crown Prosecutors so that it can make fair and consistent decisions about prosecutions. **A–002**

1.2. The Code helps the Crown Prosecution Service to play its part in making sure that justice is done. It contains information that is important to police officers and others who work in the criminal justice system and to the general public. Police officers should take account of the Code when they are deciding whether to charge a person with an offence.

1.3. The Code is also designed to make sure that everyone knows the principles that the Crown Prosecution Service applies when carrying out its work. By applying the same principles, everyone involved in the system is helping to treat victims fairly and to prosecute fairly but effectively.

2. General Priniciples

2.1. Each case is unique and must be considered on its own facts and merits. However, there are general principles that apply to the way in which Crown Prosecutors must approach every case. **A–003**

2.2. Crown Prosecutors must be fair, independent and objective. They must not let any personal views about ethnic or national origin, sex, religious beliefs, political views or the sexual orientation of the suspect, victim or witness influence their decisions. They must not be affected by improper or undue pressure from any source.

2.3. It is the duty of Crown Prosecutors to make sure that the right person is prosecuted for the right offence. In doing so, Crown Prosecutors must always act in the interests of justice and not solely for the purpose of obtaining a conviction.

2.4. It is the duty of Crown Prosecutors to review, advise on and prosecute cases, ensuring that the law is properly applied, that all relevant evidence is put before the court and that obligations of disclosure are complied with, in accordance with the principles set out in this Code.

2.5. The CPS is a public authority for the purposes of the Human Rights Act 1998. Crown Prosecutors must apply the principles of the European Convention on Human Rights in accordance with the Act.

3. Review

A–004 **3.1**. Proceedings are usually started by the police. Sometimes they may consult the Crown Prosecution Service before starting a prosecution. Each case that the Crown Prosecution Service receives from the police is reviewed to make sure it meets the evidential and public interest tests set out in this Code. Crown Prosecutors may decide to continue with the original charges, to change the charges, or sometimes to stop the case.

3.2. Review is a continuing process and Crown Prosecutors must take account of any change in circumstances. Wherever possible, they talk to the police first if they are thinking about changing the charges or stopping the case. This gives the police the chance to provide more information that may affect the decision. The Crown Prosecution Service and the police work closely together to reach the right decision, but the final responsibility for the decision rests with the Crown Prosecution Service.

4. Code Tests

A–005 **4.1**. There are two stages in the decision to prosecute. The first stage is *the evidential test*. If the case does not pass the evidential test, it must not go ahead, no matter how important or serious it may be. If the case does meet the evidential test, Crown Prosecutors must decide if a prosecution is needed in the public interest.

4.2. This second stage is *the public interest test*. The Crown Prosecution Service will only start or continue with a prosecution when the case has passed both tests. The evidential test is explained in section 5 and the public interest test is explained in section 6.

5. The Evidential Test

A–006 **5.1**. Crown Prosecutors must be satisfied that there is enough evidence to provide a "realistic prospect of conviction" against each defendant on each charge. They must consider what the defence case may be, and how that is likely to affect the prosecution case.

5.2. A realistic prospect of conviction is an objective test. It means that a jury or bench of magistrates, properly directed in accordance with the law, is more likely than not to convict the defendant of the charge alleged. This is a separate test from the one that the criminal courts themselves must apply. A jury or magistrates court should only convict if satisfied so that it is sure of a defendants guilt.

5.3. When deciding whether there is enough evidence to prosecute, Crown Prosecutors must consider whether the evidence can be used and is reliable. There will be many cases in which the evidence does not give any cause for concern. But there will also be cases in which the evidence may not be as strong as it first appears. Crown Prosecutors must ask themselves the following questions:

Can the evidence be used in court?

(a) Is it likely that the evidence will be excluded by the court? There are certain legal rules which might mean that evidence which seems relevant cannot be given at a trial. For example, is it likely that the evidence will be excluded because of the way in which it was gathered or because of the rule against using hearsay as evidence? If so, is there enough other evidence for a realistic prospect of conviction? **A–007**

Is the evidence reliable?

(b) Is there evidence which might support or detract from the reliability of a confession? Is the reliability affected by factors such as the defendants age, intelligence or level of understanding? **A–008**
(c) What explanation has the defendant given? Is a court likely to find it credible in the light of the evidence as a whole? Does it support an innocent explanation?
(d) If the identity of the defendant is likely to be questioned, is the evidence about this strong enough?
(e) Is the witnesss background likely to weaken the prosecution case? For example, does the witness have any motive that may affect his or her attitude to the case, or a relevant previous conviction?
(f) Are there concerns over the accuracy or credibility of a witness? Are these concerns based on evidence or simply information with nothing to support it? Is there further evidence which the police should be asked to seek out which may support or detract from the account of the witness?

5.4. Crown Prosecutors should not ignore evidence because they are not sure that it can be used or is reliable. But they should look closely at it when deciding if there is a realistic prospect of conviction.

6. The Public Interest Test

6.1. In 1951, Lord Shawcross, who was Attorney General, made the classic statement on public interest, which has been supported by Attorneys General ever since: "It has never been the rule in this country – I hope it never will be – that suspected criminal offences must automatically be the subject of prosecution". (House of Commons Debates, volume 483, column 681, 29 January 1951.) **A–009**

6.2. The public interest must be considered in each case where there is enough evidence to provide a realistic prospect of conviction. A prosecution will usually take place unless there are public interest factors tending against prosecution which clearly outweigh those tending in favour. Although there may be public interest factors against prosecution in a particular case, often the prosecution should go ahead and those factors should be put to the court for consideration when sentence is being passed.

6.3. Crown Prosecutors must balance factors for and against prosecution carefully and fairly. Public interest factors that can affect the decision to prosecute usually depend on the seriousness of the offence or the circumstances of the suspect. Some factors may increase the need to prosecute but others may suggest that another course of action would be better.

The following lists of some common public interest factors, both for and against prosecution, are not exhaustive. The factors that apply will depend on the facts in each case.

Some common public interest factors in favour of prosecution

A–010 **6.4**. The more serious the offence, the more likely it is that a prosecution will be needed in the public interest. A prosecution is likely to be needed if:

(a) a conviction is likely to result in a significant sentence;
(b) a weapon was used or violence was threatened during the commission of the offence;
(c) the offence was committed against a person serving the public (for example, a police or prison officer, or a nurse);
(d) if the identity of the defendant is likely to be questioned, is the evidence about this strong enough?
(e) the defendant was in a position of authority or trust;
(f) there is evidence that the offence was premeditated;
(g) there is evidence that the offence was carried out by a group;
(h) the victim of the offence was vulnerable, has been put in considerable fear, or suffered personal attack, damage or disturbance;
(i) the offence was motivated by any form of discrimination against the victims ethnic or national origin, sex, religious beliefs, political views or sexual orientation, or the suspect demonstrated hostility towards the victim based on any of those characteristics;
(j) there is a marked difference between the actual or mental ages of the defendant and the victim, or if there is any element of corruption;
(k) the defendants previous convictions or cautions are relevant to the present offence;
(l) the defendant is alleged to have committed the offence whilst under an order of the court;
(m) there are grounds for believing that the offence is likely to be continued or repeated, for example, by a history of recurring conduct;
(n) the offence, although not serious in itself, is widespread in the area where it was committed.

Some common public interest factors against prosecution

A–011 **6.5**. A prosecution is less likely to be needed if:

(a) the court is likely to impose a nominal penalty;
(b) the defendant has already been made the subject of a sentence and any further conviction would be unlikely to result in the imposition of an additional sentence or order, unless the nature of the particular offence requires a prosecution;

(c) the offence was committed as a result of a genuine mistake or misunderstanding (these factors must be balanced against the seriousness of the offence);
(d) the loss or harm can be described as minor and was the result of a single incident, particularly if it was caused by a misjudgement;
(e) there has been a long delay between the offence taking place and the date of the trial, unless:

- the offence is serious;
- the delay has been caused in part by the defendant;
- the offence has only recently come to light; or
- the complexity of the offence has meant that there has been a long investigation;

(f) a prosecution is likely to have a bad effect on the victims physical or mental health, always bearing in mind the seriousness of the offence;
(g) the defendant is elderly or is, or was at the time of the offence, suffering from significant mental or physical ill health, unless the offence is serious or there is a real possibility that it may be repeated. The Crown Prosecution Service, where necessary, applies Home Office guidelines about how to deal with mentally disordered offenders. Crown Prosecutors must balance the desirability of diverting a defendant who is suffering from significant mental or physical ill health with the need to safeguard the general public;
(h) the defendant has put right the loss or harm that was caused (but defendants must not avoid prosecution solely because they pay compensation); or
(i) details may be made public that could harm sources of information, international relations or national security;

6.6. Deciding on the public interest is not simply a matter of adding up the number of factors on each side. Crown Prosecutors must decide how important each factor is in the circumstances of each case and go on to make an overall assessment.

The relationship between the victim and the public interest

6.7. The Crown Prosecution Service prosecutes cases on behalf of the public **A–012**
at large and not just in the interests of any particular individual. However, when considering the public interest test Crown Prosecutors should always take into account the consequences for the victim of the decision whether or not to prosecute, and any views expressed by the victim or the victims family.

6.8. It is important that a victim is told about a decision which makes a significant difference to the case in which he or she is involved. Crown Prosecutors should ensure that they follow any agreed procedures.

Youths

6.9. Crown Prosecutors must consider the interests of a youth when deciding **A–013**
whether it is in the public interest to prosecute. However Crown Prosecutors should not avoid prosecuting simply because of the defendants age. The seriousness of the offence or the youths past behaviour is very important.

6.10. Cases involving youths are usually only referred to the Crown Prosecution Service for prosecution if the youth has already received a reprimand and final warning, unless the offence is so serious that neither of these were appropriate. Reprimands and final warnings are intended to prevent re-offending and the fact that a further offence has occurred indicates that attempts to divert the youth from the court system have not been effective. So the public interest will usually require a prosecution in such cases, unless there are clear public interest factors against prosecution.

Police Cautions

A–014 **6.11.** These are only for adults. The police make the decision to caution an offender in accordance with Home Office guidelines.

6.12. When deciding whether a case should be prosecuted in the courts, Crown Prosecutors should consider the alternatives to prosecution. This will include a police caution. Again the Home Office guidelines should be applied. Where it is felt that a caution is appropriate, Crown Prosecutors must inform the police so that they can caution the suspect. If the caution is not administered because the suspect refuses to accept it or the police do not wish to offer it, then the Crown Prosecutor may review the case again.

7. Charges

A–015 **7.1.** Crown Prosecutors should select charges which:
(a) reflect the seriousness of the offending;
(b) give the court adequate sentencing powers; and
(c) enable the case to be presented in a clear and simple way.

This means that Crown Prosecutors may not always continue with the most serious charge where there is a choice. Further, Crown Prosecutors should not continue with more charges than are necessary.

7.2. Crown Prosecutors should never go ahead with more charges than are necessary just to encourage a defendant to plead guilty to a few. In the same way, they should never go ahead with a more serious charge just to encourage a defendant to plead guilty to a less serious one.

7.3. Crown Prosecutors should not change the charge simply because of the decision made by the court or the defendant about where the case will be heard.

8. Mode Of Trial

A–016 **8.1.** The Crown Prosecution Service applies the current guidelines for magistrates who have to decide whether cases should be tried in the Crown Court when the offence gives the option and the defendant does not indicate a guilty plea. (See the "National Mode of Trial Guidelines" issued by the Lord Chief Justice.) Crown Prosecutors should recommend Crown Court trial when they are satisfied that the guidelines require them to do so.

8.2. Speed must never be the only reason for asking for a case to stay in the magistrates' courts. But Crown Prosecutors should consider the effect of any likely delay if they send a case to the Crown Court, and any possible stress on victims and witnesses if the case is delayed.

9. Accepting Guilty Pleas

9.1. Defendants may want to plead guilty to some, but not all, of the charges. Alternatively, they may want to plead guilty to a different, possibly less serious, charge because they are admitting only part of the crime. Crown Prosecutors should only accept the defendants plea if they think the court is able to pass a sentence that matches the seriousness of the offending, particularly where there are aggravating features. Crown Prosecutors must never accept a guilty plea just because it is convenient. **A–017**

9.2. Particular care must be taken when considering pleas which would enable the defendant to avoid the imposition of a mandatory minimum sentence. When pleas are offered, Crown Prosecutors must bear in mind the fact that ancillary orders can be made with some offences but not with others.

9.3. In cases where a defendant pleads guilty to the charges but on the basis of facts that are different from the prosecution case, and where this may significantly affect sentence, the court should be invited to hear evidence to determine what happened, and then sentence on that basis.

10. Re-starting a Prosecution

10.1. People should be able to rely on decisions taken by the Crown Prosecution Service. Normally, if the Crown Prosecution Service tells a suspect or defendant that there will not be a prosecution, or that the prosecution has been stopped, that is the end of the matter and the case will not start again. But occasionally there are special reasons why the Crown Prosecution Service will re-start the prosecution, particularly if the case is serious. **A–018**

10.2. These reasons include:

(a) rare cases where a new look at the original decision shows that it was clearly wrong and should not be allowed to stand;

(b) cases which are stopped so that more evidence which is likely to become available in the fairly near future can be collected and prepared. In these cases, the Crown Prosecutor will tell the defendant that the prosecution may well start again; and

(c) cases which are stopped because of a lack of evidence but where more significant evidence is discovered later.

The code is a public document. It is available on the CPS Website: www.cps.gov.uk

INDEX